THE
COMMUNITY OF CATTLEMEN

THE COMMUNITY OF CATTLEMEN

A Social History of the Cattle Industry in Southeastern Oregon 1869-1912

Peter K. Simpson

The University of Idaho Press
Moscow, Idaho

Copyright © Peter K. Simpson 1987

Published by The University of Idaho Press, Moscow, Idaho

PRINTED IN THE UNITED STATES OF AMERICA
9 8 7 6 5 4 3 2 1

———————

Library of Congress Cataloging-in-Publication Data

Simpson, Peter K., 1930-
    The community of cattlemen.

    Bibliography: p.
    Includes index.
    1. Cattle trade—Oregon—Harney County—History.
2. Ranchers—Oregon—Harney County—Hisotry.
3. Ranches—Oregon—Harney County—History.
4. Cattle breeders—Oregon—Harney County—History.
5. Harney County (Or.)—History. I. Title.
HD9433.U5H277 1987   338.1'762'00979595   87-5855
ISBN 0-89301-117-7 (pbk.)

To Earl Pomeroy

Contents

PREFACE

A buckaroo in southeastern Oregon who catches wild horses on the side once said, when the subject of early cattle king Peter French came up, "Oh, I suppose what they write about him is all right for the history books, but it ain't true." What he meant, of course, was that as far as he was concerned the historians of his area embellished and twisted facts in order to tell a good story. He knew, living as he did in Peter French country, that Peter French meant more than just a good story—so much more, in fact, that a book could not impart the man's true impact. That impact was at once complex, many-faceted, deep, and permanent in the ways that a "good story" is merely disembodied, abstract, symbolic, and—unless the storyteller is gifted—lifeless. Add to this a question once asked by a colleague—"Why does the cattleman always seem so hypocritical? Why does he treat the federal government like an enemy, for instance, at the same time he is using it shamelessly for his own ends?"—and there emerges a rationale for the present study.

Most histories of the cattle industry fall into three general categories: histories of the business, histories of the method, and histories of the open-range era. All of these overlap, but each serves as a focus and only in rare exceptions are these foci not central themes. Applying historiographical jargon, or trade labels if you will, one can place the first category within the province of the economic historians; the second lands in the ring with cultural historians, antiquarians, popularizers, and charlatans—a mixture of good and bad, too intricately interlaced to be unraveled here. The third category ends up in the bailiwick of the "frontierists" who attract to themselves, more is the pity, almost all the practitioners in the other two groups as well.

Some exceedingly fine work has been done in all three categories, as comments throughout this study and in footnotes are intended to show; yet in all three, if historians treat social history at all, they treat it only in terms of cultural traits and habits and rarely in terms of social relationships within the community of cattlemen itself. Obscuring still further what efforts there are is the frontierist tendency to have done with the industry at the end of the frontier period—thus dividing the history of the range-cattle industry into an open-range era up until the late 1880s and early 1890s and a modern stock-farming era thereafter. The so-called "transition period" between invites historical stitching and cutting from every scholar with a sharp scissor who happens by, until continuity becomes a thing of shreds and patches. In fact, one wonders if at any time the pieces ever made a quilt.

In truth, however, there is a clear continuity as well as a richly colored pattern of social development in the history of the cattle industry. It lends believability to a facet of American history so far transposed into myth that some serious scholars a few years back had very nearly given the subject up for lost to serious study.

What evidently was lacking was a method or methods for a fresh approach. Since that time works such as those of Gene Gressley and Robert Dykstra have shown how the case-study method on the one hand and the application of concepts from other disciplines like sociology on the other can spruce up the field and lend it new importance. Nonetheless, as with all new or, more accurately, different methods, it is the new or different assumptions one brings to them that make these methods workable in the first place. To make a fresh start in the cattle industry, one can assume with Gressley and Dykstra that the industry was a part of the business of the nation as a whole and that those participating in it shared values and habits in common with the national culture as a whole. In the history of the cattle industry as a phase of economic history, one can assume what historians of rural society assume: that what one does to make a living and how well he succeeds at it are the primary determinants of what social position he will be assigned.

From the directives these assumptions supply comes the method for the present study. The period under consideration begins well before and ends well after the transition period of the industry, on the principle that a running start and a long finish might make the interval between seem smoother and more of one piece. A recognizable, spatially defined community has been selected, Harney County, Oregon—a community with a town (Burns), a hinterland, and a system of communication between the two. More important, the community is small and therefore the total population forms, wherever and whenever data are available, the subject matter of the study on the principle that a true view of one part of a society depends upon an understanding of its relationship to the whole.

Finally, from such friendly disciplines as anthropology, geography, and sociology come particular research tools, including primarily the rather common-sense technique of participating in and observing the society being studied; finding one or two especially knowledgeable local citizens who could help interpret what had been observed; and interviewing, sometimes in a loose, sometimes in a formal way, people who had participated in the life of the community over a long period of time. Maps of the community help to make spatial sense of historical events, while perspective is lent to these events through the use of certain analogies made with the patterns of behavior told of by students of other communities—sociologists mostly, who use the phrase "analytical model" rather than analogy but who mean thereby something functionally very similar. Not that historical records were shunned; in fact, they perform two crucial functions—one in the corroborating of interviews and in providing data and the other in adding, as all historical records do, the vital element of process to the static stuff of space. The county clerk's and county assessor's offices were rich in information, even if it was sometimes incomplete. In addition, the office of the county extension agent as well as the local library, museum, and Chamber of Commerce yielded important pieces of information. Less productive repositories were fraternal organizations, churches, and service clubs, which had not kept records as judiciously as they might have. Newspapers were, as always, helpful, as were a number of published and unpublished sources—most especially the boxes upon boxes of materials of the Hanley Collection in the Oregon Historical Society Library.

These sources, distilled, filtered, and analyzed as well as they could be within the limits of the researcher's competence, helped reveal some important social facts about the cattle industry that have heretofore either gone unrecognized or, if recognized, been left unexplored. Foremost among them is the fact that the modern cattleman in semi-arid regions is the descendant of victorious would-be farmers and small cattlegrowers who won the classic feud between sodbusters and cattle barons. Implications of this fact and the story of how it came to be true may help answer the question posed by my colleague at the outset and may go a way toward satisfying the old buckaroo about the truth one finds in history books.

ACKNOWLEDGMENTS

My gratitude to those who helped me with this study is as immense as the list of those to whom I owe it. The research emerged from a project funded by the University of Oregon Institute of International studies for research in Alsace, France. I owe a debt to the institute for that opportunity and to the citizens of the Commune of Mittelbergheim, particularly my gentle informant, the Guard Champaitre, and to my Alsatian friends, the family of Pierre and Dolly Seltz.

Early struggles with the conceptual nature of the story were shared with fellow graduate students Tom Cox and Bill Robbins. The 1969 "Cowboy Project" helped me to shape pertinent ideas. I probably never voiced my appreciation to Bus Lehren and director Jack Schultz as insistently as I might have. I do so belatedly here. The cultural scope and cast of the research was the product of deeply rewarding associations with members of the University of Oregon department of geography, notably Clyde Patton, Gene Martin, and Al Urquhart, whose interest was real and whose encouragement was heartening.

The locus of the study, the community of Burns and Harney County, Oregon, became as much of a home to me as it did a subject of study and it confirmed again for me the dignity and the power of rural living. Al Brown, scion of a pioneer family, was a wise counsel. Rex Taylor, a Sod House rancher, lent me his top horse and his ear with equal generosity. Don Toelle and his lovely wife and family were the soul of courtesy. Walter and Virginia McEwen were elegant and generous hosts and the memory of Walter's library is still for me a source of admiration.

Johnny Crow, horseman, cowhand, raconteur and advisor, represented in his person much of the tradition of Harney County's rich past. The watermaster, Clarence Young, was a helpful guide through the complicated history of Harney County water rights. Joe Fine, last of the great foremen, stood as tall with me as he did with the entire community—north and south end alike.

John Scharff taught me about the valley and its citizens from a wealth of experience and showed me at the same time the man behind the prodigious reputation he enjoyed for public service and leadership in that community. Ray Novotny, county extension agent, evidenced the cultural similarities that exist among cattle-raising communities. He was as openly helpful to me in Oregon as I remembered him to be when I knew him years before in Wyoming. The "court house gang,'" the women in the assessor's office and the clerk's office, gave me time and assistance and shared with me occasional fruitcakes and cookies when they felt my energy needed bolstering. No one should underestimate the value of the county court house staff to local and community research; for me, they were keys to the material and invariably accurate interpreters of its meaning.

Many, many sources in scattered locations contributed important data to the research. A major resource was the Hanley Collection, which has considerable to offer researchers in the history of Oregon and the West. My appreciation goes to Tom Vaughan, director of the Oregon Historical Society, for his inimitable courtesy and service.

Researchers who rode the southeastern Oregon range before me provided in their work both examples and valuable perspectives, particularly Margaret Lo Piccolo's master thesis, the work of A.A. Bardwell, Dale Eggleston, M.D. Palmer, and the various treatises of local historians and students of the industry. Of overarching importance was and is the prodigious work of J. Orin Oliphant, who defines the task for us all while he illuminates the history of the cattle industry in the Pacific Northwest with intelligence and insight.

To my beloved parents, the honorable Milward and Lorna Simpson, I owe not only my western birthright but my thanks for a summer on the family ranch on the South Fork of the Shoshone River—a place for thought and contemplation and for enlisting one's will to cross that most formidable of barriers, the one between the research and the writing.

Trails into the High Desert

Cultural Origins and Dispersals

D.W. Meinig, prolific cultural geographer and historian, has put the history of the trans-Mississippi West into an illuminating spatial conceptualization that at once challenges the view of an inexorably westward-moving frontier of settlement and development and provides a spatial framework in which early indigenous and pre-Anglo-Saxon cultural influences can be seen with greater clarity. The West, according to Meinig, was a set of dynamic regions based on a series of cultural nuclei that grew independently. They were located in southern and northern California, the Willamette Valley, central Texas, Utah, Colorado, and central New Mexico along the Rio Grande. Population, culture, and circulation within each nucleus developed through stages from isolation, to a provincial system, to integration into the national culture; the history of each revealed a "gradual fading of identifiable parts into an ever more uniform whole."[1]

These nuclei, though not "radically different," were "recognizably distinct" from each other in two ways. Some nuclei differed sharply on the basis of language, race, or religion, while others, though not as clearly distinguishable on those grounds, were found to be culturally different when additional historical criteria were used to establish where the inhabitants came from, how they intermingled, what they did when they got there, and how they organized their area into functional systems. The societies that developed in those places in turn had an acculturative effect on the later populations that came in contact with them.

Meinig's hypothesis suggests that the "cattleman's frontier" was more of an acculturative force than has been acknowledged and less of the colorful, transitory phase of western development so often pictured. A brief review of the history of the cattle industry tends to bear this out. Cattle of Spanish descent—more correctly, "Moorish" cattle of Andalusian descent—were brought by missionaries from Mexico to the valley of the Nueces River in Texas in the seventeenth century and to the low-lying semicircle of land that fronted on the Pacific Ocean west of the San Bernardino Mountains between Redondo Bay and the shrub-covered Santa Anas in 1769. Surpluses of these cattle developed in both places, and by the middle of 1840 the Pacific coast from the

Los Angeles basin to Monterey was dotted with a succession of large ranchos, the equivalent of the Mexican haciendas. Even the Willamette Valley received the flow of this stream of cattle: by 1840 farming and stockraising with Andalusian blacks had supplanted the fur economy in that region.[2]

Meanwhile, over the Wilderness, Forbes', and Braddock's roads, and by flatboat down the Ohio, settlers and their cattle flooded the trans-Appalachian West. Most of these cattle were Durhams, which the pioneers claimed trailed better than shorthorns; a surplus of them built up in the Ohio Valley even before the general westward movement reached Illinois. Some of these cattle were trailed back over the National Road to eastern markets; many more were slaughtered for their hides, or salted and packed in barrels to be floated down the Mississippi to markets in New Orleans. A sizable percentage moved on toward the West, and the center of the surplus moved gradually into Illinois. By the time the railroads reached that state in the 1840s the small cattle owners of the previous decade were in a position to become the first Western cattle kings, specializing in grain-fed beef for eastern consumption.[3]

While the eastern demand for beef was increasing in the 1840s, midwestern farmers found an even more convenient, and therefore a more profitable, market among the multitude of immigrants traveling along the overland trails to the West Coast. This demand was augmented by that of the great freight companies, which needed sturdy beasts to haul goods across the prairies. The combination of these two markets was such that the focus of the midwestern cattle trade shifted to Missouri. At Independence, the jumping-off place for the Oregon Trail, great numbers of Durhams were hitched up to family wagons and to freighting drays and headed toward the West Coast. At the end of the journey the freighting teams were sold to settlers, who in turn bred them and the family "oxen" to their milk cows.[4]

A major alteration in breeds came in the wake of "Oregon Fever." By 1846 the importance of Andalusian black cattle had declined in northern California as well as in western Oregon. What stockmen called the "American" cattle of the Durham breed supplanted them, and within a decade there was scarcely a black cow north of the Los Angeles Basin. From this great Durham herd came the cattle that fed the northwestern miners during the rushes of the 1850s and 1860s.[5]

Thus cattle from Mexico were originally clustered in the regions of Meinig's cultural nuclei in the Southwest and along the Pacific Coast, while midwestern cattle were by 1850 bunched in the Midwest and in the unique cultural island of Mormon Utah. By then, too, the Moorish cattle in Texas had been supplanted by America's first indigenous breed—an accidental cross between Andalusian blacks, a few Spanish cattle of Hamitic Longhorn descent, and some scrub Durhams from Louisiana, which produced the legendary Texas longhorn.[6] This lean creature made up the herds that moved north after the Civil War; but the longhorn was a beast without a buyer in the 1840s while the midwestern breeds were coming west in increasing numbers with the settlers on the Overland trails.

Despite the small influx of midwestern cattle into northern California, there was always a market there for Texas herds. Drives in the late 1850s went north to the overland trails rather than through the tortuous Gila River country, and the entire trade was finally brought to a halt when Union troops blockaded the Confederacy in 1861. California could maintain itself on its ample local herds, but by 1865 enterprising cattlemen like Henry Miller of San Francisco could not exploit a growing national market without cheap Texas beef.[7]

The northern ranges of Wyoming, Montana, and Colorado showed great potential. Small ranches had grown up along the overland trails in the 1850s as way stations where trail-weary cattle were either fed or traded off for fresh animals. A boost was given this nascent industry by the Colorado gold rush of 1859, and Montana and Wyoming ranchers enjoyed a similar boom after the strikes of 1860 and 1862. By the end of the Civil War there were scattered throughout northern ranges substantial herds that served overland immigrants, reservation Indians, workers on the Union Pacific, soldiers, and hard-rock miners. But if ranchers of this region wished to produce beef for the national market, they—like northern Californians—had to stock the ranges with cheap Texas cattle.[8]

Cattle "demography" in 1865 indicated the potential for an eastern market. The Texas cattle population was between six and eight head per capita, while in the northeastern states of Massachusetts, New York, and Ohio the average per person was .38 head. In the southern states of Georgia, Kentucky, and Mississippi the figure was .59 head per capita. Even in Iowa and Missouri, after a generation of purchases by immigrants together with the encroachment of farmers and the demands for beef during the Civil War, the number of cattle per capita was .84.[9]

Between 1866 and 1890 the barriers separating western nuclei began to fall. In that time the buffalo were destroyed, Indian resistance was broken, and railroads were completed across the continent. In those two decades the ecology of the plains was changed. A massive migration of Texas longhorns, five million strong, crossed the Red River toward railheads in Kansas and Missouri. A large number were diverted to feeder lots in Iowa and Illinois, and a still larger number went to the waiting ranges of Colorado, Wyoming, and Montana.[10]

North with the longhorns came the open-range system, the essential ingredients of which were ample grass and accessible water. The Texas prairies, and later the ranges of the North, provided all the grass that cattlemen in 1865 could foreseeably use. As for water, the tough longhorn had the capacity to search miles for it. Branding was the only means of distinguishing between cattle on unenclosed land; this involved a distinctive set of rules for herding and marking, some of which had evolved over several centuries. Most of the methods are in fact traceable to the operations of the sixteenth-century Spanish *mesta*. Texas and Mexican cattlemen, like the California miners of an earlier period, taught the methods of the business to northern cowboys. Thus the open-range method, together with many of the tools of the trade, developed out of the Spanish heritage and were diffused along the great cattle trails north to Canada.[11] Certain tools come instantly to mind: stirrups, chaps, and the lariat or *reata*, to name a few.

At the same time a different technique for cattle raising spread from the Midwest directly across the continent to northern California, Mormon Utah, and the Willamette Valley. The stock-farming technique emphasized enclosures, the production of winter feed, and the practice of controlled breeding. Its place of origin was clearly England and northwestern Europe.

The dual heritage of the American cattle industry is attested to once again by evidence of the dispersal of major breeds. The cattle of Spanish origin dispersed from south to north along the great Texas trails, while those of English and northwestern European descent dispersed from east to west along the overland trails. The latter breeds gradually supplanted the poorer grades of cattle as eastern methods became dominant. Thus the colorful paraphernalia of the cowboy, his riding accoutrements, and not infrequently his cowpony were the features of a Spanish heritage still observable in the American cattle industry; the methods, breeds, and range techniques were all of English and northwest European origin. Thus it seems reasonable to conclude that the cattle industry was one of the earliest contacts between Meinig's various cultural nuclei—occurring, in terms of his formulation, between the stage of isolation and that of the developing provincial system.

Placed in this context, the role played by southeastern Oregon in the American cattle business takes on larger dimensions. In the first place cattle appeared there late compared with the areas just discussed. In 1863 and 1864, during the northwestern mining rushes, large herds of Durhams with some Moors moved east out of the Willamette Valley to feed miners in southern Idaho and eastern Oregon. Local markets were exploited profitably enough with these herds, but stocking of the empty ranges had to await the infusion of vast numbers of California cattle that came in the wake of the California "herd laws" of 1864 and the removal of the eastern Oregon Indian barrier in 1868. Beginning in 1869, northern California drained its surplus into a broad inland area including not only southeastern Oregon but northwestern Nevada and southwestern Idaho as well.[12]

Several thousand Texas longhorns helped expand these herds rapidly at low cost; the longhorns were never numerous enough to reduce the quality of the California and Willamette Valley herds. Gradually southeastern Oregon, where farming seemed doomed from the start, attracted the lion's share of California investment money. By 1873 the cattlemen of the area were facsimiles of the great "rancheros" of an earlier period, and the ranges teemed with their sleek cattle—cattle that began to make a mark on the northern ranges. Well-to-do western Montana ranchers, who had survived the depression of the middle 1870s, were looking for quality cattle, and, since ranchers who knew Oregon-bred cattle found them more durable than the Midwestern "pilgrim" cattle and more salable than the tough longhorns, their interest gave rise to the first great west-to-east cattle drives for stocking in the history of the American cattle industry.[13]

But southeastern Oregon was never simply a cattleman's country. From the start, groups of settlers and would-be farmers found portions of this high desert to their liking and settled down to try to farm or raise a small herd of cattle or both. The cattle they brought with them were of midwestern origin, as were the people themselves, and the areas they settled in were the best-watered areas in the north end of what is now Harney County.

In the early years there were never many people, but enough settled in the area to establish a special cultural dichotomy in this huge country—a dichotomy between northwest European cultural traditions and Spanish cultural traditions. Neither was manifested strongly in language or racial differences; the strands appeared in subtle differences between methods of cattle raising and ranching. Differing geographic conditions helped sustain this dichotomy.

A Portrait: The Setting for a Community

The major basins and valleys of southern Harney County were in 1880 the sites of minor kingdoms sealed off from each other by the fault blocks and scarps of the basin and range province. The location of these satrapies influenced not only the business methods of each but the economic and social relationships that developed later between these cattle kings and the settlers who were moving simultaneously into the open valleys and river bottoms in the north end of the county.

From Mann Lake on the north to the headwaters of Pueblo Creek just south of the Nevada state line, and from Steens Mountain on the west to the Crooked Creek drainage on the east, a vast interior basin embracing 840 square miles of rolling and level range land draws the water from intermittent streams into shallow marshes or playa-type lakes and toward a large alkaline desert lake bed of parched white clay—a sump or giant evaporating pond known as Alvord Lake. Most of the streams running off Steens Mountain drain into an even larger piece of desolation northeast of the lake called the Alvord Desert. The best soil is on the alluvial fans of these streams. The rest clings in shallow layers to uplands that mount gradually to the basalt and block-fault ranges rimming the basin.

Vegetation today is probably little different from the vegetation familiar to the earliest aboriginal nomads: native grasses, sagebrush, rabbit brush, and greasewood. There are no trees except along some of the stream courses that run out of the mountains. Two of the more prominent streams, Trout Creek and Wildhorse Creek, cut relatively fertile valleys parallel to and close beside Steens and Pueblo mountains.

Average precipitation since measurements have been made has been about seven and one-half inches per year in the basin and eighteen inches on the top of Steens Mountain, the latter mostly in snowfall during the winter months. Spring runoff from the mountains is still the principal source of water for ranching operations but is dessicated in the bone-dry air of the basin at an evaporation rate of 60 inches per year, far in excess of measured precipitation. Wind blows sharp and hot in the summer, when temperatures reach seasonal highs of 100 to 110 degrees; in the winter they hurl air chilled to 50 degrees below zero in icy blasts of up to 40 or 50 miles per hour across the frozen basin floor.

Despite these extremes, the growing season is slightly longer than in other areas to the north, and the xerophytic grasses carry more nutriment than the lush marsh grasses on the west side of Steens Mountain. Mule deer and antelope survive and propagate, as do several varieties of desert rodents and reptiles. But the region is harsh, vast, and formidable. Its chief asset was then and is now grass, and the use to which it was put by the first rancher in the area is the use to which it is put today: extensive, large-scale cattle-ranching operations carried on by a relatively few operators in an isolated and remote setting.[14]

John Devine, the flamboyant ranch manager of the partnership of Todhunter and Devine, was the first to seize control of any large portion of land in the south end of the county. In 1869 he laid out the buildings and corrals of the Whitehorse Ranch on the creek from which it got its name.[15] The alluvial fan along the stream is first-class soil, well drained and slightly acid, good agricultural land when irrigated. It is still one of the most desirable locations in the entire basin of which it is a part.

Devine was master of most of the region, but he permitted the establishment of some minor principalities near the east flank of the Steens and in the Alvord Valley along the north rim of the basin. By 1880 Abbott and Whiteside occupied the site of Camp Alvord (a relic of recent Indian conflicts) in the shadow of Steens Mountain; John Catlow ran a few thousand head of cattle on his Trout Creek holdings south of the fork of Cottonwood Creek, and Phillip Mann settled on House Creek south of Mann Lake. A few others had crept into the narrow, sheltered valleys of the Steens, particularly along Wildhorse Creek. These made up that part of the community of the south end whose distinguishing talisman was the tin white horse weathervane atop the barn of the great ranch on the south rim of the basin.[16]

The steep eastern face of Steens Mountain effectively walls off the basin just described from the Blitzen River drainage and from Catlow Valley just to the west. The only access to Catlow Valley is through a boulder-strewn, ten-mile-wide gap that separates the major fault-block system in the south end of the county into the Steens and Pueblo mountain ranges. An early pioneer in the cattle business, David Shirk, gave the first account of the valley on the other side: "A veritable stockman's paradise . . . [with] bunch grass and white sage . . . [which] stood two feet high. . . ." Shirk had other concerns that diverted him from claiming this particular part of paradise. Thus, when the legendary Peter French drove 1,200 head of cattle fresh from the ranges of northern California into the west side of the valley in June of 1872, he saw it untouched—a promising winter range and his for the taking.[17]

French was nothing if not shrewd. He arrived just after the spring runoff during what both oldtimers and modern meteorologists describe as one of the "wet cycles" in southeastern Oregon's history. None of the streams that emptied into this 610-square-mile basin cut permanent beds. The whole valley was an interior basin with no central lake, only a small marsh at the northeast end into which a large spring debouched. There were no perennial streams. French knew the valley for what it was, a summer range of indeterminate value depending on the weather. He laid out corrals at Roaring Springs and moved on to the lush valley of the Blitzen River.[18]

The original surveys and more recent analyses of Catlow Valley, together with the experiences of the years, confirm French's judgment.[19] The soil is thin, mostly second to fourth class, volcanic in nature, extensively weathered and covering sediments compacted into hardpan. Most critical of all, it is waterless. Five shallow, intermittent streams flow off Steens Mountain north of Long Hollow gap. During good years some limited agriculture is possible on the alluvium deposited there. Rock Creek and Guano Slough, however, which run from the Hart Mountain region on the western rim diminish to rivulets near the boundary between Lake and Harney counties and sink out of sight into the dry valley floor west of Cox Butte.

There is some scrub juniper; otherwise the valley has no timber. At the time Shirk and French saw it, the native grass was plentiful, as was a remarkably nutritious winter browse plant known as white sage. After periods of overgrazing and several attempts at farming, the vegetation has turned to big sage, rabbit brush, winterfat, and pepper grass (the last regarded more as a weed). The climate is as severe here as on the east side of the Steens, though the growing season is slightly longer. In the summer, during dry spells, the grass disappears; a fine powdery white dust covers the roots of the sagebrush and blows in clouds before the prevailing northwest winds or swirls up as high as 300 feet in great dust spouts that dot the valley on hot days. Winter snows paint a picture of gray-white desolation. Historically, the valley has been an illusion—or better yet a mirage—beckoning the hopeful in the wet years and turning their hopes to dust in the dry. Until recently, it was afforded precarious footing for even the large ranches like French's and the later 7T and Rock Creek spreads.

What Peter French was looking for, he found in the southern drainage of Harney Basin, in the beautiful Blitzen River Valley.[20] Nearly 80 percent of all the moisture that accumulates annually on Steens Mountain flows into this valley and sustains the gently meandering Blitzen River the year round. The total area of the drainage pattern, which includes the long western slope of Steens Mountain, encompasses 500 square miles of land. The river course itself runs due north through a rich natural hay meadow nearly forty miles long and up to seven or eight miles wide. Its northern terminus is the broad marsh of Malheur Lake. John Scharff, former superintendent of the Malheur Wildlife Refuge, describes this valley as "one of the smaller watersheds . . . and probably the most productive for its size."[21]

The soil throughout the valley is dark, rich volcanic soil, which has been deposited in deep, uniform layers for many eons. Beaver contributed to its richness during the centuries before irrigation and artificial drainage. The natural hay of the valley seldom yields today less than one and one-half tons to the acre which is about the same as the yield in the time of Peter French.[22]

The long west slope of the Steens was once covered with a dense carpet of fescue grass, but overgrazing has long since replaced it with sagebrush. Some surviving remnants of grass hug the topmost ridges at about the 9000 foot level. Even hardy sheep of more recent times have had only limited access to it. Its absence down the slope causes sheet erosion of the lighter soil. Still, various morainal deposits scattered here and there on the mountain support thick aspen groves and tangles of mountain shrubs.

Water is more plentiful in the Blitzen drainage than in most areas of the county, but stream flow fluctuates radically during the year. Glacial action has gouged out several steep gorges, particularly the spectacular natural flumes through which Kiger, Krumbo, Riddle, and McCoy creeks flow. With the exception of Kiger Creek, which has the most stable and sustained flow, these streams disgorge nearly three-quarters of their entire volume of water each spring. To complicate matters for early settlers, during the years of heavy snows and drifting on the Steens the effluent is retarded and planning consequently hindered. The Blitzen River itself is more predictable, averaging 87,600 acre feet of water per year with peak months in May and June and sharply diminished flow in July. Throughout the valley, any increases in natural productivity depend today, as they did in the past, on artificial stream diversion and control.[23]

Two tributary streams, Diamond Creek and Riddle Creek, plunge down steep walls into two narrow but highly productive valleys. Diamond Valley opens onto the Blitzen meadow south of the lava flow formed by Diamond Craters; Riddle Creek empties into an interior basin called Barton Lake, but not before it waters a rich alluvial plain named Happey Valley. Each valley is a sheltered enclave, free from the more severe extremes of cold and heat and hidden safely away from the more destructive effects of Harney County's winter storms. The whole of the Blitzen Valley, in fact, benefits from a high ridge on the west called Jackass Mountain. Winds and weather are moderated to a slight but important degree by this protective rim.

From the beginning of settlement in 1872 cattlemen, settlers, sheepherders, and Indians vied for this choice region, and the contention has continued in one form or another far into the twentieth century. Peter French faced this conflict literally from the moment he got off his horse. To be sure, settlement was sparse and widely dispersed, but there was a nucleus of families in both Diamond and Happy valleys, in addition to the increasing number of settlers moving into Harney Valley north of Malheur and Harney lakes within the protective reach of the U.S. Army's Camp Harney.

The presence of any settlers was somewhat surprising.

Aside from the surveys conducted for military wagon roads in the early 1860s, nothing much had leaked out about this region—certainly nothing that would attract anyone to come and set up a permanent home. Popular accounts before that time had held that the area was uninhabitable except for a few savages, who were welcome to it. Three wagon trains of settlers had gone through the Malheur and Harney Lake region under less than ideal conditions by 1853. The first of them, in 1848, had been attacked by Indians near the shores of Malheur Lake; the others were constantly harassed. None stayed longer than it took to fill their canteens or bed down for a night. Yet even then there were those among the immigrants of Elijah Elliot's train who remembered the glimpse they had gotten of the country at the mouth of the Blitzen Valley. Besides, the Willamette Valley was filling up—according to some of its more restless settlers. One of the earliest families to contribute to the "spillover" of population from that valley into eastern Oregon in the 1870s was the George A. Smyth clan, members of Elliot's luck-starved caravan of 1853. Despite the memory of Indian harassments, short rations, and weeks of wandering lost, Smyth, his wife, Margaret, and their eight children left their donation claim near Roseburg to settle in Diamond Valley in 1873.[24] There had been earlier arrivals: A. H. Robie had brought a small herd of cattle from Idaho and had claimed sizable chunks of land in the Blitzen Valley. His diamond brand gave the tributary valley and the stream running through it their names. Mace McCoy was there from northern California, applying himself to a claim in the southwest segment of the valley. Across the ridge to the east, the Riddle family gave their energies to setting up a home and their name to the creek watering Happy Valley.[25]

There is no indication that French might have seen the portent of the few pitiful earthen and frame huts that flecked his self-proclaimed kingdom in 1872; confident that all the Blitzen Valley and its tributaries were or at least would be his, he turned his cattle loose to forage. The settlers, for their part, neither wished for nor got trouble from French. The country was too raw and new, and Indians were still a potential threat. For the time being at least, the eagle and the sparrows would tend their own nests.

The metaphor has pertinence among Harney County people. Bill Hanley, one such eagle in his own right, a quarter of a century later often sat on the front stoop at his Double-O ranch after an evening meal to watch the great birds soar in the clear evening sky. Hanley found the sight "uplifting," and scarcely an evening passed without his being able to watch one or two float high over Harney Lake on the way to aeries in Eagle Rock, southeast across the lake from his cabin.[26] The so-called rock is actually a mesa ridge nearly six miles long, the northernmost rim of the Jackass Mountains. Jackass Creek, at most times of the year a dry gulch, runs north out of these mountains toward Harney Lake. Except during wet years, the water runs off into a marshy flat or simply collects in stagnant pools and evaporates before a drop reaches the lake bed.

The bed itself is broad and flat; before settlement and irrigation, there were times when it was full, but never over a few feet deep. Since settlement, nearly the only water reaching the lake collects in a shallow perimeter fed by the springs around the OO and by the runoff of Silver Creek to the north. A moderate wind storm out of the northwest will send the water skidding across the lake's level white alkali surface, holding it in the opposite end until the wind dies.[27]

The quality of soil north and northeast of this shallow evaporating pond is mostly first- and second-class alluvium interspersed with sandy and some alkaline soils, all deposited by Silver Creek and the several springs of Warm Springs Valley. Silver Creek itself is a perennial stream running south out of the Blue Mountains through a wide desert valley nearly forty miles long. First-class soil is distributed along the river bed in layers of irregular thickness and breadth—narrowest where the geological uplift forming Squaw Butte and its attendant ridging has forced the stream to carve a shallow defile through hard sedimentary layers separating Silver Creek Valley in the north from the Warm Springs Valley in the south.[28]

Average annual rainfall in the Silver Creek watershed is around twelve inches, with most of it falling in the form of snow in the mountains. Thick stands of ponderosa pine attest to ample moisture at higher elevations, but the Silver Creek runoff is neither as plentiful nor as stable as the water supply in the Blitzen Valley. Settlement has been more limited as a result. Local appraisers working in the area in 1957 accurately assessed its history: "Except for those lands carrying water rights and which have been suitable for irrigation, [this region] . . . has not been considered a district with appreciable agricultural land use potential."[29] Thus the bucolic scene that is upper Silver Creek in the spring—a blue stream winding through a green valley nestled between forest covered mountains—is a scene born of first impressions; after the spring runoff it is more accurately a pastoral scene. The entire length of the valley is covered today with the same natural vegetation as in earlier days; bunch grass, rye grass, bluestem, native clover, and various browse plants such as buckbrush, bitterbrush, and white sage predominate.

Warm Springs Valley, the choice region in the lower portion of the Silver Creek drainage, was claimed first by Riley and Hardin, one of the four great cattle empires of early Harney County history. Like the Whitehorse Ranch and the P Ranch of Peter French, the OO has never been subdivided into smaller spreads. Even during periods of heavy settler influx into the unclaimed segments of Warm Springs Valley, it was always Double O country under Riley and Hardin and later under Bill Hanley as it is today as a part of the Malheur National Wildlife Refuge.[30]

A handful of early settlers staked their claims in Silver Creek Valley to the north, and, as in the south, the land-use pattern has with a few dramatic exceptions remained basically unaltered since that day. Cattle kings and homeseekers, separated only by a shrub-covered, low-lying ridge, both drawing sustenance from the same imperfect umbilicus, have lived with a remarkable degree of harmony considering the potential for conflict. As in the Blitzen Valley, the sparsity of population, the newness of settlement, and the very real hazards to life and property contributed to peaceful accommodation. Camp Curry, the military outpost in Silver Creek Valley, symbolized what safety and stability there was during the first decade of settlement.[31] Its later abandonment removed both the outside threat and the symbol of harmony and placed the burden of accommodation squarely on the shoulders of the people in the two valleys. Subsequent history tells a story of forbearance not common to much of the rest of the county.

A more complex situation developed from the first attempts to settle the Silvies River watershed to the east, particularly the area of overflow land in Harney Valley. Here the river divides into two meandering forks that part and reunite aimlessly until they empty through numberless mouths into the marsh of Malheur Lake. The whole system carries the largest volume of water of the three major streams draining Harney Basin. Its source is the Aldrich Mountains in the Strawberry Range far to the north, and its course is through 1,290 square miles of some of the richest land in southeastern Oregon. An exceptionally lovely mountain valley—the Silvies Valley on the north border of present-day Harney County—comprises a small part of it, but the major part is in the south, where the Silvies emerges from a shallow canyon through which it has borne the saline and sodic soils of the Blue Mountains for ages and spread them onto an alluvial plain embracing over 26,000 acres of land. The upland rims of this plain are composed of first-class chestnut lithosol soils, but water is scarce. The vegetation is largely sagebrush interspersed with bluestem and bunch grasses. The northern edge of the valley is watered by intermittent streams that tumble out of the several parallel troughs in the low south wall of the Blue Mountain uplift. This "creek country", as its residents refer to it, provides some protection from the weather as well as limited amounts of rich bottom land and fairly stable water supplies.[32]

The region's earliest visitors saw the whole of Harney Valley either from Drinkwater Pass over the Stinking Water Mountains in the west, or framed in the "V" cut by Rattlesnake Creek as they descended toward Camp Harney from the north. Many were convinced that the green meadows at the fork of the Silvies could be made to grow grain and provide for the families of immigrant farmers. Diversion ditches and dams would be needed so that the spring floods could be checked, and the tens of thousands of acres that were sometimes awash for as long as a month during the early summer could be reclaimed and farmed. None of this, of course, could happen in the eastern half of the valley until it was opened to settlement; in 1872, the federal government had reserved this half as a part of the Malheur Indian Reservation. The eight families who squatted in the western half of the valley were hardly in a position to do more than fashion crude, inefficient breastworks, which often as not failed even to keep their shacks dry.[33]

At the same time settlers began to show interest, however, ranchers became more visible. John Devine of the Whitehorse Ranch and Tom Overfelt—soon to be associated with the largest of the big outfits in Harney County, Miller & Lux—started independently to secure control over the valley as a winter range. By 1879, the valley came to be inhabited by about ten or twelve families and fifty or sixty vaqueros herding and feeding livestock. To all appearances the picture was little different from the Silver Creek or Blitzen River drainage; but it was here in this rich valley that nearly all of the familiar types in the drama of westward advance intermingled at one time or another: Indians, cattle kings, sodbusters, speculators, town builders, and promoters, disparate elements in a complex history of adjustments and accommodation.

The boundary of the Malheur Indian Reservation removed from entry not only choice Harney Valley land but the well-watered bottomland and timbered regions of the Middle Fork of the Malheur River as well. This drainage is not a part of the Harney Basin system; it is a tributary of the Snake River and thus a part of the Pacific watershed. Several snow-fed streams flow into it from the Strawberry range and from the Stinking Water Mountains, making the Middle Fork the most stable supply of water in the county. To the Paiutes the surrounding country was ideal for hunting, with its mountain forest shelter, its long triangular parks and meadows, and its pure mountain river where deer and antelope watered in the evening. However, wherever wild game could feed and grow fat, cattle and sheep could do the same; and where water could be counted upon, hay and perhaps grain could be raised. Thus big and little operators alike ignored the boundary of the reservation from the very beginning. The country would go to the quickest if not the shrewdest, and they and their families would persist longer on their original claims than settlers anywhere else in the county.

One other minor watershed linked Harney County settlement with the Malheur drainage: Crane Creek, east of Malheur Lake. This creek taps water from both the Steens and the Stinking Water mountains, then runs through the jumbled formations where the Steens Mountain fault block ends and the Blue Mountain uplift begins. Once a sluiceway draining Harney basin to the sea, this region has become a low barrier sealing off Malheur and Harney lakes from the continental watershed. Crane Creek parallels the ancient egress over a short distance, then curves north to form the South Fork of the Malheur River. The watershed has good soil but receives less precipitation than the region of the Middle Fork; the surrounding country is more like the deserts to the south. Settlement has been dispersed and partially isolated as a result.

It is possible that there has seldom been a more striking example of the arbitrary nature of political boundaries than those defining Harney County. The six major subregions are as distinguishable today as they were in the eyes of the first visitors who left any account of them; yet they defied early attempts to define their best use. The limits of farming and cattle raising, though not really segmented, were never wholly clear. In addition, the gold deposits of the Blue Mountains never extended to that part of the range which lies in Harney County, though pyrite and quartz deposits were there and an occasional small strike was made, usually by someone who had come to farm. In the same way, the gold fields of the Sierra Nevada fault block had no counterparts in the Steens, though experienced miners refused to believe it until after the turn of the century.

Geographically, then, Harney County was not the Rocky Mountain West, nor the great interior basin, nor the Pacific Slope, though it contained elements of each. The first white inhabitants brought with them cultural traditions that could be traced ultimately from two wholly different origins. It was the same kind of meeting place for these white men it had been for the Indians: a place of little coherence, a geographical and cultural transition zone subject to outside influences.[34] Despite examples of persistence and efforts at accommodation, it has not, until recently, afforded a great measure of social or economic security, and it has always been a unified but heterogeneous community afflicted since birth with chronic double vision.

CHAPTER TWO

The Heroic Years: 1869-1889

In the three decades after Appomattox, the great social and industrial forces that were transforming America before the Civil War continued at a greatly accelerated rate. Millions of new immigrants, most from non-English-speaking countries, poured into urban centers; an even greater number of them found homes in the vast interior empire west of the 98th meridian and east of the tier of Pacific states.[1] This was the last and greatest of the American frontiers. Into it flowed much of the nation's energy and wealth, and out of it gushed profits that encouraged still greater investments and helped, in the process, to open up millions of new acres of land to cattle raising, farming, and mining—fields in which promoters and speculators mingled with cowpunchers, sodbusters, and prospectors in one of the most exuberant treasure hunts in the history of modern capitalism.

The need for transportation facilities to and from the new land offered a gold-plated opportunity to eager investors. From 1865 to 1873, 30,000 miles of railroad track were laid in America, much of it in or to the West. By 1900, 150,000 miles of track had been laid since the Civil War.[2] These advancing rails injected dynamism into other industries. Quickest to respond was the mining industry. Completion of the transcontinental railroad sent stock in western mines soaring. After 1863, more expensive equipment was hauled out west where well-organized and well-financed mining companies, using stamp mills and mercury processing plants, extracted and processed in a single week the equivalent of nearly a decade's production from a hand-powered rocker box.[3] These same railroads carried in their shiny new cars cattlemen and merchants who came to strike it rich in the service of gold-seekers.

The cattle industry was born of a rapidly expanding eastern market and was sustained by a growing transportation network that helped encourage a number of willing investors from both at home and abroad.[4] Between 1865 and 1885 the cattle industry became a bonanza of the first magnitude. Farmers, by contrast, reaped only modest rewards. Yet urban industrial growth opened markets never before available, and most farmers responded by consolidating their holdings and buying machinery when they could—or, when they could not, which was often the case, by moving out across the Great Plains to start anew. In one sense cheap land provided a way for farmers to avoid the expense of modernization, but by 1885 subsistence farming was largely a thing of the past. The railroad network, together with the perfection of the windmill, the invention of the barbed-wire fence, and later the development of modern techniques of dry farming, gave the American agriculturist most of the tools he needed to farm profitably on the treeless plains.[5]

As Americans entered the last quarter of the nineteenth century, a new generation looked forward to a future of seemingly limitless material progress. A good deal of their optimism was drawn from the promise of the West. Horace Greeley had extolled its virtues even before the Civil War; after the war, his words began to stimulate the vision of ambitious men throughout the whole spectrum of American society.[6] For the man on the make, there was more to be made and less in the way of his making it than ever before. Even political and social reformers, increasingly aware of the discrepancy between new opportunity and the number of people who were enjoying it, accepted material progress as the great new harbinger of social progress.

This tremendous national outpouring of energy and confidence influenced the settlement of remote southeastern Oregon just as it did the conquest of the Great Plains and the building of the Brooklyn Bridge. When the father of the now legendary Harney County rancher Bill Hanley told his son in 1890: "Go 'til you find a big country, for you will never get any bigger than the country you are in," he was voicing not only traditional pioneer hopes but the expansionist sentiments of an age.[7]

Prologue to Settlement

Rodman Paul has said that "of all the new regions that opened to mining during the 1860s, Idaho and Montana came the closest to making a reality of the dream of finding a new California."[8] In the Boise Basin just east of Oregon's border, seasoned "yonder-siders" from California and hopeful eastern "pilgrims" who were trying their luck for the first time in the western gold fields joined an assortment of disappointed Colorado gold-seekers, Nevada miners, midwestern farmers, and cattlemen to form a thriving community of nearly 16,000 souls by 1862. A number of the gold-seekers among them went farther west that same year to test the rumors of new strikes in Oregon's Blue Mountains.

Most of the approximately 5,000 gold-seekers who burst into central Oregon on the heels of the Canyon City strike in 1862 came from Idaho, but some came from the Willamette Valley and some from California by way of Portland or The Dalles. A few resolute California argonauts came through Nevada directly to the mines.[9]

Just as the territory of Idaho had been a child of the Boise Basin and Clearwater River mines, Grant and Union counties issued from the mines of Canyon City and the Blue Mountains.[10] County organization did not mean the advent of county services. Roads remained hazardous traces cared for perfunctorily by local citizens, and then only over short distances close to town. Early western frontier communities, despite their professed community spirit, were commonly neither willing nor able to support the kind of road building necessary to encourage more permanent settlement and build more stable economies.[11] Most of them preferred to badger state governments for their roads. Oregon politicians, from Joe Lane's time until the railroads came, knew the political value of obtaining government assistance for wagon roads, but as often as not their advocacy was a charade acted out to win votes.

Political rhetoric or no, there were only three government-surveyed military wagon roads across southeastern Oregon in 1869 and all three had been privately financed.[12] A frustrated and impatient group of Linn County cattlemen organized the Willamette Valley Wagon Road Company, hoping thereby to gain early access to eastern Oregon ranges. Later, another private concern carved a road from Eugene to the Idaho line, crossing the old Fort Haryen—Winnemucca wagon road at Camp C. F. Smith, near the site of the Whitehorse Ranch in southeastern Oregon. During most of the 1860s and 1870s both of these roads were barely distinguishable from the game trails and gullies they crossed. The third—the Dalles Military Wagon Road—sustained Canyon City even though it was impassable in the winter, while the part between Canyon City and Fort Harney, seventy-five miles south, became more passable only as it became more heavily traveled.[13]

During the mid-1860s, a number of scientists, adventurers, soldiers, and prospective homeseekers found their way into the vicinity of Fort Harney. In a short time the fort became an important hub of early traffic going either south to Nevada, or north to Canyon City, or west to the older settled areas of Oregon; travel eastward was always precarious, and Indian depredations in the 1860s made it even more so.[14]

At the same time that Fort Harney was assuming some importance as a crossroads sanctuary for travelers and hopeful settlers, Canyon City was losing population as the flush days came to an end in 1868.[15] The county seat remained in Canyon City, but its population was only a small sober residue of its boom-town beginnings. In 1868, the two settlements of Canyon City and Fort Harney, each dependent upon the other for certain complementary needs, comprised an isolated little interior community organized around the extractive industries of mining and cattle raising. The valley surrounding Canyon City provided agricultural staples of grain and fruits; the town itself provided the amenities. Harney Valley, despite its increasing population, was clearly tributary by comparison, but the fort served as both the symbol and the source of community security and stability.[16]

Several events coincided in the 1860s to change the economic and social character of this community and set the stage for the beginning of permanent settlement in Harney Valley. In 1866, General George Crook, commander of Fort Harney, brought the Bannock and Paiute Indians to the council table after a systematic campaign of intimidation and force. A peace treaty was signed in 1869 to establish a Paiute reservation but, incomprehensibly, without providing it with a definite boundary. Nonetheless, the decade that followed its signing was free enough of Indian trouble to encourage pioneers. By the time a reservation boundary was finally established in 1872, it embraced the claims of several cattlemen and settlers who quite understandably had no intention of relinquishing them.[17] Though tensions were high, no fighting occurred. Crook's superior forces, abetted by Paiute disunity, kept the peace and settlers continued to trickle in.

More important for settlement was the completion of the Oregon-Washington Railway and Navigation Company line through the Columbia Gorge to Walla Walla in 1875. In that year immigrants from the West Coast could reach The Dalles by rail and from there could travel on to southeastern Oregon with much less difficulty than the miners had encountered a decade before.[18] The economic potential of the Central Pacific Railroad, already completed along a line running through Winnemucca south of the Oregon-Nevada boundary, attracted the large cattle owners who came into southeastern Oregon from California and Nevada during the late 1860s and early 1870s. Their move was prompted also by a series of California "herd laws" passed through the influence of Sacramento Valley wheat farmers in 1864. Severe droughts between 1864 and 1868 were an added impellent, so that by 1869 the surplus cattle of northern California were becoming the stocking herds of southeastern Oregon and of the broad inland empire of open range that included northwestern Nevada and southwestern Idaho.[19]

The coincidence within a decade of all these circumstances made southeastern Oregon at once more peaceable and economically more attractive, at a time when the settlers in more populated areas were becoming more restless and when large cattleowners in California and Nevada were being displaced. The movement of both settlers and cattlemen into southeastern Oregon coincided—an exception to the general pattern of farmer "encroachments" on the open range, and one which had far-reaching social implications in the development of southeastern Oregon.[20]

Early Settlement Patterns

Settlement flowed into southeastern Oregon in the 1870s from two major sources: the Willamette Valley and California. Those who came from the Willamette Valley were largely aspiring farmers; those who came from California, primarily large-scale cattle raisers or their employees. The Willamette Valley migrants were more numerous and ultimately became the more important of the two.

The Willamette Valley had a substantial population in 1870. The Donation Land Act of 1850 had attracted thousands; the appeal of temperate climate and fertile land attracted thousands more, so that by 1870, 64,749 or Oregon's 90,923 inhabitants lived west of the Cascade Mountains. Yet there were forces at work that encouraged out-migration from the valley during the decade that followed. For one thing, the cost of improved land was becoming more than the average pioneer could pay. Larger farmers had already begun to consolidate, and the portions of land left for homesteading were considered inferior or not worth the effort.[21] Consequently newcomers in the 1870s, as well as "old-timers" who had failed to establish farms in the marginal or heavily wooded areas, turned their hopes toward Oregon's remaining frontiers in the eastern part of the state.

A small but steady stream of these people moved out of the great valley toward The Dalles. The heaviest flow went east to the Palouse district of the Columbia Basin, but a trickle found its way into southeastern Oregon. The completion of the Oregon-Washington Railroad accelerated this general movement eastward. Simultaneously, some established stock farmers from the valley were beginning to look for bonanza opportunities in the interior ranges east of the Cascades. By 1875, western Oregonians had begun a recognizable and soon-to-be extensive colonization movement into eastern and southeastern Oregon in the same manner and at the same time that the settlers of the Cowlitz, Nisqually, and Puget Sound regions were colonizing southeastern Washington.[22]

The significance of this migration into southeastern Oregon is reflected in the federal census of 1880. The region now comprising Harney County then contained 419 people. Although those of midwestern origins comprised nearly 33 percent of this population, only a small proportion had come directly from the Middle West.[23] Most had gone first to the Willamette Valley, having moved an average of three times on their way west.

These newcomers settled mostly in the north end of the Harney region, an area north of an imaginary line drawn east to west through Harney and Malheur lakes. In the manner of land-seekers elsewhere, they avoided sites where there was no water or timber and where the land was broken or seemingly infertile. Early arrivals took river-bottom land and never had cause to regret their choice.[24] Into all these areas settlers brought some cattle and at least two horses each—more if they were family men, which most of them were not, though many had wives and children or sweethearts visiting in western Oregon or "back east" waiting for news that the cattle had been sold in Canyon City or Fort Harney and that prospects looked good enough for them to come to southeastern Oregon and set up a home.

In the Oregon of the 1870s diversified farming on the large scale was supplanting the earlier Willamette Valley stock-raising industry and putting pressure on the small settlers. Concurrently, bonanza farming in northern California was putting the cattle industry and the few small settlers of that region to disadvantage. Both these circumstances affected the settlement of Harney County. Small stock raisers from Plumas County, California, and the region around Sonoma began to follow the trails of the California cattle barons into southeastern Oregon. A number settled in Pueblo Valley, while others found sites in the shadow of Steens Mountain. A few went north into the Crane Creek and Stinking Water River drainages; but more preempted or homesteaded parcels around present-day Burns and in Harney Valley. Most of these California settlers had been born in the Middle West and had gone through the same rootless pattern of migration as had their northern neighbors.[25]

Taken as a whole, the data in the Census of 1880 show that the typical Harney County homeseeker was a man between twenty-five and thirty-five years old who had started life in the Middle West and had moved with his parents at an early age to California or the Willamette Valley. In the tradition of the day, he had left home as a young man to seek his fortune by working at a number of typical frontier pursuits, such as mining, farming, and stock-raising. Generally he married in his 30s and upon coming to the Harney country took up a preemption or homestead in the better-watered sections at a time when good unappropriated land in the Northwest was becoming scarce. If he was among the 26 percent who were tenacious enough to stay more than a decade, by 1880 he would have seen two out of every three of his neighbors move away to be replaced by others. Most of these men had been farmers or had worked on farms at some prior time. Together with the great wave of homeseekers who came during the 1880s they formed the solid core of settlement that helped shape and later came to dominate the social and political life of Harney County in the twentieth century.

The history of settlement in the south end of the county was quite different. In 1868, the same year that a farmer from western Oregon, J. J. Cozart, plowed a few acres of land near Fort Harney to plant the area's first crop of grain, an enterprising immigrant from Missouri named David Shirk drove a herd of Texas longhorns into the Trout Creek country southeast of Steens Mountain. The herd belonged to English-born John Catlow of Silver City, Idaho. This drive introduced the first longhorns into the area and represented the first serious attempt to exploit the open ranges of the Harney County region.[26] Although longhorns never figured importantly in the development of the Harney County cattle business, Catlow's methods of exploitation did.

He began by claiming a homestead on Trout Creek; with it, he was able to gain control of the water of one of the two major streams flowing north out of the Trout Creek Mountains. He then hired Shirk to work his herd of approximately 800 cattle in the vicinity of Alvord Basin. The herd grew to 4,000 within seven years.[27] By these simple procedures Catlow anticipated the methods of the great "cattle kings" who came between 1869 and 1873—French and Glenn, Todhunter and Devine, Riley and Hardin, and Miller and Lux, the Oregon rangeland counterparts of the industrial tycoons of the last quarter of the nineteenth century.[28] The composition of society in what was then coming to be known as the "south end" quite predictably revealed some marked differences from that of the north.

Census data shows that the average age in the south end was slightly higher and there were fewer family men in this region, where 123 people lived in scattered clumps of settlement—mostly near the French-Glenn ranch headquarters in the upper Donner and Blitzen Valley and at the foot of the Steens to the southeast as well as in the Trout Creek drainage further south.[29] Half of these people were cowpunchers working for wages. Among them were several of the California vaqueros who had come with the cattle kings. Among the remaining half of the population, eleven listed themselves as independent stock raisers, six as farmers, and the rest as carpenters, teamsters, blacksmiths, or gold miners. There were no professional men, nor were there any merchants or other entrepreneurs such as are usually associated with more stable communities. The ratio of women to men was lower there than in the north. Only twenty-five females were listed in the census, and all but three of them were either wives or children. In short, the south end bore all of the statistical markings of a raw frontier.[30] Whatever stable or civilizing force there was was neither church, town, nor school; it was the cattle corporations, whose influence, as always, acted more to retard permanent settlement than to promote it.

During the 1870s the Fort Harney-Canyon City axis continued to serve as a linkage for society north of the lakes. In the south there was little social integration. French's interior empire was largely self-sustaining. So was Devine's. The two military camps of Alvord and C. F. Smith were mere outposts on the Winnemucca Road. Isaac Foster, the OO Ranch foreman, was more frequently in contact with his California provisioners than with the settlers and soldiers of Camp Currey, forty miles farther north on Silver Creek, or Fort Harney, just a half-day's ride to the northeast. The organization of the economy in each of the two sections, together with their differing cultural backgrounds, habits, and customs, kept the two regions distinct if not wholly apart.

The Economics of Survival

A modern Northwest scholar has commented: "Few settlers [in the Northwest] wanted to establish subsistence farms as the early American colonists had done."[31] The settlers of the north end were, however, taking up homesteads on one of the last frontiers: a dry and isolated segment of the country that was hundreds of miles from the nearest railroad. The chief task confronting them was not one of making money; it was one of survival. Their purchases at Fort Harney and in Canyon City were infrequent and largely on credit; their meager capital was mostly in the form of dwindled savings.[32] As with the first comers since the first American colonists they were subsistence farmers by force of circumstances, whatever their original choice.

Still, land was cheap and there were several ways in which a homeseeker might acquire it during the 1870s. He could file on a homestead and take a preemption concurrently. After 1873, under terms of the Timber Culture Act, he could acquire an additional quarter section of land if he met the provision to plant and cultivate some trees. Further flexibility was introduced with the passage of the Desert Land Act in 1877, which gave title to an entire section of desert land to anyone who could reclaim it within two years. Besides these federal acts, Oregon had its own land grant program. The Swampland Act of 1870, for example, offered unreclaimed swampland at a dollar an acre with ten years to pay. This was land that the United States government had granted to the state and, in places like southeastern Oregon, it was of high quality. There were abuses of these laws; but they made some good land available to early settlers in the Harney country.[33] The difficulty lay in whether they would be able to make anything out of it.

Southeastern Oregon pioneers, nearly all of whom had some farming experience, considered Harney Valley potential agricultural land; but the range was excellent, and the difficulties involved in draining marshland and damming streams led them instead to stock raising. An early pioneer, Homer Mace, described the process in the following way:

> It [Harney Valley south of Burns] looked like good farmland, but nobody was farming on it. I started my building right then and there and lived there in a kind of shack. . . . When I got located, I fenced my land and built me a house, there was plenty of game, the next season I started in to irrigate and I built as long as I was able. I started a dam to get the water out, but I let it go. . . . I used the land for hay . . . the first year and I was there and I used it for hay every year afterward.[34]

Later on, 1893, he filed on what became known as "Mace Desert," a piece of dry pastureland near the outer rim of Harney Basin. This perimeter gave him what he needed for a rudimentary cattle operation.

Mace's energies went into providing shelter, water, food, and forage for his cattle, roughly in that order. It took him six years to get established, and he worked alone. Others relied on neighbors, but the length of time was frequently as long.[35] One of the hired hands for the great Pacific Livestock Company recalled years later only that the early settlers in this region were generally a poor lot who "might have had some cattle and a few horses."[36]

Still, the 1870s saw the rude beginning of settlement in nearly all the accessible valleys of the north end. In all of them, the chief variable in the scheme of survival was the water. If one were to persist until transportation came or markets improved, he had to control at least enough stream flow to water his stock.[37] But for every Mace who acquired a water right and persisted during those early years, there were many others who gave up and moved on, perhaps to repeat the same pattern elsewhere. Bill Hanley described them poignantly:

> settlers drifting in with their little herds, looking for a likely water hole and a piece of land, settling for a while and drifting out again; couldn't stand the strain of trying to drive their crop 300 miles or more to a shipping point. Those who stayed, always dreaming of when a railroad would come through, raised their children on that hope—and their grandchildren.[38]

The larger owners in the south end had neither children to encourage nor hopes waiting to be fulfilled. For Peter French there was no struggle putting up buildings or constructing dams. At the very outset he had twelve good ranch hands cutting juniper off Steens Mountain and putting up corrals, shacks, and outbuildings at the south end of the Blitzen Valley while the rest of his thirty or forty buckaroos were pushing his cattle into the higher ranges. At the end of his first season French was ready to drive cattle north. John Devine, after only three years, was reputed to have from 15,000 to 30,000 head of neat cattle on his Trout Creek ranges. Ike Foster needed only to ask his employers for the supplies and materials to make the OO a first-class operation.[39]

Miller and Lux bought out Tom Overfelt's holdings on the Malheur River in the mid-1870s, then skillfully used the Desert Land Act after 1877 to augment this acquisition, thus foreshadowing the most extensive and enduring monopoly in southeastern Oregon's history.

From the very beginning, the economy of southeastern Oregon was principally in the hands of these four giants. While the settlers of the north end struggled with limited interior markets and chafed at the presence of the Malheur Reservation, which barred their path to the northern ranges, the south-end "rancheros" consolidated their positions behind their respective mountain ramparts and forged increasingly lucrative connections with national markets.[40]

Early Cultural and Economic Symbiosis

Despite the aspirations of the settlers, there was little overt resentment against "big men." For example, rustling was infrequent. Furthermore, the large owners did not feel constrained to organize themselves into cattlemen's associations in order to protect their rights against farmer encroachment. Not until the late 1870s was such an association formed, and then not for those purposes. In the meantime something resembling a symbiotic economic relationship developed between large cattlemen and small stock-farmers—a relationship that carried over into the social life of the region.

In order to illustrate this symbiosis, it is important briefly to describe the techniques of the cattle business. Cattle were raised on the open range, and, as David Shirk, a pioneer cattleman of the south end, described the methods, they were "simple in the extreme." Cattle were rounded up in the spring, branded, and turned loose on the range until fall, when they were rounded up again and shipped to market. Naturally, there were subtleties of management. The nature of the country, the size of the herd, and the exigencies of weather had to be reckoned with. Shirk himself admitted the need for experienced hands and adherence to some general rules of the Oregon rangeland. Still, enough has been written about open-range methods of cattle raising to suggest that eastern Oregon practices represented only minor variations on a theme.[41] Little or no hay was put up for either cattle or saddle horses, and although southeastern Oregon range barons took greater care in feeding and breeding cattle than most of their contemporaries elsewhere, the business was essentially speculative and the methods were those best suited to bringing the largest return at the least expense. Old-timers called these methods "rawhiding," and the term was apt. Cattle were wagered against weather, disease, and a fluctuating market. A bad gamble was paid off at spring roundup when the carcasses were counted against the survivors.

Large cattlemen were better equipped to survive such setbacks, yet smaller owners bent on staying survived because, paradoxically, the cattle barons themselves helped provide some real economic stability. With some significant exceptions, the clusters of settlers in the north and the occasional home seekers in the south not only gained their livelihoods but also modified some of their social and cultural habits under the influence of their large neighbors. The stories of David and Bill Shirk and the family of James Rankin Crow are good examples of these interrelationships in the south end.

David Shirk began his career in southeastern Oregon as a hired herder for John Catlow. He became manager of Catlow's interests on Trout Creek and served in that capacity until 1876, when Catlow sold his stock to Peter French. By that time Shirk had learned the business. He bought cattle with his savings and filed a homestead claim on Home Creek in Catlow Valley at the same time that his brother Bill, with whom he rarely spoke, took up a claim on 3-mile Creek a short distance to the south. The two accumulated between 200 and 600 head of cattle. Still, according to oldtimer Rankin Crow, "they were considered small operators; but they held the key to the Catlow Valley, controlling most of the water."[42]

The Shirks' only other serious rival was French. Yet no animosity emerged between them during the 1870s, even after David Shirk illegally fenced portions of the public domain. French was, of course, doing the same, but there was grass enough to go around. Besides, the mid-decade years were wet years, and Indians were still a potential aggravation. Both Shirk and French had ridden the same country and, as was the custom, had shared the responsibilities of the spring and fall roundups when all cattleowners, large and small, joined in gathering up the cattle and separating them by brands. These oft-repeated patterns bred interdependence alongside rugged self-reliance. Real friendship developed between David Shirk and French, a friendship not unlike that between comrades-in-arms. Both were young men pitting their stamina against a raw country; both worked hard and each enjoyed his rare moments of leisure in the company of other men who worked alongside them.[43]

When it came to enjoying the company of respectable young women, the two young ranchers were lucky, for such company was for south-end swains like them. Even so, visiting was only possible upon formal invitation to a "social" or a dance at the home of the girl's parents or guardian. There the young man of substance was compelled to put forward his best manners. His cowhands had to console themselves with looser kinds of women—drifters themselves—who could be found near Fort Harney or in the bar at Egan. French and

Shirk might drink in that same bar, but the democracy of the saloon never extended into the parlor.

In the 1870s there were few young ladies of quality who wished to stay for long in southeastern Oregon and fewer still who wished to live there. Shirk and French both paid court to the vivacious Frances Crow, a girl accustomed to the rugged life and at home in southeastern Oregon. They competed for her hand without rancor until she consented to marry Shirk. Even then the two got along peacefully until changing social and economic circumstances in the 1880s drove them apart and transformed the memory of their mutually amicable courtships into a source of spiteful hatred that ended in tragedy.

The Crow family was one of the few families homesteading on the east side of the Steens. The original property was located between Mann and Juniper lakes about a morning's ride north from old Camp Alvord. James Rankin Crow, the patriarch, was Frances' uncle and the father of a family of five, three girls and two boys. Crow's eldest son, David, worked for French, first on the Roaring Springs spread in Catlow Valley and then on the Blitzen River property. James himself and his other son, John, hauled freight from Ontario for the big outfits. Later, James became foreman of the Whitehorse Ranch under John Devine.

A homesteader friend, John Witzel, having then located on a piece of French's "accustomed" range in Blitzen Valley, worked for the great man as buckaroo and "rango" in order to keep food on the table while he built his crude home and improved his land. In fact the small homesteaders were a regular enough source of labor to make the big owners reliant upon them during peak seasons.[44] In the summer season the small owners could build fence while their meadow grass grew into winter pastures. They followed the same seasonal directives as the large outfits and in many ways they replicated, on a modest scale, the lifestyles and habits of the large owners. Those lifestyles could be high: Shirk even built his new home with a billiard room, and Crow rode a Spanish mare.[45]

Similar conditions prevailed in the north end, with some significant differences. Here, there were pretensions of farming, and here too there were small communities of settlers gathered in nascent towns like Harney, Burns, Lawen, and Narrows, each of which consisted of fifty people, and the town of Crane, destined to be an important transportation hub, numbering about seventy-five inhabitants. In addition, a straggling line of fifteen or twenty squatters claimed small parcels along the lower Silvies drainage. Several actually built rustic diversion works along the river, either to irrigate the natural hay crop or to raise a stand of grain.[46] The larger owners who shared this area with the settlers were French on the lower Blitzen, Devine on Oregon swampland claims near Camp Wright, and Henry Miller on pieces of ground east of the Silvies. All fell into the basic rhythm of cattle raising already described. Here, however, the method was called "swamping."[47]

The cattle were wintered in the marshes on both the public domain and the Indian reservation on the east side of the Silvies River, where cattails and tules afforded some extra protection from winter winds. North-end cowhands, like their counterparts in the south, lived a life close to hibernation during the winter season. When spring came and the ice broke up on the slow-moving Silvies, cattle were moved north toward the Blue Mountains. By mid-summer Harney Valley mosquitoes helped drovers push the herds high into the mountains, where the cattle fed until fall. Then roundups were again jointly organized; the cattle belonging to settlers were cut out and the big herds driven south to Winnemucca.

Markets for the small men were almost exclusively the small northern communities and the forts. What little they made from yearly sales to these outlets was augmented by wages they earned working cattle for some of the large owners.[48] There were a variety of other opportunities open to them as well. A. H. Robie operated a crude sawmill for local settlers, but his best customers were always the cattle barons—particularly French. Others who were handy with tools, like Homer Mace, found there was money in building corrals and outbuildings. When irrigation of the Silvies River drainage began in earnest in 1878, both settlers and cowmen found profit from this new work: the settlers through employment on the construction of simple dams and gates and the cowmen through the increased productivity of the natural hay.[49] In a very real way settlers who sold hay to the fort were helping it to sustain itself, thereby benefiting the large as well as the small owners who were protected by it. This may or may not be the reason why the settlers were not bothered much by bigger owners when they diverted small amounts of Silvies River water to irrigate their hay land, but it cannot be doubted that while settlement remained sparce, a general harmony of interests helped promote a flexible and rational working arrangement between big and small men over the use of the Silvies River.[50]

This same harmonious interdependence extended to relationships along Silver Creek and the other stream beds of the north end. Tom Allen, ranch hand and later foreman of the OO Ranch, tells of the yearly cycle of cowpunching, roundups, fall marketing, and, by 1880, summer haying. "You see," he begins, "we were all of us working together with the cattle."[51] For him the entire recollection was a social phenomenon. Herding cattle, battling the elements, attending a dance

at Egan: all were descriptive of a way of life, a pattern of personal interrelationships remembered as a whole. It may be reasonable to assume
that even those who did not move up the ladder as Allen did remembered these days with the same fondness.

The center of this society, and of the whole region for that matter,
was Fort Harney. It was news bureau, market, medical center, and
refuge where the tired sodbuster or cowhand could shake off the dust
of a hot summer's trail drive or the cold snow of a stormy winter's
herd-check. The town of Egan was not too far away to get a drink of
whisky, but the first stop was usually the fort. Every bachelor in the
area knew he could get his laundry done there and that the laundress,
Mrs. Kennedy, would have it folded neatly for him when he got back.[52]

On several occasions throughout the year, parties and balls were
held at the fort. Again, supposed drifters or riff-raff were not invited,
but Peter French usually was, and he apparently mixed with the sons
and daughters of midwestern prairie farmers as easily as he did with
his own vaqueros. Most such occasions were holidays accompanied
during mild weather by horseraces and parades, a potpourri of thrills
for young and old alike. Devine invariably entered his horses in the
races and French attended the balls wearing dancing pumps that went
carefully back into his saddle bag when it was time to put on his boots
and ride back to the Blitzen.[53]

At no time, however, were distinctions of status and wealth per-
manently erased, at either the urging of fiddle music or the sharing
of a convivial drink. When the more community-minded citizens of
the Egan-Burns area met in 1875 to organize a school district supported
by voluntary subscription, none of the cattle barons was approached
and none contributed. With the exception of French, the same was true
of the early drive to bring churches and ministers into the area.[54] One
of the few diaries extant, that of David Shirk, reveals many of the prejudices of the agricultural middle class. Shirk condemns on the one side
the large owners who were too often corrupted by wealth and power,
and on the other the irresponsible drifter and transient homeseeker
who was "born in a wagon—here today, there tomorrow."[55]

Though exceptions would abound, a rough outline of social group-
ings based primarily upon wealth and influence in the community
would include cattle barons and military leaders at the top, successful
firstowners and ranch foremen next, then laborers, cowboys, and
drifters in roughly that order, with Indians at the bottom. With the
exception of the Indians, the position of the groups cannot be interpreted as a simple pecking order that all respected. For one thing there
were other cultural criteria that cut across this simple social
schematic—such criteria as the way one rode, or the degree of range
"savvy" one possessed. Nonetheless, Indians and their habits remained

contemptible to whites, and the threat they posed to white security was partly the cause of harmony between the other social groups. Again, Shirk revealed the sentiments typical of white pioneers in general. Indians "work when hunger compels, are subject to all the vices and none of the virtues of the dominant race, and but a few years hence will live alone in song and story."[56] Thus, beneath the surface of harmony there were basic prejudices inimical to it. With the coming of new settlement and the ending of the Indian threat, these potential enmities were stirred up to the boiling point in the 1890s.

Removal of the Indian

According to a U.S. Army report of 1879 on posts in the Division of the Pacific, there were about 750 Paiute Indians on the Malheur Reservation when it was established in 1874.[57] Almost from its inception, pressures mounted to have the reservation abolished. Both large owners and settlers united in a common cause. "[White men] in general . . . considered the difference between governmental land they could use and land they could not use because some Indians were not yet exterminated to be a lawyer's distinction . . . that is, one without a difference."[58] Three-quarters of a century later, in the brief submitted to the Indian Claims Commission on behalf of the disinherited Paiutes, pioneer Mart Brenton remarked: "early settlers [and] stock growers practically pre-empted the reservation land right from under the Indians. There were 13,000 cattle on Indian land before the end of the '70s."[59] Local residents casually referred to the method of stockraising in this region as "the reservation system."

In the spring of 1878, the citizens of Grant County petitioned the federal government to set aside that portion of the Malheur Reservation lying east of the Silvies River. No one acted on the petition. The activities of a conscientious Indian agent, W. B. Rinehart, who was determined against popular pressure to keep the reservation intact, compounded settler discomfort.[60] A few of the bigger men who wished to avoid trouble approached him with a leasing plan. Rinehart seized it as a drowning man would a straw. His strategy had largely been one of guarded retreat in the face of antipathetic local courts and a U.S. Attorney who considered grazing merely a "technical" violation of the law. But even this hopeful plan was dashed when it ran afoul of federal regulations against alienation or leasing of reservation lands.

The whole sordid story is told in great detail in J. Orin Oliphant's impressive work on the early cattle industry in the Oregon country. It needs only to be noted here that the tangle of government regulations emanating from a confused Indian policy helped seal the fate of

Indians in the Harney country as inexorably as it did elsewhere. Rinehart's career was capped with the ultimate frustration for a man of his peaceful convictions—a war between a Bannock-Paiute alliance and the aggressive white settlers of the region. In the summer of 1878, a group of warriors under Chief Egan set out upon one of those desperate campaigns so typical of the Indians' last stand in the late 1870s. The U.S. Army, which had not moved to prevent trespasses, moved swiftly enough to put down the uprising. The Paiutes were removed from the reservation, and the peaceful Winnemuccas, some of whom had allied themselves with the whites, were taken north to a Washington reservation along with the rest.[61]

The war itself—actually more of a raid—had been too precipitous and disorganized seriously to threaten the large cattle herds, much less white settlement.[62] Even before it was over, reservation land was being preempted at an unprecedented rate by previous settlers and some early newcomers who got wind of the impending removal. By 1882, the best land was gone. The following year, the government officially condemned the reservation and "returned" most of the land to the public domain. When the remaining Paiutes wandered back in the mid-1880s as fee-simple "owners" of a few fragments of the old reservation, one old brave spoke for the rest when he asked Milt Davis, who was standing at the door of his newly built cabin, "whose land?" Milt answered, "Mine," to which the old Indian replied, "No! No! All Paiutes"—a cry of resignation rather than a challenge, for by then the Paiutes knew the white man's medicine was irresistible.[63]

From Military to Commercial Province

The years from 1878 to 1882 were in many ways transitional years in the economic and social life of southeastern Oregon. A number of circumstances, both national and local, combined to alter the dynamics of the local economy. There was no radical change in the fundamental pattern of settlement, or in the structure of the livestock business itself. The change was quantitative, involving decisive shifts in land ownership, marketing, and transportation and in the flow of incoming settlers. It was marked by the abandonment of the military posts in the south and the reduction of the garrison at Fort Harney. The decade of the 1880s saw the Harney country change from a military to a commercial province.[64]

With the abandonment of the army posts went one of the most reliable markets for settlers' cattle and hay. If there was any consolation, it was in the empty acres of the Malheur Reservation; but the big cattlemen had the same idea at the same time. The vast surpluses of cattle that subsequently accumulated went far beyond the capacities of these new ranges to absorb them.

Relief from overproduction and its attendant calamity, overgrazing, came in the perverse way of the open-range livestock industry: the two winters of 1879-80 and 1880-81 wiped out the great surpluses entirely and created a deficit from which profits eventually emerged during the nationwide cattle boom of the early 1880s. The range recovered quickly in 1882, but many stockmen did not. Some big owners suffered along with smaller owners, but as a group the latter were hardest hit. Partly as a result, homestead sales were heavy during the early 1880s. The buyers were the big owners, some of whom by that time were reaching for control of the grass and hay land as well as the water.[65] Thus began a period of unprecedented land purchase and consolidation that helped give the large owners of the region nearly complete dominance over the production and marketing of cattle during the 1880s.

A countervailing trend challenged and undermined the dominance of the monopolists at the time of their greatest success. An in-migration of unprecedented proportions occurred between 1880 and 1890.[66] This movement was part of a larger nationwide westward migration spurred by the return of good times after the depression of 1873; these people brought not only ready means and a firm commitment to build anew but the anti-monopoly bias and rhetoric characteristic of those who had lived through the depression in the agricultural communities of the midwest.[67]

Both trends bred more frequent clashes between settlers and cattle barons, especially during the mid-1890s after hard times returned. A detailed look at them reveals the complex interworking of national and local forces in the development of a fringe society striving to enter the mainstream of the national life.

Land Consolidation

Several pressures led the large cattle owners of the 1880s to consolidate their holdings through land purchases of one kind or another. Capital outlays increased with the number of settlers who contended for the range. Higher cattle prices in Chicago, together with the development of better transportation, attracted a larger number of investors, and these factors in turn increased the amount of competition between cattle raisers who sought the available land. The solution for many partnerships and independent owners was to change a corporate form of doing business, which gave them the advantages of limited liability and pooled resources. With capital from new investors, larger owners could buy more land, raise more hay, and improve their methods of cattle raising. The exceptional partnerships—those founded on mutual trust between the financing partner and the manager and blessed as well with competent men in both capacities—entered this competitive, boom phase of the business without severe dislocations. The great partnerships of southeastern Oregon not only persisted but prospered during the decade of the 1880s; but what was true of the business as a whole, was equally true of the partnerships in southeastern Oregon. Their first and major capital outlay after the purchase of cattle had to be for new land.[68]

There were many ways to augment holdings in the 1880s in addition to buying out defeated homesteaders. The plethora of confused and contradictory land laws, together with a corrupt and dilatory land office, conspired in favor of the large owners. Chief among the land laws they used in southeastern Oregon were the Preemption Act, the Desert Land Act of 1877, and the commutation clause of the Homestead Act. Another local inducement was the Oregon Swamp Lands Act of 1870, which was applied to the rich lands north and south of Malheur Lake near the mouths of the Blitzen and Silvies rivers. All of these laws, used sometimes separately and sometimes in conjunction with each other, led to huge engrossments of the public lands before 1890.[69] Each of the great baronial partnerships had its own methods of engrossment, depending upon the financial structure and resources of the partnership, the area being engrossed, the quality of the land, and its intended use.

The partnership of Miller and Lux began in 1858 as a San Francisco butchering firm. Henry Miller's method was to purchase swampland and springs in the San Joaquin and Sacramento valleys, then expand his acreage at the expense of smaller owners during dry years when they were most likely to sell. A local associate of Miller's bought out settlers on the former Malheur Reservation who had given up after the winter of 1880-81. He also bought a large amount of property along the North and Middle forks of the Malheur River encompassing all of what is now called Agency Valley.[70]

Miller and Lux had acquired most of their land up until that time through the purchase of homestead claims and entries as well as through the use of government scrip. The partnership used the Desert Land Act to help it expand southwestward out of Agency Valley into present-day Harney County. By 1880, Miller's boast held that he could drive cattle from the Blue Mountains to San Francisco and stop each night on his own land. In that year along his butchering firm in San Francisco processed 11,000 beeves, 400 hogs, and 2,600 sheep (40 lambs per day in peak season), all raised on ranches owned by the partnership.[71] In all of this expansion the partnership was able to maintain its early reputation for fair dealing. Miller and Lux had stretched the provisions of the Desert Land Act, but they had not resorted to crude or flagrant frauds. The secret behind the Miller and Lux empire was its capital resources, combined with Miller's shrewdness and his thorough knowledge of all aspects of the business from the selling and processing of livestock to the raising of cattle on the open range—a combination of assets few other partnerships could claim.

Todhunter and Devine, another butchering and cattle raising partnership, was not as well capitalized as Miller and Lux. Devine's methods in Harney Valley were legitimate as long as settlement was sparse, but as population pressures gradually increased, he apparently employed more guile. One report has it that Devine bought a piece of land in someone else's name, then had it notarized by a notary in his own employ and transferred the title to his partner in San Francisco with neither the original seller nor his partner being the wiser.[72] The story of his manipulation of the Oregon Swamp Land Act is better documented. Under the provisions of this act, the notorious "Hen" Owen had established claim to thousands of acres of arable land around Malheur Lake. In 1884, Devine purchased about 34,800 acres of this land for $37,069.[73] Original surveys show there were at least 15 squatters already on the land by then. The fraud had been Owen's in misrepresenting the land as swampland, but Devine was considered guilty by association. Out of his purchase came a multitude of bitter and protracted law suits involving individual settlers, the state, and Devine himself. Thus Devine emerged as the archetype of the ruthless monopolist. Settlers' suspicions clung to him even after he had been forced into bankruptcy and had lost his influence in local affairs.[74]

Devine's downfall came from profligacy and land hunger, a fatal combination in an era of rising land prices. The Oregon legislature declared "Hen" Owen's patents illegal in 1887, and speculators snapped them up, forcing the partnership to put its strained resources into the business of buying out these new claimants. In the dry years of 1888-1889, Devine's herds ate the sparse grass to the dirt and sucked the mudholes dry. Thousands of his cattle perished. The partnership went into bankruptcy in 1889, its vast holdings reverting to a receivership of its bankers. When bids were asked, there was only one person there to buy: Henry Miller of Miller and Lux. The price was reputed to have been one million dollars. With this acquisition the Miller and Lux enterprise was reorganized into the Pacific Livestock Company, the largest cattle company in American history.[75] It also acquired in the bargain much of the ill will associated with John Devine.

The saga of Peter French took on significant new dimensions in the 1880s. French had become an integral and permanent part of Harney County society during the previous decade. Henry Miller, by contrast, had never stayed for more than a week or two at any one of his ranches. Miller's control, in fact, was exercised through foremen and, later, through superintendents who oversaw the work of several individual foremen. Devine made his home in the south end and was better known; but neither he nor Miller was in such close proximity to the settlers as French, whose headquarters at the P Ranch was only thirty-five miles south of Malheur Lake and Harney County. If Devine seemed the archetypal monopolist, it was not only because of his ruthless methods, but because he lived farther away and seemed to represent more clearly outside interests and foreign power. French, on the other hand, personified the local pioneer cattle king. His activities were as visible as his vast holdings, and his decisions seemed to emanate from his own will. The P Ranch was Peter French.[76]

French had obtained the swampland claim of A. H. Robie in the Diamond Valley in 1877. In 1882, the partnership bought the John Catlow holdings in the area of Steens Mountain for $102,000. Throughout the remainder of the 1880s—particularly the dry years of 1888-1891—and up until his death in 1897, French acquired smaller properties piecemeal in the vicinity of Malheur Lake.[77] This entire area, like the lower Silvies region north of the lake, was usable chiefly as winter pasture and hayland.

In Catlow Valley to the south the claimants were far fewer; only one, David Shirk, was a serious competitor, and the land in that area was primarily summer range. During the boom of the early 1880s, French sought to expand into this region. His techniques were generally illustrative of the large holder's methods of acquiring range and grasslands. In the fashion of the day, French hired dummy entrymen to make claims under the Desert Land Act, but his use of government scrip land was more ingenious. Shirk described the technique as follows: "[French] . . . laid a string of 40 acre scrip lands around [my claims]: then . . . put up a 5-wire fence." He also hired men to contest Shirk's holdings and backed them with sufficient money to prosecute their claims, buying them out if they failed.[78]

The whole process was as effective for French as it was harrowing and annoying for Shirk. In order to expand his holdings, Shirk had to avail himself of similar weapons in the same arsenal of land-law loopholes that was open to French. In Shirk's words, this meant "filing on all sights [sic] the law afforded under the laws as then interpreted by the Interior department."[79] This meant a homestead, a desert claim, a preemption and a timber culture entry, all of which combined to give him title to 1,240 acres. To Shirk's great discomfort, French contested each of these claims. Shirk's resentment later led him to shoot one of French's hired claim jumpers.[80]

The means and process of consolidation were generally duplicated by Riley and Hardin of the OO and S. W. Sisson, another California investor who bought out the main portion of Catlow's holdings on Trout Creek in the south end.[81]

One other big owner just coming into his own was the colorful self-made stockman Bill Brown, who filed on a coveted water hole northwest of the OO range. This vast, dry area near present-day Wagontire, was largely unclaimed during the 1880s. Most of it was public domain, but across the middle of it lay the lands that had been granted to Willamette Valley and Cascade Mountain Wagon Road Company. With proceeds from the sale of sheep, Brown purchased a small portion of this land. He also filed on a homestead near Wagontire Mountain, but a OO hand was hired to contest it, and Brown summarily shot him. He was acquitted, as Shirk was, by a jury that had identified him as a small man forced to defend himself against a grasping giant.[82]

The pressure to consolidate lands was greatest on the big cattlemen like Riley and Hardin who girded themselves against men like Brown, whose exploitative tendencies threatened their own. But the pioneer homemakers or firstcomers of the 1870s also brought a particular brand of pressure to bear on large owners. Assessment records of the 1880s reveal a small but significant percentage of firstcomers still on the land by 1890.[83] The large owners could not stake out every water hole, engross every swamp, or claim every section of good land; for firstcomers expanding their claims, the public domain was still vast and land was still available. Besides, many of those who came and failed during the 1880s were sufficiently prejudiced toward big owners to want to sell to small settlers as long as the latter had the resources to make cash bids. Also, as with the large owner, there were other means open to firstcomers besides cash purchase: hiring entrymen, making claims under the several available laws, or contesting a neighbor's legal right to the land.[84] The large owner may have monopolized much of the early cattle trade in Harney County, but he had no monopoly on the varied techniques for acquiring land; the well-located, persistent firstcomer with a foothold in the country was just as shrewd and sometimes just as ruthless.[85]

Among the more persistent firstcomers were the Smyths and Riddles, who augmented their holdings in the Diamond and Happy valley regions at the same time French was trying to expand into that area. New settlers were not nearly so formidable an obstacle to French's plan as were these early families. Similar cases were those of the Cecils and Shieldses, who acquired additional acreage in the Silver Creek drainage under the very shadow of the OO. At the same time, Jones and Poujade formed a partnership in the creek country near Fort Harney in 1888 and added 2,280 acres of deeded land to their combined holding in just two years.[86] On the reservation lands, the people who were bought out with Henry Miller's money were relatively few compared to those who stayed; in all, fifty-three settlers established choice individual water rights on the major rivers and streams in that area. Over half of those families persisted well into the twentieth century, long after the P.L.S. Co. had dissolved.[87] For firstcomers, consolidation was the best hedge against an uncertain, albeit apparently prosperous, future.

Transportation

The development of transportation in pioneer communities has been treated as both a cause and an effect of social democracy; but either way, new roads could and did benefit some while at the same time they hindered others. In southeastern Oregon, the distinctions lay between heterogeneous elements searching for economic and social betterment. Heterogeneity, after all, was a mark of Harney County society from its birth. Interests were always factionally ordered. Vigorous disputes arose among these factions over the advisability of new roads and the promotion of railroad connections with the "outside" world. These disputes erupted at various times from the efforts of one group or another to promote or discredit some new transportational scheme, and they have continued in one form or another until the present day. In the 1880s, it was the well-established firstcomer who stood to gain the most in the long run.

Cattle barons worked against the smaller owners to thwart railroad transportation. They had some vital interests at stake. Burns, Harney City, and the town of Drewsey, a small but growing transportation center on the Malheur River, were connected with each other and with John Day and Canyon City by a few well-traveled wagon roads. Supplies for a winter could be gotten at Canyon City or in Ontario on Oregon's eastern border. For the big cattlemen this necessitated tedious, costly, and time-consuming trips to Winnemucca and to Ontario and east or occasionally to The Dalles. Yet they could bear this inconvenience better than they could the prospect of an army of settlers that would inevitably follow a railroad.

Partly because of this threat, the big owners tended to put all transportation into a lump, opposing the construction of local market roads as vociferously as they did the promotion of railroads. County road petitions rarely included any of the big names. Indeed, the petitions often proposed rights-of-way through a piece of "accustomed" range or some deeded land owned by a cattle baron. Occasionally

French's or Devine's name would appear on a petition, generally because the road stood to serve their own interests in some way. In such a case it was only a matter of weeks before complaints began to flow into the road supervisor that cattle were beating the roadbed to pieces.[88]

This does not mean that big cattlemen opposed modern transportation facilities; in fact they relied upon them, but as market facilities, not as internal improvements designed to "develop" the country. As their attitudes hardened, range barons soon gained the reputation of being retrograde influences—a reputation that went with their title of monopolists. In the "official" history of Grant, Baker, Malheur, and Harney counties published in 1902, the cattle kings were openly chided for "opposing . . . anything having a tendency to promote settlement."[89] Clearly, the harmony of the 1870s was breaking down.

None of the efforts of big men, however, could halt the inexorable. In 1884, the Union Pacific built its spur, the Oregon Short Line, through to Ontario and linked it with the Northern Pacific at Huntington. The threats that big men of southeastern Oregon most feared—immigration and the alteration of southeastern Oregon society—both rode in on the same rails that opened up the "Chicago market" and introduced the range baron to the last great boom of the nineteenth century.

The Market of the 1880s

The frontier livestock business contained an element of risk similar to that of the frontier mining industry. Indeed, the similarities are instructive. The element of chance operated for both the prospector and the stockman, and both industries drew a high proportion of speculators and adventurers. Even during the boom years of the early 1880s, when livestock interests were being absorbed into the corporate structures of large eastern and foreign investment concerns, the element of risk was always present. The price of cattle continued to fluctuate not only with the seasonal market but with changing consumer preferences—with drought and cold, and with ever-shifting ratios of supply and demand. Even the best-capitalized mines ran into major faults where their veins of gold were lost, or they experienced costly cave-ins or were heavily mortgaged on rich lodes that quickly petered out. But transportation facilities, when they came, tended to help stabilize the mining business and to reduce the risks involved.[90]

Here the similarity ends. When the railroad came to the cattle country, new risks were added to the old ones. Transportation placed the cattlemen of the 1880s even more "at the mercy of both national livestock and money markets . . . the dangers [of which] . . . dwarfed the menaces of rustlers and redskins of tradition . . .''[91] Yet the national market of the 1880s promised big returns for the barons of southeastern Oregon, and they reached out for it hungrily.

In a commercial stock-raising economy, marketing significantly affected the social order. It was a matter of which groups or individuals had better access to market outlets. The most direct outlets were the packing houses of eastern and far western terminal markets, which bought beef for slaughter. The major ones were in San Francisco, Omaha, and Chicago. A cowman could choose to ship directly or indirectly through a livestock commission agent to any one of these markets, which promised the greatest profits but also carried the greatest risks.[92] By shipping directly, a cattleman could avoid many middle-man costs, but he had to feed and fatten his own cattle before shipping them; once they were shipped, all he could hope was that some temporary fluctuation in the price of cattle had not wiped out his anticipated profits before his cattle arrived at their destination. In the late 1880s, these national markets were used only as last resorts when falling prices forced cattlemen to hold onto their herds longer in order to avoid feeder costs.

Feeder lots, located mostly in the midwest, were the second group of outlets. These concerns commonly bought full-grown steers, three to four years old, fattened them, and sold them to the packers. Thus the cattleman's price for feeders was not the full price he could have received at the packer's terminal; but selling to feeder lots offered the cattleman somewhat greater security, partly because cattle carried only to maturity were less of a burden on the resources of the cattle owners, partly also because the feeder lot took over some of the responsibility for calculating profits at the terminal markets, and partly because the feeder lot specialized in the sedentary business of feeding. This does not mean that the feeder market was a great deal more stable. It was nearly as susceptible to price fluctuations as the terminal market, and buyer capital was just as likely to dry up abruptly. The producer again risked absorbing a major burden of the losses.

The third group of outlets were regional markets among fellow cattlemen who were either expanding old herds or beginning new ones. These markets were outlets for stocker cattle, and the demand among buyers was for a functionally wider variety of animal. The cattlemen of Oregon and Washington sold mostly one- and two-year-old replacement heifers, bulls, and steers to Montana and Wyoming stockmen. This stocking market had many advantages. It put a relatively slight burden on the producers' resources; the market was less seasonal and the handling period much shorter. Profits were therefore easier to calculate, and the calculations were more reliable. The chief disadvantage was that these markets were, by nature, short-term markets.

Stocker cattle could not be sold year after year to the same buyers in the same region. Such markets could be the source of ready capital for a producer in a position to take advantage of them, but unless that producer was exploring terminal and feeder markets as well, his profits would be short-lived. There were, of course, also local markets, which became more and more important to small owners. The historical development of and interrelationships among all of these markets—local, regional, and national—from 1876 to 1890 tells a story of growing economic conflicts and deepening social rifts between major elements of southeastern Oregon society.

Social Aspects of the Market

The Pacific Northwest, particularly eastern Washington and eastern Oregon, produced cattle that were superior in size and fleshing to range cattle of longhorn ancestry, and superior in endurance to the "pilgrim" cattle of midwestern origin. These cattle were range-bred animals of Shorthorn and Durham stock whose reputation was widely recognized by 1878.[93] From that year until 1882, a massive migration of Oregon country cattle went to the northern plains of Montana and Wyoming, making this area temporarily a more important market for cattlemen of the Pacific Northwest than were the markets of San Francisco. The whole movement hastened the end of the Texas migrations and helped create a near cattle famine on the northwestern ranges after the winter of 1881-82. Even before the building of the Oregon Short Line, these drives released the Oregon cattlemen from their dependence upon local markets.[94]

The situation in the Harney County area of southeastern Oregon was generally the same except in some significant details. The large cattlemen there had always been independent of local markets. Theirs had been the regional market in San Francisco. The west-to-east drives in the late 1870s merely widened this regional market, but true integration with the Chicago trade came only with the Oregon Short Line in 1884. The large owner continued to drive cattle to Winnemucca even after 1884, but by 1885 Ontario had become an outlet of equal importance and most of the large owners availed themselves of it as well.[95]

Thus, the Oregon Short Line Railroad stimulated the southeastern Oregon cattle industry. At the same time, it caused the decline of that industry in the Columbia Basin, where the area was susceptible to more intensive agricultural uses. Farmers from the Middle West swarmed into the Palouse until, in 1884, the entire Columbia Basin, which had been the largest cattle-producing region in the Northwest, produced fewer cattle for northern ranges than did southeastern Oregon alone.[96]

As the Columbia Basin filled up with farms, southeastern Oregon filled up with livestock—most of it sheep. In 1880, that part of Grant County which is present-day Harney County carried on its ranges 13,743 sheep and 46,250 cattle. There were only forty stockmen recorded in the census. By 1890, the same area carried 56,698 sheep and 27,328 cattle, or a net increase of 15,628 head of livestock. There were 344 livestock producers. The relatively small increase in the number of livestock compared to the number of livestock producers does not mean there was a heavy shift to small farm holdings. During the mid-1880s a tremendous surplus of cattle built up, which the census does not reveal. The number of cattle recorded on the assessment rolls of Harney County precincts during the peak year of 1885 was 52,835, and the number of sheep was 61,470. What is more, the five big cattle and sheep owners owned nearly 40 percent of all livestock produced in the region. Even more significantly, the three big cattle owners still owned over 60 percent of all the cattle despite an 83 percent increase in the total number of livestock producers.[97]

As to the 341 smaller producers, both firstcomers and new settlers had to reach out for a new market to take the place of Fort Harney. The search made life hard. Most holdings were family-size operations, which meant that the burden of raising beef and of trying to sell what was raised forced the head of the household, or one of the older boys, away from the ranch for long periods of time. The family members who stayed behind, including the wife and able-bodied daughters, were left with seasonal duties, such as the routine of herding, feeding, branding, and rounding up the cattle, as well as the cultivation of hay and of whatever garden crops could be grown.[98] Meanwhile, the family marketing agent would probably have gone first to Canyon City, which was the closest settlement of any size. But he needed to guard against high hopes, for the cattle raisers of that vicinity competed strongly against anyone who had to drive his cattle over the Strawberry Mountains. If he made a sale there he was "double lucky," because he could return sooner to the ranch, where his services were always needed. More often than not, however, there was no market in Canyon City, and he would end by driving his cattle to the railhead at Huntington or Ontario or even to The Dalles, picking up along the way any additional cattle he might be in a position to buy.

Conditions such as these placed tremendous power in the hands of large owners, who themselves were the closest and therefore the most desirable potential market outlet for the small owner. Range barons always bought cattle from the small owners each year, but the prices they paid were never as good as they might have been at the railheads; worse yet, the large owners might become concerned over their own surpluses and buy sparingly from these potential competitors when times were hard. As the number of cattle on the range increased during the late 1880s, a large owner could ruin a small one simply by refusing to buy from him, though the sense of community prevailing at the time helped prevent such eventualities. Nonetheless, the cattle baron was able to tighten his grip on the ranges of southeastern Oregon, and in the process he came to control the grazing on public lands.[99]

Between 1885 and 1890, the southeastern Oregon livestock industry suffered some of the setbacks experienced by the national livestock industry as a whole. Cattle prices began to plummet in 1886, and cattlemen dumped market stock onto the dying range. By 1888-1889, the southeastern Oregon surplus was again in danger, and by 1890 it was gone. Prices began to go up once again that year, but not in California, only in the Chicago market. As in the preceding decade, big owners survived these troubles without great hardships, but so did many more of the small operators. One reason was that buyers from the eastern markets began to come west onto the producer's home ground, a trend beneficial to smaller stockmen. The important qualities of the 1880s—the qualities which hold it together as a subject of study—were peace, prosperity, and internal development. During this decade, opposing economic interests prospered and put off the threatened showdown between them for as long as profits could be maintained without it. An analysis of each group will illustrate its economic and social position relative to the others, important knowledge when it comes to sorting out winners and losers in the decade that followed.

The Pioneer of the 1880s

According to figures taken from the U.S. Census of population for the two decades between 1870 and 1890, the percentage of increase in the population of the United States was greater during the 1870s than the 1880s, and the two decades taken together marked the greatest numerical increase over a like period in United States history. Still, internal migration westward was not as extensive during the early 1870s as it was later, after the effects of the depression of 1873 had worn off. Post-depression prosperity spurred the nation into the activity which led to the boom of the 1880s.

There is a definite correlation between good times and increased internal migration, particularly within agricultural populations. Economic slowdowns traditionally affect agricultural and laboring segments of society more adversely than others. During the 1880s, agricultural markets expanded enough to allow depressed farmers, mostly from the midwest, to sell their land, pay off their debts, and move on;

thus, homeseekers of the 1880s had enough money to ride the railroad rather than a wagon and to bring their families even if they had to leave their hunting dogs behind. They came west with more money, took fewer risks, and stayed in one place longer than had their predecessors.[100]

Unique factors operated in the Pacific Northwest to select a distinct element of this migration: a more conservative, more practical, rather more intelligent, or at least more literate settler, who was generally even better off than migrants moving to other western areas. Oregon migrants were "self-chosen" in that they came in response to others who wrote home in value-laden terms about both the potential advantages and the hardships of living in the Oregon country. Certainly local newspapers were discreet and promotional articles were usually hedged around with practical advice.[101]

But this does not mean that the immigrants of the 1880s were politically conservative. As a group they exhibited traits of political radicalism that had a profound effect on the state as a whole and on southeastern Oregon in particular. These traits helped tip the social and political balance in favor of the small landowner against the speculator and land monopolist. The location of this new political and social force is revealed in patterns of settlement.

Population and Settlement Patterns

Southeastern Oregon, and particularly the southern part of Grant County, was the very kind of marginal country that the settlers of the 1870s tried to avoid. During the 1870s they could afford to be choosy, but by 1883 there was little to choose from in the way of first-rate agricultural land. Consequently, immigrants took to a longer, harder look at the semi-arid regions of the Harney country and at last began in earnest to settle this vast, unclaimed stretch of Oregon's last frontier. Thus, while the state's population increased by 81.8 percent during the 1880s, the population of the Harney region increased by over 600 percent, or from 419 to 2,559 people—a remarkable increase considering also that part of that increase made up for the loss of military personnel stationed at Fort Harney and Camps Curry and C. F. Smith.[102]

Sources of population during the 1880s were the same as during the 1870s: the Willamette Valley, the Middle West, and California. But there were differences in the relative proportions from each area as well as in the kinds of people who came and in the routes they chose to travel. Vital statistics of all incoming groups showed there were still more males than females, but the disproportionate ratio between them was not nearly so great. The ratio of family men to single men was higher than in the 1870s, although average ages for both men and women remained about the same. The 36-year-old married man represented the mean age for his group, as did the 22-year-old bachelor for his. Married women were mostly in their early thirties, and single girls, still a rarity, in their late teens or early twenties. The average number of children per family was about typical of farm populations in America at that time.

As a group, those who were either born in the Midwest or had lived there a good part of their lives outnumbered those of other backgrounds by a ratio of four to one.[103] Twenty-seven percent of the midwesterners came to the Harney country by way of California; most of the remainder came directly by rail to eastern Oregon, a change from the travel pattern of the previous decade. As a group, only 10 percent of all those who came from California had been born there. A higher percentage (30 percent) had been born in the East. Far fewer California miners came to southeastern Oregon than in the 1870s, but the mobility of the Californians as a whole was as high as it had been then and was the highest among the three groups that came during the 1880s. Indeed, Californians were in the vanguard of migration during the 1880s, most of them coming in 1882 and 1883.[104]

Unfortunately, the original census schedules for the year 1890 are not available. There are, however, a number of detailed biographical sketches in the history of the four southeastern Oregon counties published in 1902. The sample is small—only 5 percent of the total population in 1890—but the subjects' appearance in the publication indicates that they were among a group of substantial citizens who could afford to pay to have their biographies published. These men were proud pioneers who had put their roots down successfully and wanted to see a record of their accomplishments preserved. Naturally, their accounts must be treated with caution. But a detailed analysis of the information paints an illuminating picture of what the better-off settlers from each of the three major source areas of immigration were like, and something of how they fared with respect to each other.[105]

According to the published sketches, Willamette Valley immigrants did not arrive in any appreciable numbers until 1886, most of them not until 1889. As in the 1870s, those from western Oregon tended to be the most substantial citizens to begin with. Thirty-six percent of them had been donation claimants in the Willamette Valley. Whether the sale of donations had been their source of capital or not, the Willamette Valley immigrants had among them enough men of sufficient means to establish a sawmill, two general merchandise stores, a hardware store, a livery stable, two saloons, and a bank. They also had a higher percentage of professional men. From their ranks came two attorneys and an appointee to the position of receiver in the local land office, titles and emoluments neither of the other two groups could claim. There were fewer homesteaders among them and more who purchased land outright. Most brought with them herds of 20 to 100 cows; some brought in herds as large as 500 head, a very respectable number for anyone wishing to start in the cattle business during that period. In general, most of the Willamette Valley settlers in this sample seemed to know something of the capabilities of the country and came prepared to take advantage of that knowledge.

Californians stood next in line as community leaders, entrepreneurs, and men of means. Among them were freighters, merchants, a hotel owner, and a hardware dealer. Two of them came as foremen for the big outfits and stayed on as independent cattle owners. Midwesterners, the majority of whom were homesteaders, were in general the youngest group in the sample. They were also the least well off and the most agriculturally oriented. During the decade that followed, they produced the smallest number of county leaders despite their numbers, but it was precisely because of their numbers that no one in a position of leadership could afford to ignore them. They gave a decidedly reformist cast to local politics in the 1880s.[106]

The most striking of the patterns of settlement within the whole population is the high rate of turnover among settlers of the 1870s. Fully three-quarters of all those who had come during that decade had moved out by 1890.[107] The nineteen Californians who had settled in the south end on scattered parcels extending in a great arc north from the Pueblo Valley, then around the rim of the Alvord Desert and on through Burnt Flats as far as Crane Creek, left those arid wastes within a very few years of their arrival. Twenty-two new Californians came there during the 1880s, most of them young laborers or men of small means. Among them, those who came to settle staked their claims on Crane Creek or, Wild Horse Creek or in Catlow Valley, the three most promising places in the region. No one settled the places where firstcomers had already tried and failed.[108]

The area around present-day Burns and in Harney County lost as many people proportionately as did the south end, but the location of new settlement was simply superimposed on the older pattern: along the eastern shore of the East Fork of the Silvies River (the area of newly "redeemed" Indian land) and on the broad, tull-covered delta where the river empties into Malheur Lake. Most of the river settlers were Willamette Valley or midwestern migrants who engaged in a mixture of speculative crop raising, "swamping," and speculation in land. Earnings from any one of these strategems could and often did provide a grubstake for investments elsewhere in the county. Many of the early names reappeared in other areas after settlement on the Silvies thinned out. In fact, a sizable proportion in the twentieth century bore the names of progenitors of prominent cattle-raising families. For the settlers of the 1880s the lower Silvies River was clearly the area of the main chance.[109]

In the Blitzen River drainage to the south, 85 percent of the settlers who had come during the 1870s were gone by 1890, and the area showed a small net loss of twenty-seven people by 1890. Newcomers went mostly into Diamond and Happy valleys. Of the total of fifty-eight people who came during the 1880s, however, only three family names appear again in the assessment records of 1890. This can be taken as statistical evidence of the social and economic instability of these fertile valleys during the era of Peter French.

By contrast, the region of the Malheur River showed remarkable stability from 1880 to 1890. Those who came in 1878 and 1879, before it was officially opened to settlement, were squatters, but nearly one-half of them were still occupying the same land in 1890. In addition, sixty-nine more families moved into the Drewsey region during the 1880s, making the net population the largest in the county outside Harney Valley. Although settlement in this region was comparatively late, seventeen of the fifty-three names of settlers who established water rights during the 1880s are represented on the tax rolls of the county today. In the only other comparable river basin, the Blitzen, only nine names from the list of vested water rights appeared on the tax rolls in 1890, and there were far fewer water-right petitions per settler than in the Malheur River region. The region's physiographic features partly account for this. There were no swamp lands in the Malheur River region, and therefore there was no haggling over claims under the Swamp Land Act. Both the dominant P.L.S. Company and the individual settlers seemed to accept the doctrine of prior possession, so that those who had acquired parcels along the riverbed were not threatened by adverse claimants, whether bona fide settlers or hired entrymen. The P.L.S. Company contests were all in Harney Valley, not in the Malheur River drainage. From a geographic standpoint, this region provided the best conditions for permanent settlement, and it consequently produced a more stable, more closely knit society than did the other areas.[110]

One region that had not attracted much settlement during the 1870s did so during the 1880s. This was the Silver Creek region in what was then called the Riley precinct, an area that had been the accustomed range for cattle from Riley and Hardin's OO Ranch. Only four settlers, including two brothers, Logue and Carl Cecil, had taken up claims in the Silver Creek Valley during the 1870s. The Cecils' claim was near the site of Camp Curry, where a big spring gushed out onto the valley floor; the other two claims were located farther down the creek toward

the southern end of the valley. Of the thirty-eight newcomers who
came to join these early claimants during the 1880s, about twenty of
them chose land along Silver Creek between Camp Curry and the
present-day town of Riley. Most of these people came from California. When they arrived they found the oldtimers raising horses on the
range, a practice to which both the Californians and the Silver Creek
country itself were well suited. The remainder settled in the lower
Silver Creek drainage on swampland located in Warm Springs Valley.
Judging from the sample in the history of southeastern Oregon counties, midwesterners tended to avoid the area, choosing the better
watered drainages; and although a few of the Warm Springs settlers
were from the Willamette Valley, most western Oregonians shared the
preferences of midwesterners.[111]

The majority of settlers in the Warm Springs area moved on within
five to eight years after their arrival, but a few of their names appeared
elsewhere in the county later on—mostly in Silver Creek Valley just
to the north. Although the soil was not as fertile or the water as plentiful, the conditions of land ownership in Warm Springs Valley were
similar to those in the lower Silvies and lower Blitzen regions, where
instability and confusion arose out of conflict over swampland grants.
The grant in Warm Springs Valley was in the name of Isaac Foster,
a manager of the OO. Had agricultural prospects been as bright as they
seemed to be in the other two swamp areas, and had the OO owners
been less pliable with those who moved in, there might have been more
trouble. As it was, the dry years of the 1890s pretty well made up the
settlers' minds before any court actions or like proceedings were
necessary.[112] By 1900 the valley was so sparsely settled as to look
almost like just another hay meadow on the OO spread.

Making a Living

The heavy sales of homesteads and preemptions during the poor
years at the beginning and end of the 1880s were, as has been asserted,
an indication of the equally heavy consolidation of land carried on
by big owners. What is not so often mentioned is that such sales were
also a source of capital for small owners. It is difficult to measure
precisely either the extent or the effect of this source of capital on the
early economy, but by analyzing county deed records, together with
assessment rolls, one can see that a number of homesteaders and
preemptioners who had "sold out" to their larger neighbors got title
to other lands within the county later on. What is more, the assessment rolls carry many of these names year after year, sometimes with
expanded acreages picked up after the original sale had been made.[113]

It is reasonable to infer that these people obtained some economic leverage through the sale of their original claims.

Not all sales of land were sales to big owners, and big owners were not the settlers' only source of capital. Settlers themselves provided a rather more considerable share of capital than might have been expected. Among those who came during the 1880s, fully 30 percent showed a gross worth of $1,000 or more, and the number of land purchases and recorded deeds in Harney County other than homesteads shows that a brisk land sale business went on among them.[114]

This does not mean that there was consolidation of land going on among new settlers. That practice was reserved almost exclusively for big men and firstcomers. It does show, however, that small parcels of land were acquired and held by a number of settlers who used a variety of means to do so in addition to and including homesteading. It also alters the picture of the big men as "masters in the tactics of freezing out settlers"—a stereotype that is simply not true.[115] The era of consolidation did not mean a headlong flight of settlers any more than it meant a restriction of their sources of capital. The range barons provided some of the funds for purchase of settlers' claims; firstcomers and newcomers of modest means provided much of the rest. There were underlying conflicts, but the history of these conflicts is complex. The principal competitors lived in a functioning society where conflict was latent. The enterprising newcomer, even in the absence of transportation and in the face of consolidation, had opportunities to provide for himself and his family, and even in some cases to prosper.

A striking example of the complex interrelationship between simultaneously integrative and divisive forces in early Harney County society is the story of the relationship between two small men, J. C. Foley and William Hudspeth, and one of the Harney County giants, the partnership of Todhunter and Devine. A major part of the story comes from a lawyer's brief prepared for a case involving the Pacific Livestock Company and a local irrigation and development company. The brief, prepared in 1916, was slanted to show that harmony existed between the partnership and early settlers over the matter of water usage. Actually Miller and Lux used the water primarily for their own purposes, but the testimony does indeed show a surprising degree of harmony in the midst of conflict; the symbiosis of the 1870s had not entirely disappeared. Other peripheral parts of the story have been pieced together from assessment records, deed books, and the county history or "mug book" of 1902.[116]

The Green Hudspeth family came in 1884 and filed on a school section on the Silvies River two miles south of the present site of Burns. This land included a valuable piece of river property from which

Devine had planned to irrigate his Island Ranch ten miles to the south. The land was also on a part of the road over which Devine drove his cattle to the summer range. Green Hudspeth sold his claim to Devine in 1885. His son William moved to Catlow Valley with a part of the proceeds, leaving his father and mother, four brothers, and two sisters on property they had acquired by combining a homestead claim with a purchase farther up the Silvies River near Poison Creek. This purchase was made from their share of the proceeds. Green later appeared among the favored faces in the county "mug book," while William was assessed in 1890 for taxes on 25 horses and 250 cattle valued at $7,420.[117]

Foley and his wife arrived in Harney County with some cattle in 1883, one year before Hudspeth. He set out a homestead claim on the Silvies River five miles north of present-day Burns. In the manner of knowledgeable settlers throughout the valley, Foley began improving his property by constructing some breastworks on the river for irrigation purposes. In order to obtain the capital he needed, he went to work for Devine, who needed someone to build works on the Hudspeth section. In 1887, with the help of a local speculator and a few neighbors who stood to benefit, Foley formed the Harney Valley Dam and Ditch Company and built a rather extensive dam onto his own original breastworks, materially altering the flow of the river below him. Devine immediately brought suit contesting Foley's right to the water. While the case wound its way through court hearings on the water rights and land titles involved, Foley continued to manage Devine's irrigation works on the original Hudspeth section. An injunction against the main dam was issued after Devine's property went to the P.L.S. Company in 1889. In the meantime, Foley had worked as chief irrigator for Devine during the springs of 1885, 1887, and 1888 and for the P.L.S. Company in that capacity in 1889-1890. In that last year, his tax assessment showed him the owner of 160 acres of what was by then improved land on the Silvies River valued at $640, together with 10 horses and 100 head of cattle, making a gross valuation of $2,840.[118]

Hudspeth's and Foley's cases were not uncommon in the valley. Several newcomers had similar experiences, and, though the court dockets were full, open conflict between parties was avoided and something of the earlier symbiosis maintained.[119]

Newcomers in parts of the county more remote from the neighborhood of a big owner's winter pasturage found there were other opportunities to acquire needed capital. Sheep raising was one, although it was not as common in Harney County as in the north central counties of the state. Still, with very little money, a man could buy and graze sheep on the open range, shear them for a few years, and then sell them for enough either to augment his herd or to get a start in the cattle business. Most nontransient sheepraisers settled in the Diamond Valley area, which was only two days' herding from the Steens Mountain summer ranges—ideal ground for lambing and shearing as well as for grazing.[120] There were always transient bands of sheep, but in the 1880s they were not so numerous as to cause the kind of friction they did in the 1890s and again in the 1920s.

The tax rolls show only nineteen sheep raisers among the newcomers living in the county in 1890. Few as they were, the men who raised sheep were men of some substance, at least according to assessment records. Their combined worth represented 5 percent of the gross valuation of the county, excluding the five big cattle owners—a figure one and one-half times their number as a percentage of the taxpaying population. When the three previously established sheepmen who came during the 1870s are added, the figure is 6 percent—double the proportion of sheepmen in the taxpaying population.[121]

Harney County had no early history of range warfare between cattlemen and sheepmen. This is partly explained by the fact that the ranges of Harney County grazed only 10 percent of all the sheep in the three counties of southeastern Oregon. But it was difficult to tell who had priority on the range. Cattlemen and sheepmen came at nearly the same time; each staked out accustomed ranges, and a significant though small number of sheepmen appropriated land and water rights that ostensibly constituted an investment in the locality and in its future. Of the nineteen newcomers who came to raise sheep during the 1880s, the families of five persisted into the twentieth century and up until the present. Four sheepmen appear among the ninety-two prominent citizens in the county "mug book."[122]

Horse raising provided yet another source of capital and required not much more operating capital than sheep raising. For one thing, the initial expense for stock was no higher. Horse breaking and herding, which were confined to roundups in either spring or fall, were the chief activities. During summer and winter months horses needed less attention on the open range than either cattle or sheep, but the outlay for labor, though less than that for the cattle raising, was a good deal more than that for sheep raising. Whereas one sheepherder could care for an entire band of sheep—from 1,000 to 2,000 head—a horse raiser had to hire anywhere from two to ten "bronc-busters" depending on the size of his herd. The market for horses was, like the cattle and sheep markets, subject to fluctuations on a national scale, but such fluctuations were offset by a stable and extensive local market that was not dependent upon the wealthy cattlemen.[123]

During the 1880s, while settlers were flooding into the area, a man with from $200 to $500 to invest could buy six to fifteen horses, brand them, turn them out on the range in the summer, round up the horses and new colts the next spring, break the ones to be sold, and, with the proceeds from sales no farther afield than Canyon City, double his herd the following year. He could do all this on nearly a part-time basis and by himself. If by the third year there had been little or no winter-kill or foal loss, he would be in need of one or two hired hands at roundup and branding times. In all likelihood it would be no more than six or seven years before he could save enough to expand, or to buy other livestock as he chose. The Cecil family in Silver Creek Valley built a herd of over 260 horses in a little over fifteen years. Several others in the same area built up herds of 90 to 100 in the space of fewer years.[124] Well-established families in this region like the Oakermans, Freemans, and Williamses all started by raising horses. The business continued to be profitable well into the first quarter of the twentieth century.

Nor were the country's resources limited entirely to grass. There was timber close at hand in the Blue Mountains, and enough customers were coming in during the 1880s to make lumber milling profitable. Between 1880 and 1890, five lumbermen took over where A. H. Robie left off. In addition, gold and copper in the south end still attracted a number of miners. The beginnings of a relatively extensive trapping and fur-trading business began in un-Turnerian fashion after the peak of settlement late in the 1880s, booming in the 1890s and declining rapidly thereafter.[125] Each one of these pursuits could be followed by newcomers part-time. Thus a newcomer of the 1880s might, upon arrival, do as his predecessor in the 1870s had done and hire out to a large operator in any one of several capacities, from corral builder to horse-breaker, mostly on a temporary basis depending upon the availability of work. He could then care for his own property, knowing there would probably be an opportunity for working at the round-ups or trapping, mining, or doing odd jobs as his talent and time permitted. If he was shrewd and tenacious enough, he could accumulate both land and stock in a relatively short time.

This does not imply that all newcomers enjoyed equal opportunities. Not all came with equal amounts of capital, nor did all have either the requisite talents or the persistence to overcome hardships. What is more, Harney County was by no means a garden of Eden; those who came solely to raise grain or farm—and many did—were inevitably discouraged.[126] Yet, despite the handicaps of transportation and limited natural resources, there were more opportunities available and more people taking advantage of them than historians of the region have indicated. Writers who have looked at the period through the eyes of local newspaper editors and with the extensive records of the big owners to guide them have sometimes fallen into the trap laid by frontier antimonopolist rhetoric.[127] The tendency of editors to glorify all pioneers who survived, combined with most editors' biases against the big owners, made the story of the triumphant pioneer sodbuster seem even more inspiring as he was seen to win over gigantic odds. It conforms with the American doctrine of self-help, and there is no denying that the myth of the self-made man had a basis in fact in Harney County during the 1880s. But there were more self-made men during good times than bad, and there was more opportunity in a nation like America where the ratio of land to people was high than in European nations where it was not. In other words, external forces such as the economic climate were as instrumental to success as personal character, and anyone who started with coins in his jeans was that much ahead of the game.

The decade of the 1880s was one of the heavier than normal rainfall in the West and rising prices in the East. The circumstances of good times worked to produce a substantial core of solid citizens in Harney County as well as a number of opportunities for a wave of newcomers who would have passed over the landscape like a light fog had it really been altogether inhospitable. Besides, the weight of both numbers and public opinion was in their favor. The settlers who stayed won in the long run because they were struggling against surmountable, not insuperable, odds; they were clearly formidable contestants, and, although the disparity between them and the cattle barons was great, they were not the downtrodden poor often pictured.

Signs of Stress

While most settlers were able to provide for themselves and their families, the large owners were enjoying unprecedented prosperity. The relationship between the two groups was symbiotic and interdependent in the early 1880s. As long as times were good during that decade, the big men were tolerant, even paternalistic, toward the small men. They could afford to be. As the decade ended on a rising tide of settlers and a falling barometer, the latent competition between them began to surface—competition emanating from the crucial matters of land tenure and water rights and extending over into everyday stock-raising methods themselves.

Even before the end of the 1880s, cattle barons in Harney County perceived that conditions in the industry were changing, and they moved in ways other than consolidation of land to accommodate to those changes. In so doing, they were ahead of many range tycoons in other western states and territories, anticipating the techniques of stock-farming by as much as a decade. For example, French experimented with alfalfa as early as 1874.[128] During the mid-1880s, Miller and Lux and Riley and Hardin raised irrigated alfalfa on small portions of their best acreage. Before the legendary winter of 1886-87 covered the northern plains, Harney County range barons and a growing number of their smaller imitators were putting up surpluses of hay each year. When the southeastern Oregon version of that winter—the winter of 1889-90—settled over Harney County, none of the cattle barons was frozen out, nor, according to assessment rolls, were the vast majority of firstcomers.[129]

Big owners even anticipated marketing trends and began upgrading their herds well before the mid-1880s. There were 3,678 purebreds and 39,965 head of half-blood cattle or higher in Oregon in 1890. Of these, the Harney County range barons owned 1,586 of the purebreds and 36,317 of the half-bloods or higher—an extraordinary 88 percent of all significantly upgraded stock in the state.[130] Before he retired in 1879, Devine was noted for his Devons, shorthorns, and Durhams; Miller had already experimented with Herefords, and French had imported carloads of "fine Durham bulls" from California as early as 1882.

The chief student of the era gives two reasons for all of this: One was that the range barons of southeastern Oregon had firmer control over the cattle industry in their individual areas than did other tycoons in other states and territories. The second reason was that there was a great amount of ready capital behind the southeastern Oregon managers with few, if any, confining strings attached.[131] Anyone familiar with the local records and with Gressley's study of large corporations on the northern and southwestern plains can see that the relative harmony which existed among the partners of the large southeastern Oregon concerns as well as the skill of their individual managers contrasted with what Gressley reveals of the prevalent disharmony, not to mention distrust, between corporate directors and incompetent managers in much of the rest of the range-cattle business. By 1890, all of the big men in southeastern Oregon had learned what the smaller men learned later: other things being equal, the difference between profits and losses was good management.[132] The chief difficulty was that the cattle barons' ideas of good management conflicted with the settlers' views of what constituted their vital interests. In the absence of coherent land and water legislation, efforts by the big owners to upgrade their management clashed violently with settlers' interests during the 1890's, a situation aggravated and, in part, caused by the onset of dry weather and the return of hard times following the depression of 1893.

CHAPTER THREE

The Struggle for the Range: 1889-1897

The Transitional Period

Recent scholarship has quite adequately dispelled the notion that the range cattle industry died in the winter of 1885-86. During the whole period from roughly 1880 to 1900 ranchers made continuous changes in the methods of stock raising that eventually ended heavy reliance upon the free, open range and ushered in the modern era of stock farming. Neither the open range itself nor dependence upon it disappeared, but the way in which cattlemen used it and the relationship it held to other resources at their command changed markedly. These changes were represented by a general shift from investment in cattle to investment in both land and cattle, an increased effort to produce forage crops such as hay and alfalfa on privately owned or leased land, and an emphasis on upgrading stock and on improving methods of animal husbandry. The result of all this was to reduce the operating size of most cattle spreads while increasing the amount of their privately owned land in relation to open range and often improving the efficiency of the whole operation.[1]

Many of these changes were already under way early in the 1880s. Large cattlemen, particularly, were looking for ways to maintain large-scale production while minimizing the ever present dangers of overproduction. Overproduction in the early 1880s stemmed from a multitude of interrelated causes. Among the most important were the rapid expansion of transportation facilities, the lure of rising prices and easy credit, a surge of foreign investments, and the development of new marketing techniques—particularly the growth of middlemen who carved out whole new market areas through skillful organization, advertising, and efficient processing, making the domestic market seem infinitely receptive to more and more beef.[2] Given also the two or three wet years on the plains in the early 1880s, and growing hopes of green years for decades to come, it is easy to see why many new investors crowded into the industry and many old investors pressed to buy more cattle. Yet, when bad times and poor weather returned, bursting the bubble in 1886-1887, those who had paid off debts and expanded their

land holdings in the era of plenty survived, while those who had spent
carelessly and had increased their herds without increasing their forage
reserves failed. Ernest Staples Osgood's assessment of the process is
a true one: "The bad winters of 1886 and 1887 hastened the process
already under way toward stock-farming."[3]

Prices rose somewhat in 1888; credit eased, and consolidation advanced. When the market sagged again from overproduction in 1890,
cattlemen were for the most part able to adjust. Consequently, the panic
of 1893 and subsequent depression, though they checked land values
and depressed prices, did not hurt the cattlemen as much as they did
other segments of agriculture. Beginning in 1897, the market expanded
once again, and from that time until just after the First World War cattlemen shared in an era of prosperity unprecedented for its duration.

Many factors converged in the mid-1890s to bring all this about.
The worldwide depression of the early 1890s came to an end late in
that decade, as did the long dry spell on the Great Plains.[4] Immigration was swelling American population faster than agriculturalists could
produce for the new market. Gold flowed into America from strikes
in the Klondike, adding to the supply of money and helping to decrease
the burden of fixed costs through inflation.

Cattlemen prospered after 1897, but the period of transition had
been painful and far from smooth. Where they had made efforts to
stabilize the cattle industry and to improve management of their
ranches, confused and chaotic governmental policies often thwarted
their efforts. Despite the fact that much of the potential farmland in
the West had been claimed by 1890, the federal government persisted
in keeping large remaining portions of the domain open for incoming
settlers. Fred A. Shannon put it forthrightly:

> The federal government would have been doing the small farmer a favor
> if, instead of forbidding . . . enclosures and encouraging homesteading,
> it had adopted a national leasing act, dedicating the range country to
> cattle and sheep, under strict limitation as to the number that could be
> pastured in any area. Thus, the grass and the land might have been
> preserved, the industry legalized, and the rancher compelled to pay his
> rent. Also, the farmer would have been prevented the harrowing ex-
> perience of trying to make a living where nothing but . . . starvation
> could ensue.[5]

But the United States Congress, following the midwestern agricultural tradition, supported the small farmer in the delusion that the
ranges of the West were only temporary pastures waiting to be plowed.
The case has been made that the government's uninformed, *laissez
faire* approach to western problems actually provided a fertile field
for conflict between settler and cattleman.[6] Certainly much conflict

occurred during the 1890s; but as western states gained in number and political strength, they began to force needed reforms so that some stability was achieved. The Carey Act of 1894, designed originally to encourage state or privately financed irrigation—something large cattlemen both feared and needed—was expanded into a full-fledged federal reclamation program in 1902; forest reserves were established with regulated grazing in 1905; homestead sizes in the arid lands were increased in 1909; and adequate formulas for assessing the legality of western water rights were developed in nearly all of the rangeland states by 1910.

None of these laws, nor others to be discussed, entirely solved the problems of adjusting to a modern industrial economy; they did, however, help ease the severities of change and they illustrate the fact that the so-called "transitional period" was a function of both the changing methods of cattle raising and developing federal policy—two inseparable processes.[7]

If the idea of a transitional period is to be at all useful, it should be applied to the migrating farmer whose attitudes and habits were shaped by events during this period and from whose ranks came the small cattlemen of the new century. All areas of agriculture were undergoing rapid changes during this period. The cycles of wet and dry years and boom-and-bust business affected midwestern wheat and corn growers as fundamentally as they did cattlemen, except that the farmers probably suffered more. It is not necessary to repeat their travail in detail; it need only be said that the small farmer, in both the West and the South, was subject to enough natural and economic pressures to become convinced that a great conspiracy was under way to uproot him and to smash the last hope of American individualism and yeoman democracy.[8] The most obvious conspirator was the monopolist, specifically the railroad, but generally it was all large combinations of power and wealth.

During the 1880s, the farmer's position as a producer was competitive in the truest sense of *laissez faire* competition while his position as a buyer was not; in neither case did this work out to his benefit. He sold on an unprotected market for what the traffic might bear, and bought industrial goods on a market hedged around by protective tariffs. Since middlemen and the industrialists—large corporations in most cases—made profits at the farmer's expense, the farmer's sentiment against them became increasingly radical, especially when he saw the futility of legislation designed to curb privileged industries while they doubled and tripled their size under the aegis of the very acts by which they were supposedly bound.[9]

Political radicalism was the inheritance of the farmer of the 1890s along with the older legacy of mobility left to him by the tradition of the moving frontier. It was a radicalism tinged with desperation, since the line of the frontier itself had disappeared. The farmer's special cry for reform, the Populist crusade, shook the entire nation; yet it was less Populism than the return of good times after 1896 that brought him a degree of stability. Forced in the 1890s to the farthest reaches of the farming frontier, a place of unregulated, semi-arid pasturelands, this fiery-eyed son of calamity faced off against the range barons for control of his own destiny. The ensuing conflict extended into every corner of the frontier, exploding with nearly equal force on the ranges of Harney County and in the mountains and plains of Colorado and Wyoming. The farmers presence on the plains constituted a force as strong as bad winters and hard times in the transition of the cattle industry.

Sources of Conflict in Southeastern Oregon

The relative importance of agriculture, compared with other growing industries in the Pacific Northwest, declined after the boom of the 1880s. The range-cattle industry retreated almost entirely from the Columbia Basin and came to be centered in the semi-arid frontier regions of southeastern Oregon and east-central Washington. Although there was no winter in southeastern Oregon comparable to the calamitous winter of 1885-86 on the high plains, hard winters did strike this area in 1884-85, and again in 1890. After that, "cattle raising no longer held its early promise for those who had to start from scratch."[10]

Capital requirements grew in southeastern Oregon as elsewhere. The winter of 1889-90 brought a relatively prosperous decade to a close and forced out many of those who had failed to specialize or to intensify their operations. Some got rid of their cattle in time: Peter French was able to take advantage of the decimated ranges of Montana to unload his cattle preparatory to retrenchment; Ike Foster took several thousand head to California, as did the P.L.S. Company. Hay prices soared from $20 to $40 per ton by the end of the winter. Estimates made at the time put the death rate of cattle around Harney Lake at 100 per day.[11]

Hardest hit were the small men who either had not been in the area long enough to establish themselves securely or had not moved to meet the demands of changing times. It is difficult to show the extent of failures among small men through census and assessment figures. The Grant and Harney county records are combined for the decade of the 1890s. Furthermore, that decade was one of large population increases in both counties, and the original United States census schedules for 1890 upon which a comparison could be based are not available. Still, some important comparisons can be made between gross census and assessment figures for the 1880s and the 1890s. For example: The average size of a herd in 1880 was nearly 1,000 head of cattle. The number of owners increased from 40 to 341 during the 1880s, but the number of cattle decreased by 41 percent, making the average size of a herd in 1890 only 80 head. Despite the decade-long decrease in the number of cattle per owner, until the winter of 1889-90 twelve of the original forty owners in the Harney region still owned over 1,000 head. After that winter only six outfits owned that many or more, and three of those were the erstwhile giants of Harney County who owned between them over 16,000 head.

Most striking is the fact that the three large owners who in 1880 owned 60 percent of all the cattle in the county, despite the liquidations of 1889-1890, owned in the last year 61 percent of all the cattle in the county. Even with the trend toward decreasing herds, the disparity between large and small owners remained great. Still, 26 out of 341 cattle owners, or 8 percent of those who owned less than 1,000 cattle, owned over 100 head—within the range then considered to be a good-sized herd for a small owner.[12] Among those who owned less than 100 head, the vast majority were newcomers. Thus, in addition to the disparity between big men and small men, there was a distinction between newcomers and firstcomers—a distinction that became more pronounced as more newcomers came into the area and tried to gain a foothold on marginal lands. Gene Gressley has hinted that there was a struggle throughout the West between the "have somes" and "have mores" which was as important as that between "honyockers" (settlers) and cattlemen.[13] In Harney County the "have somes" were definitely the newcomers; the "have mores" were oldtimers and firstcomers.

While newcomers may not at the outset have represented much of an economic threat to those already there, they did represent votes and a certain crusading conscience that made them a clear political threat. The population of the Harney region grew by over 600 percent between 1880 and 1890.[14] Big cattlemen knew the dangers of such an increase just as well as their predecessors and contemporaries had known it elsewhere. French, Devine, Miller, and Riley and Hardin all voiced concern over growing settlement, and all moved in their own ways to deal with it; but no matter how often these special interests tried to control the machinery of burgeoning democracy, it ran inexorably by the weight of constituencies. In the fight between "have somes," "have mores," and "have the mosts," the less well off banded together against the priviledged few. In that alliance, which will be explored later, the newcomers provided the numbers while the firstcomers provided the political leadership.

As important as these factors of increased population and disparity of ownership were in creating cleavages within Harney County's society, they were only two sources of conflict among several. The most severe and persistent problems were those of land tenure and water rights, the two major variables of production for stock raisers in the semi-arid regions. The shortcomings of United States land laws before 1900 applied to southeastern Oregon as well as other rangelands. Nowhere in the laws at that time was there any recognition of differences in quality of land, nor was there any provision for using land in common, or in large blocks, or any legal method for acquiring rangelands of sufficiently large size at reasonable cost, or recognition of special water problems like those in southeastern Oregon, to which the English doctrine of riparian rights simply could not be applied. Finally, there was no agency of management or control over public rangelands. Consequently, in the face of increases in population in the 1890s, the cattle barons of southeastern Oregon continued to respond as they and others had responded before—by acquiring lands or control of lands through manipulation and sometimes outright countervention of existing laws, often using ruthless tactics against those who stood in their way. These tactics, whatever their justification, proved to be a "hot running iron" for the increasing numbers of settlers in Harney County.

Aggravating this situation was the presence of the speculator and absentee landowner, those inevitable figures of opprobrium in the West who were epitomized in southeastern Oregon in a single corporation— the Willamette Valley and Cascade Mountain Wagon Road Company. One million three hundred ninety-two thousand acres of eastern Oregon land had been granted to this company in 1866. By 1900, almost none of it had found its way into the hands of settlers, nor had the road itself ever been completed. A forfeiture suit was finally brought in 1889, but the company won on the basis of completion certificates issued by the Oregon governor that, it was later discovered, were based upon a fraudulent construction report. The land remained unimproved, a visible symbol to Harney County residents of the cupidity of Oregon officials and the evils of speculation and absentee ownership.[15]

More rankling still were the claims of big men based upon the Oregon Swamp Lands Act of 1870. By the terms of the act, the prospective purchaser was both witness to the quality of the land and selecting agent for the state. Settlers became convinced that only those with an "in" in Salem could buy; the *Eastern Oregon Herald* stated their prevailing discontent: "Thousands of acres, which have been claimed by corporations, have never been earned. We believe we can safely say that three-fourths of the land given to wagon road corporations and approved as swamp land should now belong to actual settlers."[16] Action followed these complaints, and a group of settlers working through a local attorney was able to gather enough evidence of fraud to give public credence to its accusations. When state officials failed to act, the settlers took the initiative and instituted several contests in the local land office. Litigation dragged on through the 1890s, causing bitter feelings and much personal animosity. Settlers won some of the cases, but following a contest through to its conclusion exacted a stiff price. In most cases, they either ran out of funds and accepted a partial settlement of their claims or simply wearied of the fight and quit.

Big owners were additionally suspect by virtue of their having fenced off large acreages of the public domain for summer ranges. It was estimated in 1880 that French alone had put 30,000 acres of public land under fence. Original surveys show several miles of partial fencing on public lands in Steens Mountain, Catlow Valley, and the Alvord Desert—the bailiwick of the large operators. With only a mile or two of such fence, a range user could "bunch control" the cattle on eighteen to twenty square miles of land.[17] Thus the fencing issue injected yet another active source of controversy into the growing quarrel between big men and little men over land use and tenure in the county.

The area of potential controversy extended beyond questions of land tenure to include the closely associated questions of water rights. When it came to sorting out these rights, the English common law and western American precedent diverged; consequently neither offered a firm precedent. Oregon practice and Oregon court decisions on water usage had already worked to undermine the common-law doctrine of riparian rights; yet water-control legislation based on prior appropriation had not been passed. In the absence of any state or federal regulations, any change in the status of water usage usually meant a new and volatile situation in which lawsuits generally had to be brought to determine the validity of each appropriation. As more settlers crowded the banks of the Silvies River, the older downstream owners, particularly the P.L.S. Company, found themselves in repeated lawsuits to protect their vested rights. Accustomed usages were challenged nearly every year; since there was only so much water to go around, the need for adequate regulation became more and more critical with the passage of time.

The most troublesome and potentially the most volatile situation combined the questions of land and water rights. Beginning in the late 1880s and during the dry years thereafter, particularly as irrigation became more common, large areas of the Malheur Lake bed were exposed—leaving a sort of administrative and legal no-man's land over which settlers and cowmen fought for years.[18] Big men, particularly French, who claimed ownership of the exposed lands did so on the basis of the principle of riparian ownership; squatters who came to settle on the rich soil of the lakebed contended that the doctrine of riparian rights had already been abrogated in practice in Oregon, and that the exposed land should be considered public domain eligible for entry and settlement. The state of Oregon entered the picture, not as an arbiter but as a litigant claiming that the exposed lands could be neither privately nor federally owned because, in fact, these lands belonged to the state under the terms of the federal swamp land grant of 1860. The state's case might have been more popular with the rank and file had not Oregon officials already jeopardized the state's claims by allowing the fraudulent disposition of much of the land.

Between 1888 and 1895, two separate federal surveys were made and five major cases were contested. Still, in 1908 the issue of the lake bed was as much a legal morass as ever. As in the water rights cases between The P.L.S. Company and its upstream neighbors, the courts made their decisions on the basis of precedents borrowed from midwestern cases, deciding, in effect, only temporarily on each individual complaint.[19] Not until 1909 was a water-control statute finally drafted and passed. By then, however, the picture had been blurred even further by a presidential proclamation setting the Malheur and Harney lake lands aside as a wildlife refuge.

Taken separately, all these sources of contention might not have proven too serious. At least the courts were operating on them, and officials could be moved in specific instances where they were confronted with enough petitions or where they perceived concrete political benefits. But the burr under the settlers' saddle blanket was the cumulative effect of all these complaints, a list of grievances that together seemed to make an unbearable wrong. The 1890s were years of stress throughout the nation; and while it is true that hard times were not felt nearly as acutely in Harney County as elsewhere, the victims of hard times who came from the Middle West brought with them vivid memories of their experience. This combination of factors forced into the open the latent competition between small and large owners that had been building up for two decades. The growing towns in the north end of the county constituted the catalytic force in the controversy, and their role is critical to its understanding.

The Role of Towns

Frontier windfalls of any kind—gold, grass, or timber—attracted mostly a rootless sort of immigrant looking for quick returns. Consequently, any social organization was makeshift at best. Only with the advent of people who had come to stay did towns, in any sense other than that of temporary camps of bonanza-seekers, begin to grow. These towns, in turn, rapidly worked a stabilizing influence on society through an assortment of familiar institutions designed to protect property and establish order as well as advance educational and spiritual life.

This, at least, is the pattern Louis B. Wright speaks of in his study of the development of frontier communities.[20] But Wright was looking for some basic rules of frontier community behavior. Though he did not emphasize it, he probably would not quarrel with the idea that frontier towns varied widely, that they sustained different kinds of societies depending both upon the towns' sources of income, or "economic base," and upon the attitudes and habits of their people. Wright's generalizations apply mostly to frontier farm communities, whereas "urban historians" of the frontier (although the designation seems anomalous) have revealed wide variations in Wright's basic theme. Richard C. Wade's analysis of frontier cities along the Mississippi and Ohio rivers presents a unique frontier pattern of settlement in which city life was not the product of an evolutionary continuum but an actual concomitant of early frontier exploitation. Lewis Atherton chronicled the failures of midwestern towns, and Robert Dykstra, in *The Cattle Towns*, used the concepts of modern sociology to discover new dimensions in the social process by which frontier cowtowns strove for stability and adapted to change.[21]

Dykstra's approach provides some helpful analogies. His central theme is the "urban impulse": the process by which towns attempted to acquire the paraphernalia, status, amenities, and economic stability of urban centers. "Despite the advertised appeal of collective intimacy with nature, most American small towns would be cities if they could."[22] This impulse was sustained more easily in the railroad cattle towns of the Midwest because the towns were essentially commercial, not agricultural, centers; yet the "urban impulse" also meant reaching out for the main chance whenever and wherever it might appear. Not surprisingly, the community's pulse-takers were the entrepreneurs who stood to gain or lose the most. Thus, in the towns of Dykstra's study—Caldwell, Abilene, Dodge City, and the rest—there was a well developed instinct among local businessmen for reading the signs of economic attrition and decay. If cattle were not to provide the kind of long-range economic support needed for growth, then there were those who would as quickly look for ways to attract settlers and farmers.

This is an oversimplified summary of Dykstra's model of frontier town behavior, but the parts of the model that deal with the role of entrepreneurs in directing the "urban impulse" can lend insights into the behavior of the towns in Harney County at the turn of the century. All Harney County towns played a role in the struggles of the

1890s and again in the troubled search for stability that followed that decade; but it was the town of Burns that exerted the greatest influence.

Burns never really came close to being a frontier cattle town except, perhaps, during the first five years of its existence. Its first building was a general store and saloon built by the Fitzgerald brothers in 1878. A larger saloon and a hotel were in operation just west of that spot near the hot springs on the site of present-day Hines. Both settlements were little more than frontier camps where transient cowboys could find the deathless attractions of all-night poker games and women of easy virtue.[23] In that sense Burns conformed not only to Dykstra's model but generally to the frontier stereotype of most western towns, whatever their location or economic base, during their first few years of existence. Family men and women were certainly far too scarce to have forced any alterations in this atavistic community, but there were enough settlers in the vicinity of Harney Valley to encourage George McGowan and Peter Stenger to build a large general store in 1882. By 1885 there were three stores selling sundry items to a growing number of would-be farmers and north-end cattle raisers. The town's chief drawback, then and later, was its inaccessibility to the outside world. Mail came in twice a week, but there was no railroad or cattle market to draw the big herds from the south end. Burns's commercial opportunities were limited nearly from the beginning to supplying and servicing the settlers, immigrants, and firstcomers who had settled in the better-watered regions of Harney Valley near the townsite.

The parallel between Dykstra's cowtown entrepreneurs and the enterprising merchants of Burns is more striking. As commercial men they both knew the economic advantages of permanence and stability. Despite setbacks to farming the notion was not a far-fetched one at the time. The mid-1880s were wet years during which crops in the so-called "Ryegrass District" southeast of Burns were successful more often than not. Optimism ran high and store owners stocked their shelves. The hard winter of 1889 was a blow to many, but even then Burns's businessmen who stayed decided that their investments would bear fruit sooner if they encouraged farming, whatever the odds, rather than promoted markets in the south end or spent their energies promoting railroads in the face of conditions and against odds that seemed nearly insuperable.

McGowan and Stenger gave liberal credit to newcomers, as did the firm of Durkheimer and Brown. Nathan Brown actually cleared sagebrush for sodbusters himself and helped them build a gristmill for their grain.[24] It is impossible to assess the extent to which the efforts of local merchants accounted for the high growth rate in and around Burns during the 1890s, but the Burns figures show the beginning of a settlement resembling more the pioneer farm communities of the

Middle West and central California than the cattle towns of the midwestern prairies. This fact bears significantly upon the struggle between small men and large owners during the 1890s, for Burns helped fuse the alliance among the small owners of the north end—an alliance that would become the dominant social and political influence in the county after the turn of the century.

Much of Burns's growth came after 1895, when prices were rising and the United States was moving out of the depression of 1893-1895. Total assessed valuation in the county was just under $1,500,000 in 1890, increasing to only $1,794,000 by 1896. In the remaining four years of that decade it grew to a substantial $2,241,655. At the same time, the total county-wide population increased by only 1.5 percent, but population in and about Burns increased by 31 percent.[25] In the voter registration book of 1900, 79 of Burns's 297 voters listed their occupations as farmer; another 30 claimed they were stockraisers, and an additional 54 labeled themselves laborers, a category that excluded all skilled workers and actually meant farm or ranch hands. Roughly 25 percent of the farmers listed were newcomers who came to Harney County between 1890 and 1900, whereas only 9 percent of those who listed themselves as stockmen were newcomers. Not surprisingly, newcomers constituted 78 percent of the laborers.[26] Those calling themselves farmers were mostly of midwestern origin, while stock raisers were mostly from Oregon and California. The men who listed themselves as laborers were frequently of foreign origin, and most of these were German and Irish. All of these people listed their residence as either in town or on sections of land within the three townships immediately surrounding Burns. Only six of the other seventeen precincts in Harney County listed as many farmers, and all but one of those six were precincts in the north end.[27]

Burns also showed a configuration of professional services that indicated considerable specialization and extensive economic interdependence with the surrounding countryside.[28] For example, a person living less than a half a day's ride from Burns could put up his horse in one of four livery stables or have it shod at one of three blacksmith shops. If his own shoes needed repair he could have them fixed at the local shoemaker's shop. There were two town dentists, a tailor, and five saloons all of which served locally brewed beer. On his way out of town, the visitor could duck into the saddle shop either to dicker for a saddle or to avoid someone he did not wish to see, such as one of the town's eleven lawyers. Before he left he might get a prescription filled at the drugstore, or even buy his wife an inexpensive bracelet at the jeweler's. The chances that he would visit the local insurance broker were pretty slim, but enough of his neighbors were clients to keep the broker a resident of the community.[29]

The big cattle owners in Harney County neither needed nor used all of these services except selectively and only at their convenience; in fact, there was some status involved in not relying upon local services at all. Bill Hanley, for instance, bought his hats from a firm in Chicago. He allowed his foreman to be treated by local doctors when he was seriously ill, but he himself trusted only Portland physicians. John Devine continued to buy his Madeira and have his saddles made in San Francisco. As for Peter French, he was drawing more and more apart from the community in nearly every way as the years went by.[30] Indeed, with no local banks and with merchant capitalists like Brown reaching out to small settlers, there was little commercial intercourse between Burns and the large owners.[31] This may or may not have been by the design of merchants, but many similar divisions appeared between the growing Burns-centered community and the south end. For example, in 1896 there were two fraternal organizations of great social importance in Burns: the Masonic Lodge and the I.O.O.F. Many small cattle owners appeared on the rolls of both these organizations, but relatively few, except those living close to Burns, appeared on membership lists of any of the local churches, although there were four denominations to choose from: Catholic, Methodist, Baptist, and Presbyterian. More important, none of the big owners belonged to either lodges or churches, though French claimed to be a Mason and he and Devine reportedly attended some meetings.[32] It is not known if they made contributions to any of these institutions; if they did, there is no record available.

This pattern was repeated in the history of education in Harney County. The first school district was formed in 1875. At that time Harney County had not yet been formed, and even though the district had official sanction from Canyon City, there were no county funds available. Local citizens assessed their land and property, paid a voluntary tax, elected a school board, and built a two-room school house. Such zeal was evidently not uncommon among family men and women in frontier communities, and the five or six men who had families in that vicinity contributed most of the support. Others became interested when teaching jobs were opened for local people. F. L. Mace, a small stock raiser in Harney Valley and a bachelor, taught during the winter season for three months at roughly $65 per month. Funds for 30 percent of school support finally came from Grant County and the state in 1877, but early local support was the work of the "civilizing" elements of society and not of large cattle owners, who neither contributed financially nor lent men or equipment to help with the building. There was no more help when school districts were organized in cattle barons' own neighborhoods.[33]

These divisions, while they deepened the chasm between north and
south, contributed conversely to a growing sense of community pride
and a feeling of social cohesion in the Burns area. In this, Burns
newspapers played a decisive part. There were three newspapers in
town by 1893, and all three were printing a massive amount of information concerning federal, state, and county policies affecting
agriculture and stock raising. A good deal of this material was politically
slanted, but much of what was left was educational literature designed
to keep local citizens aware of current agricultural trends, prices of
farm and ranch commodities, the status of eastern markets, newly
developed methods of farming, and improvements in equipment and
machinery. The *Harney Items* even instituted a serialized column entitled "Agricultural Notes" in 1887.[34]

The papers took upon themselves a promotional function as well.
The *Items*, the *Times*, and the *Eastern Oregon Herald* vied with each
other to promote a railroad, to boom the agricultural potential of
southeastern Oregon in general, and to appeal to federal officials for
the establishment of a land office in Burns. In a less tangible but equally
powerful way, Burns exerted a centripetal force on an ever widening
circle of social relationships. Again, newspapers played a prominent
role. All fraternal meetings, dances, parties, and special occasions were
announced and covered in detail, the emphasis always on the extent
of community participation. Winter months were turned over to such
affairs, which meant, again, that people from the south end had less
opportunity to attend especially when snow clogged the roads south
of town for most of the season. In time, most of Harney Valley, including Harney City, eleven miles east of Burns, was included in these
functions. One such occasion, a dance, drew such a crowd that late
arrivals were pressed to find room in a home in the valley. This "helped
relieve pressure on the [dance] hall so that by the second half of the
night after supper at Fry's Hotel, the dancing progressed nicely until
4:30 A.M."[35] Information taken from the "mug book" of 1902 testifies
to the social preferences and divisions encompassed within these affairs. Unlike the situation at the dances held at old Fort Harney a quarter
of a century earlier, there was no room in the almost endless round
of winter parties for the south-end barons whom the book labeled
"enemies of civilization and settlement."[36]

By 1900, there were other towns in the north end where divisions
along these lines were less apparent and sometimes nonexistent. The
post road east and west from Burns bound four northern communities
together—Riley, Burns, Harney City, and Drewsey—along a single, thin
umbilicus leading in both directions to the outside world. Farthest east

was the town of Drewsey, orphan child of the Malheur Reservation, born at the hour of the reservation's demise.[37] It served as a freighting and loading center for small cattlemen along the Malheur River and for the P.L.S. Company ranch in Agency Valley. Postal authorities ignored the appropriateness of its original name, "Gouge Eye," which was changed to Drewsey in the interests of "good taste." In Drewsey, the price of bacon and flour was higher than it was in Burns, and the stock of whiskey sold to wagon drivers and cowboys under the tent of Jim Ragley's saloon required more regular replenishment than anywhere else in the county despite being five to ten cents higher per quart. By 1902, the town had grown to 104 persons and was acknowledged to be "the center of a stockraising and agricultural community of no little importance." Drewsey, was, of the four towns, most clearly a cowtown in the tradition of the Midwest.[38]

West of Burns, at the opposite side of the county from Drewsey, lay the nondescript little settlement of Riley. In 1890, it had only a post office and a small store. The community it served was less compact and more sparsely populated than the other three. The settlement's main function was to disperse mail; only later were there enough people with enough community feeling to support a school. Dispersed settlement and the gradual improvement of the post road made Riley a social and political satellite of Burns, twenty-eight miles to the east.

This was not true of Harney City, the vestigial remnant of old Fort Harney, eleven miles east of Burns. On the contrary, Harney City experienced a heavy increase of population during the 1880s and became Burns's chief rival for power and prestige. The large cattle owners found Harney City more congenial, even though the town was more agriculturally oriented and registered an even greater percentage of farmers than Burns. In the county assessment records, Harney precinct included only forty fewer taxable units than Burns, yet the town's configuration included far fewer occupations than Burns.[39]

The explanation for such rapport between a farm town like Harney City and the larger cattle interests can again be found in the role played by merchants and entrepreneurs. A political issue gives it focus. Community leaders were striving to get Harney City selected as the new county seat; to them it seemed that the only effective counter to Burns's voting supremacy was the influence large owners could marshal with legislators and officials in the state capital at Salem. The rural voters of the north end exhibited Populist leanings on national issues. The trick was to balance their political and social preferences with the economic motives of the merchants on the local issue of the county seat. The voice of the town's leaders, the *Harney Times*, showed the kind of pronouncements that had to be made. "We are in favour of letting the small stock farmer and rancher thrive and populate the country . . ., but killing off capitalists who spend their money in the country is not the way to accomplish that end."[40] Harney City ultimately lost, but not before its bid for prominence contributed a divisive political issue to a growing number of economic and social rifts between settlers of the north end and cattle barons of the south. The issue, its attendant causes, and its results are best perceived in the context of national and state politics that inevitably helped shape political loyalties at the local level.

Origins of Political Conflict

At a time when other regions of Oregon, and for that matter other western states and territories, were involved in controversies over range leasing and fencing and were torn by conflicts among cattlemen, sheepmen, and farmers, southeastern Oregon was at least on its surface less troubled and more at peace internally. For example, there was none of the hostility that attended the fence-law controversy in the Palouse country during the 1870s, very likely because there were far fewer opportunities to farm the Harney region anyway. Oregon had not followed the precedent of the California herd law; instead, the cattle interests were allowed to send their stock out onto the public lands and were liable only if their animals trespassed on enclosed private land. Thus, wherever cattle interests were predominant—especially where potential opposition had not crystallized, as in the Harney county—peaceful conditions obtained even though federal, state, and local policies generally much favored the cattlemen.[41]

The reformist surge in the nation's capital during the 1880s failed to produce any really equitable alterations in the use of western ranges. President Grover Cleveland ordered all unlawful fences on the public domain pulled down; yet the police power in states like Oregon was used to protect the cattleman's interests as well as his property. Fences came down where federal inspectors could find them, but the big men of southeastern Oregon continued to herd their cattle on accustomed ranges or simply replaced fences once the inspector had gone.[42] State officials turned the other way.

The arrogance and the success with which the big men thwarted attempts at reform helped force smaller men into more cohesive groups to protect their own interests. In the Harney country, a formal cattleman's association was formed in 1879, and even though the big owners steered clear of it, its chief function was to press not for fencing regulations but rather for state aid in control of predators and for cooperation in helping to bring occasional rustlers to justice. Besides, to go on record opposed to fencing might cramp the style of a would-

be cattle king who contributed to the maintenance of the new organization. The big owners' personal political connections were powerful
enough to maintain their interests without resorting to collective action. Besides, the preeminent tradition was still that of independence
and self-help, which was not seriously disturbed in all this region until the 1890s.[43]

Those who were better able to help themselves were those who
made the greatest impact politically, working largely on their own.
Oregon's bigger cattle interests were individually powerful enough to
promote legislation against incoming railroads in 1887, making the
railroads liable for damage to cattle on the open range. Sheepmen, on
the other hand, were totally unsuccessful in their efforts to promote
laws for their own benefit. In addition to the reasons already mentioned, there was the simple fact that sheep interests, though often
as well entrenched, were not as well organized nor as well thought
of as cattle interests; no large sheep owner ever had the political influence traditional with the cattle baron. Still, despite the open resentment of sheepmen, cattle and sheep interests in southeastern Oregon
continued to avoid, for the most part, serious controversies.

By 1890, Oregon cattlemen had acquired nearly every protection
the state's police powers could provide, including a brand registration
law. A county brands inspector was appointed, and though enforcement was always difficult, enforcement procedures were provided to
protect cattle owners from unlawful slaughtering, rustling, and misap-
propriation of strays, putting the burden of proof on the ostensible
culprit.[44]

The political climate in Salem was definitely favorable to cattle interests during the late 1870s and 1880s; but at the same time a growing reform-mindedness was beginning to develop among Democrats
in the state legislature. On the national level the Democratic standard-
bearer, Grover Cleveland, had already demonstrated in 1884 the vote-
getting power of the issue of political reform. In Oregon, Sylvester Pennoyer followed his lead, tailoring his stance to a growing tradition of
independence among Oregon voters and to the decidedly agrarian cast
of sentiment for reform in Oregon politics. Midwestern immigrants
provided increasing numbers of reform-minded voters, but the state
land frauds provided the major issues. The Granger movement found
ample room for growth in both the Willamette Valley and the eastern
part of the state, as did the Farmers' Alliance, which organized over
150 "units" in the state in the late 1880s.[45]

Pennoyer exploited these forces with skill, reaching out to discon-
tented agriculturalists with promises of direct elections, recall, initiative, and referendum and, most prominently, a call for investigation of the state land board and its role in the sale of swamplands in

southeastern Oregon. In so doing he splintered what Republican unity there was in 1886 and temporarily neutralized the political power of the urban centers. In his inaugural address in 1887 Pennoyer declared: "a thrifty yoemanry is a far richer endowment to the state than a few thousand dollars in our treasury."[46] As it turned out, he was pitching more political hay than he could feed. An investigating committee, which he appointed, was thwarted by lack of recorded evidence; records of sales were practically nonexistent. One thing did emerge clearly from its findings, however: The big boys of southeastern Oregon were among the chief beneficiaries of the swamplands act.[47] When the Salem Convention—a collection of dissident agrarian voters mostly of Granger and Knights of Labor persuasion—met in 1889, Pennoyer was quick to endorse their cause; and in the campaign of the following year he squarely established himself as a reform candidate. His reelection to the governorship attested both to his perspicacity and to the extent to which a mood congenial to reform was spreading among Oregon's voters.[48]

This mood was not parochial, but rather the reflection of a changing temper in the national electorate as a whole. Its causes were rooted in the increasingly apparent abuses of industrialism. In Oregon, as in a good part of the American West, the crusade against such abuses was focused on the supposed source of most of the trouble—the monopolist—in all his protean forms. In the East he was the financial genius, the big banker, and the shipping magnate; in the Midwest he was the railroad tycoon who charged exorbitant and inequitable rates to helpless farmers. Labor unions fought against the former, Grangers against the latter. Speculators and land monopolists were decried in the West; and in Oregon the most visible monopolists were the swampland and wagon-road swindlers, men whom the settlers of southeastern Oregon could identify plainly enough even before the law caught up with them. The small men of the Harney country could not be said to have been preoccupied with industrialism, but they were indoctrinated by politicians like Pennoyer, prompted by growing numbers of newcomers in their midst, and harangued by the newspaper voices of their own town merchants and businessmen, so that they came to reject in the political sphere the symbiotic relationship they had had with their bigger neighbors during the 1870s.[49]

The County-Seat Issue

Locating the county seat in Harney County was the first real political test of the extent to which the settlers and large cattlemen had grown apart. It provides an example of community conflict that some consideration of community conflict theory might help illuminate. Large cattle owners and settlers formed a loosely knit, heterogeneous social and economic community; any argument between them can be regarded as an internal community struggle.

Latent conflicts between agricultural groups, specifically between farm owners and farm workers, tend to "rise to the surface . . . either as individual and personal grudges or as mass action in the form of strikes, and are most apt to appear during times of stress."[50] More generally, any event that leads to conflict in a community must touch upon some aspect of the life of the community that the community itself deems important—in this case, the apportionment of political power between potentially antagonistic groups; affect different members of the community in different ways, as the first factor implies, and be an event upon which action can be taken—in this case influencing the state legislature's decision on the location of the county seat. The divisive issue itself must affect the economic relationships of the community, or its power structure, or its cultural values in order to engender conflict. The county-seat issue, in varying degrees, affected all three, but conditions were such that the county comprised a "self-contained" community—where people both lived and worked—and as such was particularly sensitive to issues arising out of economically related incidents. In fact, a very "intense response" was generated by the economic ramifications surrounding the question of which of the two towns, Harney City or Burns, might become the county seat.[51]

Harney County was settled mostly by midwesterners whose traditions were complex and diverse enough to include, but certainly not be limited to, political radicalism. It can be assumed that their attitudes, like those of all midwesterners to a greater or lesser degree, embraced traditional beliefs in self-help, individual independence, equal opportunity, yeoman democracy, and patriotism—long-standing American values that by the late 1880s and early 1890s, at least some of them believed, could be preserved only through radical political action. In Harney County these same attitudes helped shape the county-seat fight into a struggle between small independent yoemen and big monopolists.

Certain "cultural values" also helped to define the fight as one between towns as well as between divergent economic and social classes.

One added dimension is that the monopolists in Harney County were ensconced in isolated principalities, mostly in the south end, while the majority of citizens were congregated around the small towns in the north. This gave the struggle the quality of town-country split. Yet this split, though real enough, was not as important a factor in the quarrel as it seems to have been in similar conflicts elsewhere or, for that matter, in conflicts between Burns and its rural environment later in the twentieth century. One reason seems to be that Burns never really was a cattle town in the same sense that the towns along the Kansas and Missouri railroads were cattle towns. Burns had neither the market nor the facilities to handle the cattle trade. Its functions were service functions, designed to supply and maintain a growing population of farmers and small cattlemen. Nor were these functions so specialized that the town in any way encouraged social associations along specialized economic lines. In turn, the cattlemen of the south end were only partly identified with outside interests. They were visible and stable, indeed omnipresent, parts of the Harney County community. When the more threatening aspects of the big cattlemen's presence became apparent during the county-seat fight, the important divisions between the town of Burns and its close country neighbors of the north end, and those divisions within the town between newcomers and oldtimers, were both submerged in order for the town and its surrounding community to make common cause against the monopolists.[52]

In the light of these considerations, the fight itself assumes greater meaning. There were many compelling reasons for the proposed division of Grant County, but the most compelling one for residents of both the north and south ends was the problem of transportation. The two-day trip from Burns to Canyon City was time consuming and difficult; and time and distance from the south end of the county were even greater. Petitioners accumulated figures to show that the cost of serving a summons in Burns was $18.00 and in Catlow Valley $54.00.[53]

The record of circuit-court certificates shows a number of requisitions for over $20, a high cost for county court requisitions, but necessary to compensate people who had to travel from the south end to serve as witnesses or jury members.[54] Both north and south-end citizens felt that justice was curtailed for them, especially if a case involving their interests came up during a winter term of court.

Still, had the issue been simply one of transportation, the matter of the county seat might properly have merited only a passing mention in locally printed histories and reminiscences. But talk of division began, predictably enough, at the time Burns was beginning to feel its potential power in county affairs. Burns, a town that started from literally nothing in 1882, became the biggest town in the region during its first decade—surpassing even the older established town of Harney in the shadow of the old fort. Coincident with this shift, Burn's leading citizens began to agitate for a separate county organization with Burns as the county seat. Harney City, which had also continued to grow, immediately followed Burns into the struggle. Its local organ, the *Harney Press*, began in 1887 to promote Harney City for the county seat. A new paper, the *Eastern Oregon Herald*, was established in Burns that same year, and, though it was avowedly Democratic, it aligned itself with the *Items* to support Burns's bid to become the county seat.[55]

Opposition to the whole idea of making two counties out of Grant County came from the large cattlemen who feared a hike in their taxes and who deplored any expenditures that might benefit growing numbers of settlers and townsmen. The officials of Grant County itself opposed division, calling it "premature." Attacks from both camps were focused on "a few designing men" in Burns who, it was said, were in a position to gain a disproportionate amount of power should the division take place. The opposition forces were strong enough to take the opening round, so that despite what the *Items* called "considerable interest" no action was taken in 1887.[56]

The proponents of division in Burns judged rightly that the split would have to come; yet rather than wait, they took direct action, and chose a delegation of fourteen citizens to take their case to the state capital at Salem. The lobbyists had a twofold mission: to counter the efforts of a lobby in the service of the large cattlemen, and to use whatever means they could to influence the legislature to vote on the issue at its spring session in 1889.[57]

The cattlemen's own case was undermined significantly during the spring and early summer of 1888 by the flood of petitions that poured into Governor Pennoyer's office from settlers north of Malheur Lake pleading for nullification of swampland claims and asking for relief from a growing number of eviction suits that settlers were in no position to contest. Part of their complaint was associated with the time and expense it took to appear in court in Canyon City. By the time the lawmakers met in 1889, public sympathy was generally in favor of county division, and the new county was formally established on February 25, but the power of the large cattlemen was great enough to make Harney City the temporary county seat.[58]

All of the potentially divisive forces lurking beneath the surface were unleashed by this decision. Town merchants had never been deluded; the cattle barons, they said, bought and sold elsewhere to the ultimate detriment of local businesses. Thus, farmers and small cattlemen were persuaded that their large neighbors were merely the representatives of absentee landlords who drained local wealth away to California. The fact that these same representatives were taxpayers in the county and a valuable source of income for the small men was evidently forgotten. Whatever the case, events of the winter of 1889 strengthened immensely the political fusion of Burns with the settlers of Harney Valley in the north end.[59]

An ominous series of events followed. In the spring the new land office came to Burns. Soon big cattlemen were complaining that they were not being treated fairly. Henry Miller publicly accused the office of partiality. Within a month, the big cattlemen had arranged for the office's transfer to Drewsey. At the same time the partnership of Todhunter and Devine won its case against settlers squatting on the so-called "red-S" field south of Devine's Island Ranch. Devine had purchased this valuable piece of spring-irrigated natural hay land from swampland claims that settlers contended were illegally acquired. When the decision was announced, Devine demanded that the federal marshal, Broady Johnson, evict the settlers. Reports vary, but somewhere between twenty-five and sixty people were driven from their homes, their shacks pulled down and their fences cut to kindling.[60]

The conflict had reached threatening proportions. An *ad hoc* Settlers' Home Protection Society was organized in the early summer. By July, a secret group known as the "101 Society" had also been formed. Rumors circulated about its size and membership, but little was known except that a sudden wave of haystack fires and burglaries broke out, directed mostly against the property of the big men.[61]

In this troubled atmosphere, the circuit court heard for the second time in as many years the case against David Shirk for the murder of James Isaacs. The first trial had resulted in a hung jury, about which Shirk had complained bitterly, claiming that Peter French had tampered with the jury members and had even influenced the editors of the *Blue Mountain Eagle* to print defamatory articles about him. What Shirk had not mentioned was that in 1888 the settlers of the north end had not been friendly to him even before the trial. Shirk was, after all, a relatively well-to-do cattleman from the south end. Two prominent "south enders," one the pioneer cattleman John Catlow, paid Shirk's bill. To most of the people of "del Norte" the whole affair had looked like a squabble between rapacious land grabbers.[62]

By the next term of court, which was held in Harney City in October of 1889, popular sentiment had changed so markedly that the Burns papers, particularly the *Harney Items*, set out to transform Shirk's image into that of an ordinary, hard-working cowman fighting for his life against a ruthless cattle baron. When Shirk was acquitted, the *Harney Items* carried a front-page article extolling his virtues and praising the justice of his acquittal. Shirk later claimed in his diary, that "people of the county . . . had by that time seen through the machinations of the land-grabbing cattle barons, and the announcement of my acquittal was hailed with great satisfaction, not to say rejoicing among the common people, especially among the settlers."[63]

The lines of community conflict were etched so deeply by the fall of 1889 that some despaired of the future. The *Harney Items*, usually an uncompromising supporter of settlers' rights, fearfully stated, "it is certainly unfortunate that such a state of affairs exists in this county, but it seems as time rolls along the line between settlers and monopolists becomes more distinctly drawn, and it is difficult to tell when matters will be finally settled between the contending parties."[64]

The county seat election would not be until June, 1890, but in the meantime, contending parties suffered through the bitter winter of 1889-90—a winter that was one of many sources of conflict between large and small owners because the damage that it inflicted added an element of desperate resolve to the anger building among smaller owners. Some small cowmen and settlers tore the grass roofs off of their outbuildings to feed their stock, and when that feed was gone dumped their cattle onto a glutted market where prices plummeted. The number of sheriff's sales and foreclosures rose markedly that winter. Several beaten settlers moved out, but those who stayed held a new resentment against big men who were better able to survive.[65]

Almost as soon as the spring thaws came, the Burns papers mounted a campaign to win the election for Burns and for people of "del Norte." The tone of the campaign was calumnious, but there was no violence. When election day came, the turnout represented one-half of the entire recorded population of Harney County—a high percentage considering distances and travel conditions and the fact that women could not vote. In the Burns precinct alone, the turnout was 86 percent of the total population.[66] Certainly voter interest had been peaked by this issue, indicating again its importance to the entire community. When the votes were counted, Burns won, but the margin of victory was surprisingly narrow. What is more, there was a disparity between the number of votes cast for county officials and those cast for the location of the county seat: enough voters had left their ballots blank on the proposition to give Harney City officials an excuse to contest the vote. The ensuing investigation revealed some repeat voting and voting under age, but even with the questionable votes thrown out, Burns still came out the winner by ten votes.

Clearly it was a time for cool heads, but the issue had now polarized the community. Town leaders in Harney City refused to give up the county court records and swore they would appeal the circuit court's ruling. Citizens of Burns were equally adamant. On a midnight late in June, a group of unidentified riders broke into the temporary court house in Harney City and stole the court records. Next day the building Burns had prepared to house the county records was opened for business.[67]

This high-handed act of vigilantism produced such animosity that even after the appeal was decided in Burns's favor in 1892, relations between big and small men and between Burns and Harney City remained hostile. It was the kind of issue that can permeate a community's collective consciousness and influence internal relationships long after the original issue itself has gone. It poisoned the atmosphere in Harney County and helped produce the social situation in which Peter French was killed six years later, and the county has borne the scars of these two incidents substantially until the present day.[68] Yet the killing of French was a separate act, and to understand it fully, the question of just how well or ill the courts were administering justice and to what extent they affected community attitudes must be explored in detail.

Fraud and the Courts

Two years after the "rape of the records," Oregon supreme court justice Erasmus D. Shattuck handed down a decision on the results of the election of 1890 showing Harney City to be the winner. A routine recheck of his figures turned up a mathematical error of six votes, which actually gave Burns the election and forced the judge to reverse his decision.[69] The whole episode was embarrassing for the judge, but his blunder was one of the least culpable acts committed by state officials during the entire period. State officers disposed of Oregon's swamplands with callousness and duplicity, but state land frauds went far beyond swampland manipulations. Oregon school lands were scandalously mismanaged during the 1890s, so much so that an investigation in 1901 revealed a large defalcation of school funds and implicated such prominent public servants as General W. H. Odell of the school land board; George W. Davis, the board clerk; Canyon City's native son Phil Metschan; and even Governor Pennoyer himself.[70]

Graft, subterfuge, chicanery: this, after all, was the style of the gilded age. Indeed, the ethics of business had become the ethics of government; political favoritism, bribes, kickbacks, and payoffs were the bond between political aspirants and businessmen. Malfeasance among state officials in the administration of public lands was merely a reflection of a more general corruption at higher levels. The United States General Land Office Commissioner was a political appointee, as were his assistant and all local land office officials under him. The primary criterion for selection of these officials was whether they had been among the politically faithful; seldom, if ever, was it merit. That fact alone was enough to thwart even the best-intentioned commissioners, and there were only one or two of these during the entire period from 1880 to 1900.[71]

Both the federal government and the courts moved slowly when it came to bringing rich and powerful offenders to justice. The cases initiated by the Department of Justice against the Oregon wagon-road companies were typical. The Attorney General of the United States had been authorized to bring suit against all five companies operating in Oregon in 1889. These suits were instituted to force the companies to show evidence of completion of the roads or forfeit their grants— grants that had already been patented through an act passed in 1882. Unconscionable delays followed, resulting in transference of the lands to *bona fide* purchasers who were then immune from any cause of action. In most cases these purchasers were themselves speculators; thus the lands were not available to settlers until well after the turn of the century.[72]

As with the wagon-road lands, many acres of Oregon swamplands had already passed from the hands of the original claimants into those of *bona fide* purchasers. The delays were more understandable in these cases, where there was great difficulty in defining the nature of the land itself.[73] With the increase in settlement on the Silvies and the Blitzen rivers there came a corresponding increase in the number of water diversions along those stream courses. Consequently, the water levels of the lakes were lowered as more upstream users diverted the water. Malheur Lake had been a lake in more than just name even after settlers moved in in the 1870s, but sometime in the spring of 1881 the thin sand reef separating it from the flat bed of Harney Lake broke through, and the sand melted away in a torrent of water that dug a channel through the reef nearly ten feet deep and lowered the level of Malheur Lake irretrievably.

The exposed land revealed much new and usable soil, but the newly formed channel made the shoreline of the lake much more unstable than before. It some years silt gathered in the channel, so that the water in the lake rose; in other years the water from heavy spring run-offs washed the silt away, causing the lake to drop to very shallow levels.

The ordinary cycle of dry and wet years added further fluctions, as did normal seasonal variations in upstream flow. In order better to control their cattle, some settlers built shacks on the exposed land. During the early 1880s families actually lived in these shacks except in the spring when flood waters were too high.[74]

Since there was no clear precedent for establishing the legal status of this land, settlers moving onto it did so at their own risk. Irrespective of that fact, they handled their holdings like property: settling, conveying, and willing the land, all with the use of standard instruments such as bills of sale and deeds made up in the county courthouse.[75]

Inevitably owners of swampland who held the parcels that reached down to the original lake shore came into conflict with these squatters, many of whom were by the late 1880s cutting hay off of the new land below the old shoreline. As has been noted, the first attacks launched against the owners were based upon the settlers' hope of showing that they had acquired title by fraud. W. A. J. Sparks, a truly dedicated and reform-minded United States land commissioner, moved to disallow all swamp claims in Oregon. Several indictments were brought, but evidence of fraud was hard to obtain, and relatively few questionable claims reverted to the government.

Regrettably, Sparks lost some of the initial popularity he had gained by his bold policy when he placed the burden for initiating administrative action upon the settlers. In 1888, Sparks declared that Oregon's questionable swampland claims were eligible for patenting and that a settler's claims would be honored if the claimant attached an affidavit corroborated by two witnesses attesting to the character of the land—and if after an investigation by a commission appointed for the state by the General Land Office it proved in fact to be dry land.[76]

It was Sparks's ruling that brought Todhunter and Devine into conflict with the settlers of the lower Silvies River and led to the evictions in the "red S" field. As local spokesman Archie McGowan commented: "decisions were uniformly against [the settler]. Everything seemed to be against him."[77] Later that year, the General Land Office suspended this ruling, and in 1889, the Secretary of the Interior, L. Q. C. Lamar, ordered some of Todhunter and Devine's patents canceled. When Henry Miller's Pacific Livestock Company bought out Todhunter and Devine, it obtained both the remaining claims and the ill will associated with them. By the mid-1890s, the three big cattle owners—French, the P.L.S. Company, and Riley and Hardin—were joined by a fourth, the Hanley Brothers, who appeared on the tax rolls owning 4,398 acres of land. Above the Hanley Brothers' names in a list of landholders by size were Riley and Hardin with 8,612 acres, the P.L.S. Company with 82,689 acres, and French and Glenn with a total of 105,831 acres.[78] Each of these owners had built up his holdings with sizable portions of swampland acreage. The P.L.S. Company and French and Glenn were the big swampland owners around Malheur Lake and as such were the most deeply concerned. In the suits that followed, it was the P.L.S. Company that pressed first for a settlement. The company brought an eviction suit against one Armack, and this in turn brought the question for the first time before the Secretary of the Interior. The secretary then ordered a new survey establishing a new meander line upon which all subsequent claims were based.[79]

As it turned out, the P.L.S. Company litigations were mostly with upstream neighbors over questions related to the flow of the Silvies River. French, however, owned most of the Blitzen Valley. He fought his legal war with the settlers mostly over exposed lands around the southern rim of the lake.[80] French instituted three eviction suits between 1890 and 1895, but the key cases were those of French–Glenn vs. Springer and French–Glenn vs. Sarah E. Marshall, instituted in 1896 and 1897. In both of them the defendants had appropriated exposed land "below" French's swampland claims. Their legal claims rested upon the common-law doctrine of accretion and reliction of lakeshore land which held that lands exposed by a receding lake were public property and thus could be settled and filed upon as part of the public domain. French's claim was also based upon English common-law doctrine, the doctrine of riparian rights under which he claimed ownership of the land from the boundary of his swampland properties to the center of the lake.

Since the federal government had given the state of Oregon all of the lands designated as swamplands under Oregon's swampland act of 1870, Oregon too had a claim to the exposed or "relicted" land under its "laws and declared rights." Although there was no statute governing Oregon's rights until the Act of 1921, the rule in Oregon had been that all navigable streams or lakes be considered public property. Oregon had consistently applied this rule to all large lakes in the state. Thus, the state could have pressed claims to the exposed land on the basis of the lake being navigable, or having been navigable before the water level fell. This was a tenable position, but the state chose not to press it. Therefore, in French–Glenn vs. Springer the state Supreme Court allowed the litigants to consider the lake non-navigable for purposes of their private contest.

Although the state did not formally withdraw its claims, the court noted that the state had not asserted them, and this alone made it appear to settlers that the state judiciary was making room for the big interests. If there was collusion, it is not evident, but at least the move was inauspicious, since these two cases held the key to the future of many other squatters and the future of settlement in Harney Valley.[81]

The court finally handed down a decision in French's favor in 1899. While the decision disallowed French's claim based on the riparian rights and automatically repudiated that doctrine as a basis for future claims, it awarded him the land on the basis of the western doctrine of prior appropriation and beneficial use. Thus, the relicted land, since it was considered contestable by default, went to the prior owner who had used the water: French. The case was appealed and returned to the state supreme court on a writ of error. A final decision was not handed down until 1902.[82]

In the meantime, the Marshall case, on appeal to the United States Supreme Court, established a precedent for the court's consideration of the essential public nature of the relicted lands. This ruling, in effect, reversed the basis for the award in the Springer case. Accepting the view of the judge in the Springer decision that the doctrine of riparian rights was generally inapplicable, the court then awarded the claim to Sarah Marshall as a *bona fide* claimant on the public domain. It was this decision that ultimately gave the President of the United States some basis for declaring unclaimed lands around the lake government property and using them to establish a wildlife refuge there. At the same time the decision opened the door for the state to lay claim to the land under its subsequent Act of 1921 defining Oregon's rights to lake and lake-shore land within the state.

The immediate result, however, was the confirmation of settlers' claims at long last, after eleven years of bitter conflict. Thus, as far as land claims around Malheur Lake were concerned, settlers obtained a breather after 1902. The lake shore was still unstable, and the decisions of the court applied only to conditions existing in the 1880s and 1890s. When a severe drought changed those conditions later, the entire question was reopened in a bizarre replay of the events of this earlier period.

The problems the courts faced in trying to make final decisions on the basis of conditions that were fluid and changing showed up pointedly in the P.L.S. Company's suits against the Harney Valley Dam and Ditch Company, James Foley's concern. These again involved a number of claims and counter-claims, but in these instances there were no land claims involved only the fact that the Harney Valley Dam and Ditch Company had markedly changed the flow of the Silvies River to the detriment of the P.L.S. Company's downstream usage. The latter asked for an injunction against Foley's concern. The case itself took nearly five years to settle, and then it was settled in favor of the P.L.S. Company on the basis of the company's having a prior right. Still, this was not what anyone could call a final decree. It was simply decided that the company would receive all the flood water from the Silvies River from March through the first part of May, during its maximum run-off, after which time upstream settlers could divert it from mid-May through June—the months during which the P.L.S. Company had never really used it at all. The problem was that the period of maximum run-off was also the period for its most efficient use for irrigating natural hay, but since there were still relatively few settlers who were ready to cooperate in using the water, this arrangement amounted to a temporary compromise of interests, which was seriously questioned when the conditions of settlement and the demands on the water changed again after 1900.[83]

The circuit court's dockets were full of cases relating to land and water claims, and the newspapers continually reported related trespass and ejection suits, but the cases just discussed caused perhaps the greatest amount of ill feeling. It was not so much that judges and courts were blatantly biased in favor of the big cattlemen. The crucial part of any case was the selection of the jury; for every injustice that highly paid lawyers and their appeals might have brought upon small men, there were like injustices brought upon the big men by the selection of "settlers' juries."[84] Perhaps the chief problem was that legal precedents taken from the East and Midwest did not fit conditions on the western frontier. In addition, there were omnipresent confusions resulting from piecemeal, parochial legislation that filled the void where comprehensive regulatory statutes ought to have been. Consequently it was an era of contention: a lawyer's field day, when an attorney played his client's cards "close to his vest" and used the procedures of common-law pleading like a foil in a fencing match, more to confound the adversary than to settle differences with him. In fact, one could again draw a parallel between institutional values. Big business, in the spirit of private enterprise as a whole, was essentially an adversary system—a competitive, sometimes brutalized system geared primarily to turning profits. The judicial system partook of that same character when it favored parties well equipped for battle in open court as though justice was a product of the Darwinian principles of survival of the fittest. To the settlers of Harney Valley, who supported eleven lawyers in their community (approximately one lawyer for every twenty-five citizens), and who watched many more of their own kind move out rather than submit to the costly legal fights that often merely postponed their ultimate defeat and restricted their chances for starting again elsewhere, the judicial system appeared to be a unique villain indeed. As a letter to the *Harney Items* put it: "The *Items* is to be praised for its stand in behalf of the poor settler whose money is poured into contest after contest with rich companies."[85]

From the time the French-Glenn partnership first brought suit in 1891 to contest the claims of settlers around Malheur Lake until a final decision was handed down in 1902, both parties to the quarrel lived side by side, not knowing what the precise nature of their rights were, but bitterly opposed to each other's claims and vehemently convinced of the correctness of their own. This was the stuff of which violence was made, the violence that resulted in the death of Peter French.

The Killing of Peter French

The killing of Peter French was both a symbol and event in the life of Harney County. One of the most powerful beliefs in the pantheon of American myths is the "myth of the garden"—"The image of [a] vast and constantly growing agricultural society in the interior of the continent . . .—[an image] that defined the promise of American life."[86] Indeed, in place after place where the land was more desert than garden, as in southeastern Oregon, men felt they were destined to transform it with little more than what one publicist called the "prayer of their own labor." There was nothing unusual about the waves of immigrants that persistently rolled over the same land where the experience of others had been only failure. Not until the mid-1890s when the line of the frontier was gone and American industrialism had produced one of the worst of its periodic depressions was the dream in any way shaken.

The depression seemed to indicate that the disappearance of the frontier might also mean the disappearance of economic opportunity in America. Even then the dream lived on. Like all myths, the myth of the garden was sustained by men's desire to believe it, and the role of reason was, as always, to shape the myth to fit changing circumstances without sacrificing its vital heart.[87] By the 1890s the myth showed its power when after a history of agricultural failure in semiarid regions, settlers persisted in the belief that the culprit was not so much the poor quality of the land or the settler's use of it, but the monopolist who exploited it. According to mythological auguries, once this monopolist was removed, American purpose and destiny would be fulfilled and the true promise of American life vindicated. In the cattle business at least, the ranges would be gardens once again. It was this sacred purpose that gave the killing of French its symbolic cast and made it the best remembered and, from a popular standpoint, the most important single incident in the history of Harney County.

The symbolic nature of the killing of Peter French helped also to make it the most controversial single incident in the county's history. French's killer, a homesteader named Ed Oliver, lived on a claim located in the middle of French's holdings near Malheur Lake. The quarrel between him and the cattle baron was over the homesteader's annoying habit of riding through one of French's better fields to and from his house. When French, who was unarmed (he rarely wore sidearms), saw Oliver riding through the field on the day after Christmas in 1897, he accosted him; as French turned away, Oliver pulled a gun and shot him. Oliver was acquitted in the trial that followed, but he left his family soon afterward and ran off with the contributions made to them by sympathetic local citizens.

Thus the symbolic killing of a range monopolist by a yeoman farmer was also the killing of an unarmed man by a man of questionable private character. Intertwined with these less praiseworthy aspects was perhaps the pull of an earlier day, when relationships between French and his neighbors had been closer and when French was the much admired builder of an empire who could ride and shoot with the best of them—a figure to be reckoned with, even emulated, and certainly not destroyed.

One thing was sure; French himself was no abstraction. How one felt about his death depended upon one's predilections, socio-economic group, and contacts made with French, if any. Yet, regardless of what these relationships were, French's death jarred the entire community deeply. Times were hard during the mid-1890s. The nation-wide panic of 1893 had widened into a deep depression by 1894, and Harney County, though immune from it in large part, felt the pinch along with the rest of the country. Cattle prices declined in that year and the specter of overstocking threatened once again when a cold winter nipped the high ranges late in 1894.[88] Rustling increased sharply but "more often . . . as a part of the local conflict between the big companies and small settlers rather than professional, outside thievery."[89]

Nothing as blatant and costly as Wyoming's Johnson County War between cattlemen and settlers broke out anywhere in Oregon. But the problems that prompted that open clash of interests were the same as those that moved Peter French and the settlers closer to violence in the early 1890s. Choice ranges, water sites, and streambeds were being contested or taken up by homesteaders. Fencing, whether legal or illegal, whether put up by cowboys or sodbusters, was reducing the cattlemen's freedom of operation. With the growth of population, the privileges and immunities of large cattle interests were challenged more and more frequently in the courts and in the political forum.

Wherever and whenever they could, large owners changed their methods of doing business to meet the needs of changing times. The French–Glenn partnership was typical. In 1894 the partnership itself dissolved, and, in order to bring the business the advantages of the more streamlined corporate form, Peter French became one-fifth owner of the new French–Glenn Livestock Company and received complete control of the operation. Given the conditions in southeastern Oregon at the time, this was no cause for rejoicing. The company was clearly a business on the defensive by the mid-1890s. The location of the company's holdings—the Blitzen drainage all the way to its mouth and land around the south shore of Malheur Lake—thrust French into close contact with the pioneers of Happy and Diamond valleys and with the milling, unstable groups of settlers around the meander line of the lake. The French–Glenn properties became, in effect, a salient in the battlefront across which little men and big men faced each other.[90] Like the prince of a beleaguered nation, French tried at first to negotiate with his neighbors. He encouraged settlers on the lake bed to work for him while the courts were ostensibly work-ing out a settlement of both their claims and his. This took some restraint on French's part: he had been one of the chief targets of the "101 Society" and had lost 800 tons of hay by arson in the summer of 1889. The following October a range fire erupted on his land, forcing him to bring several hundred head of cattle out of the high country to feed early on the already short rations in his valley pastures.[91]

Restraint was not one of French's personal qualities. Though he was unable to bring the arsonists to justice, he was quick to prosecute those he thought were threatening his rights. More and more frequently his name appeared as plaintiff on the docket of the county court: in a trespass and damage action against his chief antagonist, D. H. Smyth, in 1889, and in an ejection suit against Smyth's brother George in 1891. Thus "negotiations" with the settlers began to break down. Despite his employment of squatters by 1893 they were accusing him of hiring them in order to squeeze them out. They came to that conclusion on the grounds that the time they spent working for French was a sacrifice of time that they could have spent improving their own property. There was an impression abroad that French's apparent generosity was merely a pose to cover some more sinister motive.[92]

In 1892 relations between the parties deteriorated further. French beat up two of his opponents with his bare fists. When the snow began to melt in the spring of 1893, he found the irrigation ditches he had built into the Diamond area trampled down by one J. H. Kidd, who said he felt he had sole right to the water. French again took his case into court; but this time, unlike most previous trials, his neighbors' testimony went almost wholly against him, and some of it was intermingled with ill-tempered, ugly aspersions on French's character. Unfortunately, there is no record of the disposition of this case. The next fall Harrison Seaward claimed French shot at him from ambush when he rode through the area. In 1894, a grand jury brought two true bills against French; grand larceny and assault with a deadly weapon, both of which were dismissed by the district attorney for lack of evidence. The dismissals in turn gave rise to ugly rumors about French's influence over the district attorney.[93]

By 1895 French stood alone, his potential friends among the bigger owners drawn off by their own concerns and his enemies more vociferous and united than ever. Whatever the basis for the rumors of his power over county officials, French himself felt he was not being given a fair shake in the county court. A petition for a road through his land to Catlow Valley had been approved over his opposition. An easement requested by Ed Oliver for a right-of-way through one of French's pastures was allowed in spite of French's complaints that consumption of forage could not be controlled in that pasture if someone was allowed to cross it at will. In the matter of the easement, French instituted another of what must have seemed an endless series of lawsuits to defend his rights.[94]

The litigation was costly. During that period of economic distress, it was a drain on French's assets that he could ill afford, since his creditors both in Burns and in California were growing more and more restive. There were also problems stemming from his personal life, which had been complicated by the death of his partner in 1883 and by his divorce from Glenn's daughter in 1891. After that, there was a cooling of relations between him and the Glenn family that carried over into business affairs. In his isolation, French became a brooding, threatening figure, quick to argue and quick to find fault.[95]

Certainly one of the most exasperating problems for French was that involving Ed Oliver, perhaps because Oliver was among the least significant of his opponents in terms of political power; and yet, as a nuisance homesteader on land surrounded by French's property, Oliver constituted as formidable an obstacle to French's designs as older and more entrenched enemies like the Smyths. French fought with Oliver the first time they met on an open field near Malheur Lake at the time John Neal was surveying the new meander of the shore line in 1887.[96] From then on Oliver's "ranch in the field" was a source of constant friction, and French threatened him often over access to it even after the county court granted Oliver his easement.

In 1895, French told Bill Dunn, a settler near the narrows between the two lakes, "Oliver's . . . riding in the field has got . . . to stop."[97] But nothing French could do for the next two years put an end to it, not even the sudden change of tactics in which French hired Oliver to work during the peak period of 1896. So when Oliver wandered across the field during a winter roundup of local cattle the day after Christmas in 1897, French rode over to him and, within sight of several witnesses, dismounted and accosted Oliver. Accounts vary, but French made his points in an angry way; and as he walked away, Oliver drew a pistol and shot him in the head.[98]

There is little available evidence to make an accurate, clear judgment about Oliver's motives, but he apparently felt he had the backing of the community at large. The transcript of the ensuing trial bears him out; the testimony reads like a study in social alienation.[99] French's hired hands were the only witnesses brought to the stand by the prosecution, and all of them testified that French had been unarmed. The defense witnesses did not contest that fact even though the formal plea was self-defense. Instead, they told of French's increasing animosity toward settlers and reiterated the stories of his hot temper and fistfights. Oliver's four lawyers were all men from Burns who knew their neighbors well; they hoped that popular resentment against French would gain Oliver an acquittal. Defense witnesses were a cross-section of the northern community; homesteaders from around the general areas of Malheur Lake and Diamond, including Alva and L. B. Springer, with whom French had fought in court, and Pres Smyth, scion of the redoubtable Smyth family. In fact, Oliver's bail of $10,000 had been raised by local businessmen including Burns general store owners R. H. Brown and Fred Lunaburg and tradesman Byron Terrill. As might be predicted, the jury acquitted Oliver of murder and justified his act as self-defense.

Oliver's act had been popular, and the ends of justice had apparently been served. But deeply disturbing elements remained. In order for such an act to be of value to the social structure, the dangers to community solidarity and safety had to be removed. Yet the French–Glenn Company holdings were not destroyed, nor were the methods by which the company operated changed in any fundamental way. There were still the same cases in the courts concerned with the same questions of the meander line, water rights, and land patents. The other big owners were still the leading cattlemen of the area, dominating the county's economic picture as thoroughly as ever.[100] But, most disturbing of all, Ed Oliver, who had been made to appear an ideal homesteader and family man, left his wife and children and made off with most of the contributions local citizens had given the family to sustain them during the trial. A casual, irresponsible newcomer had killed the most towering and imposing member of the community. This was not the story of David and Goliath, but the parable of the slain vintner.

The two incidents—the fight over the county seat and the killing of Peter French—form a continuum: a single cataclysm that has worked on the community's memory like a low-grade infection, abating and recurring throughout the years, but essentially incurable. Indeed, every major argument between big and little owners since that time has drawn in some way upon the justification of the rights of one side or the other as they were formulated in the wake of those events. It is not likely that even the memory of an all-out war could have operated more banefully on the health of the community.

CHAPTER FOUR

The Last Beginnings

Moving into the Twentieth Century

The relationship between the struggles of the 1890s and the currents of change that flowed beneath their surface was probably not altogether apparent to the men and women who lived through the turmoil of those years. Yet changes were taking place within every aspect of Harney County society, changes that promoted more community solidarity and portended more social maturity, less violence, and more sophisticated modes of community behavior. The more prosaic indices of these changes—public policy, methods of livestock raising, transportation, settlement, habits of living, and social relationships of all kinds—though not as dramatic as the death of Peter French, help produce a more comprehensive picture of southeastern Oregon society as it moved toward stability at the turn of the century. Raw frontier conditions still existed; but the community that greeted the new century was the prototypical community of a new and more orderly, if more complex, age. The forces that made for these changes, and the impact of these forces upon the structure of the community itself, will be the subject of the remaining chapters.

Transportation and Communication

When Peter French died, the county coroner rode out from Burns to look at the body. Since there was no undertaker in Burns, French was laid in a tin-lined casket, which two of his most trusted hands, Mart Brenton and David Crow, loaded into a buckboard and hauled over the rough road to Baker City, where the body was embalmed. Everyone in Burns knew the casket was on its way twelve hours before the undertaker in Baker City got word and nearly twenty-four hours before the Glenn family even knew French was dead.

On the afternoon of the killing, riders were dispatched from the scene to ride to the two nearest telegraph points, Winnemucca and Canyon City. From Wright Field on Malheur Lake, where the body lay, to Burns, the closest settlement of any size, it was a hard four-hour ride alone on horseback—six hours by buckboard or wagon. The road to Winnemucca was impassable for any wheeled vehicle during most of the winter.

Five days after French was shot and three days after his body arrived in Baker City, the range baron's embalmed corpse was sealed into a suitable casket and loaded onto a railroad freight car for the trip to Red Bluff, California. The whole process took nearly two weeks and tells a macabre but graphic story of the slow progress of transportation in Harney County by the last decade of the nineteenth century.[1]

Throughout that period the functioning of countywide social and political institutions was impaired in almost direct proportion to the poor conditions of travel. This is not surprising. As many writers on western travel and pioneer life have noted, the degree to which both internal and external communications became regular and predictable was directly proportional to the degree to which any pioneer locality ceased to be pioneer. Stable institutions derived their stability from permanent settlement, which, in all areas of the West, depended upon a permanent and dependable system of transportation.[2]

The promise of permanence in the Harney country came from the presence of major railroad lines that rimmed it for a radius of 150 miles on the south, east, and north. The contrast threats of impermanence, which left the region in a twilight of frontier instability for more than a decade, came from primitive internal communication along ill-kept roads that any passing storm, winter or summer, could obliterate, rendering a rancher and his family or an entire small community literally helpless in the wilderness.

Until 1901, the railroad terminal closest to Burns was Ontario, 150 miles to the east. Yet the late 1890s saw prosperity and increased settlement in Burns, indicated by growing markets and a greater demand for goods. To meet these changes, pack mules were replaced by wagons drawn by jerk-line teams of horses. As Herman Oliver commented in his reminiscences: "Machinery, stock salt, fencing for farms; pianos, windows, doors, and bricks for houses; pipe, hoists, and carts . . . these things didn't work too well on pack horses."[3]

When the Sumpter Valley Railroad was extended to a terminal in Whitney in 1901, thirty-five miles were cut from Burns's distance to a railhead. However, despite hints in the local papers that the new line would make a lucrative commercial link between Burns and the Boise Valley, the major flow of commercial traffic continued to go by freight wagon east to Ontario and north to Canyon City and The Dalles. The Blue Mountain mines were still more dependent upon Portland for goods and services than they were upon Baker City, Ontario, and points east.[4] The main trouble then as now was the lack of good roads between Canyon City and Whitney.

Well into the twentieth century, Harney Valley's connections with the outside world continued to be by wagon road east and north. These connections improved in quality and service only insofar as freighting outfits could afford to add a new span of horses, buy a new wagon, or hire an extra driver—improvements that came more frequently as sheep raising came more into its own, adding thereby the profits from hauling wool on the outbound leg to those from hauling finished products on the inbound journey to interior communities. This wool trade went by way of Shaniko and The Dalles and increased even more southeastern Oregon's dependence upon The Dalles-Portland market.[5]

Passenger travel from towns off the railroad to any of the railroad terminals was of course difficult as well as inconvenient. Tom Howard, one of "the best whips on the road," described what it was like for a stage-coach driver to go from Burns to Ontario in a winter storm. "I could not see any trace of where I came through . . . so that there was a unbroken trail before me and wastes of snow drifts in the rear."[6] But winter was the time when merchants, farmers, and stockmen could take care of business matters they had postponed during busy summer months. Often such business would take them to The Dalles and to Portland, less often to Ontario and farther east. Wool buyers congregated in The Dalles during the winter or traveled the railroad between there and Pendleton until spring. Consequently, there was a fair traffic in passengers traveling from southeastern Oregon to The Dalles during winter months. The Burns-Canyon City-Dalles stage run offered sleigh trips across the frozen Ochoco Mountains by 1901. Once travelers reached The Dalles, those who had business in Portland could either continue down the Columbia River by rail or choose the slower but often more comfortable trip aboard an Oregon Steam and Navigation Company steamship, which left The Dalles pier at 7:00 in the morning and slipped alongside a wharf on Harbor Street in Portland at 4:30 in the afternoon.[7]

Travel south or west from Burns remained the unpredictable venture it had always been. Those who took the trip to Winnemucca were mostly cattlemen and miners.[8] From the west came Willamette Valley immigrants and livestock buyers. Occasionally state or federal officials traveled through on official business. The leader of an official party from the United States Department of Interior remarked before leaving Burns for Eugene during a tour of southeastern Oregon in 1887: "We are all in good condition but have a terrible road to go over this trip."[9]

Difficult as travel to and from railroad terminals could be, travel between Burns and other towns in the region—Harney City, Drewsey,

Juntura, Lakeview, Vale, and Canyon City—and from the isolated ranches and farming communities into any one of these towns was equally difficult and sometimes hazardous, especially in the winter and early spring. In 1897, a fast thaw closed Burns off from almost all eastern traffic for more than two weeks. Mail was boated across the floodwaters of the Silvies River until they subsided in early May. Church services in communities east of Burns were canceled for nearly a month, and the price of whiskey went up with the prayers of the clergy.[10]

Such incidents could be multiplied nearly endlessly; the Harney County commissioners' journals and other early records contain a number of references to the breakdown of official county functions because of poor roads and bad weather. The entire winter term of court in 1892 was postponed because of "an unavoidable failure," explained further in the notice to have been a "failure" of good weather.[11] It was just this sort of problem that had led to proposals to divide the county only a few years before. Understandably, the issue of adequate roads remained a political issue into the twentieth century.

For many reasons, the county court could not meet the demands for improved roads. The court was only newly formed, and it took time to find good road supervisors and to raise the money to pay them for often thankless work. Moreover, the big cattlemen, whose influence in the state government was always strong and toward whom the county commissioners always cast a deferential eye, were not in favor of any improvements in transportation that could mean increased settlement. Thus efforts to improve county roads made little headway against divided loyalties, inadequate resources, and limited personnel.[12] Besides, what Harney County really needed was a railroad: In the minds of the vast majority, the ultimate solution to the county's transportation problems. Even the south-end barons conceded it would operate in the way that businessmen and settlers predicted by opening up the region to unprecedented development and by adding something of that elusive permanence and stability wanted by most settlers and thought already too prevalent by most cattle barons.

Settlers' hopes gave rise to rumors that in turn fed upon growing amounts of promotional propaganda put out by land developers and speculators. Land development schemes were begun in earnest in the 1890s; all of them in this period rested upon active promotion of a railroad. Despite the distinctly practical bent of local businessmen, there was a growing air of anticipation among them and a tendency in the local papers to puff the county's national resources out of proportion to what they actually were.[13] None of this led to community action such as county land grants or financial aid. But the vision of a silver lining of shining rails, moving toward Harney Valley from somewhere out past Stinking Water Pass, persisted in the county's collective consciousness from that time until it actually became a reality in 1916.

A railroad connection often seemed very close, almost palpable. It is difficult to trace the influence local promoters had on railroad officials, but coincident with their efforts some tangible plans were made by prominent railroad men to forge a link with southeastern Oregon.[14] The company that took the lead was the Oregon Railway and Navigation Company, which at the time had been forced out of its dominance in Portland traffic by the resurgence of the Northern Pacific. The O.R. and N. was looking for new markets and by 1901 had established within its organization an office for a livestock agent. In March, 1902, ten carloads of Hereford bulls—among the first to be brought into Oregon—were shipped to the ranges of southeastern Oregon as a part of the company's plan to expand into that region.[15]

The Portland Chamber of Commerce lent its support to these plans for fear that the Oregon Short Line might build a spur from Ontario to Vale and drain "over a fourth" of the state's resources off to the east. The concern was unrealistic; but in February, 1903, the chamber formed a "committee to inquire into a Central Oregon Railroad." In April, the O.R. and N. announced plans to build a line into central Oregon, and in May, officers and engineers of the company were swarming over the region like flies. Their efforts continued sporadically throughout the summer but fizzled into nothing by fall.[16]

One can only guess the reasons, although two seem more plausible than others: the previous winter had been a bad one, and to the planners, livestock looked poor. Also Union Pacific magnate E. H. Harriman's great interests were beginning to consolidate, with tentative offers of a merger already being made to the O.R. and N. Given these and other conditions, the company retreated to its earlier position of active interest but no specific action.[17]

The O.R. and N. thus came tantalizingly close to fulfilling southeastern Oregon's dreams as early as 1903. Other larger companies would come as close in the years to come. Small wonder, then, that land speculators always lurked in the wings and local businessmen and developers always seemed to be able to convince a number of potential investors and settlers that there was good fortune awaiting them should they opt to become citizens of Harney County.

The Promise of Equal Opportunity

Permanent settlement and growth depended upon something more than good transportation, as important as that was; it depended, too, in some inestimable but real way, upon the kind of future that awaited settlers once they arrived. Early studies of westward migration assumed that the frontier offered roughly equal opportunities to all comers. While recent studies have modified that view considerably, unquestionably pioneer settlers came west expecting to find something better than the social inequities they left. To them, the West meant greater equality of opportunity, and their expectations were bolstered by lawmakers in Washington whose constituents, even in the East, felt the same. During the period between roughly 1895 and 1907, the national government began to exert its leadership to promote conservation of the West's natural resources and to protect the individual's right to win a living therefrom. These were irreconcilable aims, but the one goal that gave them some coherence was the curbing of exploiters and monopolists.

In the Revision Act of 1891, Congress with one stroke repealed the two most flagrantly abused land laws then on the books: the Preemption Law and the Timber Culture Act. It also modified the provisions of the Desert Land Act to make it easier for settlers with limited capital to "prove up" on their claims. The commutation clause of the homestead law—which allowed homesteaders to buy their claim at a minimum price after a certain time—was extended from six to fourteen months, and forest reserves were authorized to be withdrawn from land "wholly or in part covered with timber or undergrowth, whether of commercial value or not." The act was designed primarily to "curtail some of the advantages of men and wealth." After all "there still remained some hope that the homesteader might succeed . . . and that the small stockman could succeed in case the homesteader did not. . . . If on this last frontier, the government remained true to its proclaimed purpose, there was reason to expect that should the common man fail to work out his own salvation the government would come to his aid."[18]

Some provisions were made to protect equal opportunity, and southeastern Oregon was the very sort of "last frontier" to which these provisions applied.

Such, at least, was the promise. In fact, however, the government was unable to enforce its reforms. Paradoxically, so long as some settlers could see benefits for themselves in the loopholes in the old land laws, they begrudgingly accepted their inequities as well. There was a bit of the aspiring monopolist in all settlers, and, like most other westerners, they wanted to see the public lands alienated without really caring much how it was done.

Though the failure of the Revision Act of 1891 did not appreciably change settlers' attitudes, certain other events did. The revulsion of Wyomingites against the Johnson County War was not unlike the sobering influence of Peter French's death on Harney County, or the disgust with which many Oregonians contemplated the cattle and sheep wars in Lake and Crook counties. Many western livestock owners were anxious to see an end to uncertainty in the use of public lands. The American Cattlegrowers Association supported President Theodore Roosevelt's appointment in 1902 of a commission to investigate continuing abuses of the Timber and Stone Act, the Desert Land Act, and the no-fencing proclamation. Evidently livestock producers ultimately hoped for some kind of leasing system for the rangelands; but before they could get it, scandals and abuses associated with the extant land acts had nurtured sentiment in Washington opposed to leasing as well as to headlong alienation in general and in favor of some meaningful regulatory legislation.[19]

The year that the Roosevelt-appointed commission met, the *Harney Items* gave its support to the formation of the Blue Mountain Forest Reserve as a means of protecting the rights of small farmers to use timberlands for their homes and cattle. When in 1905 the Bureau of Forestry was transferred from the General Land Office to the Department of Agriculture and a grazing-permit system was finally established, the settlers of southeastern Oregon began to concede that perhaps the federal government was taking the correct steps to protect them.[20]

If would-be settlers needed further indication that the wind in Washington was blowing in the direction of more rather than less equal opportunity on the last frontier, it came from the government's support of irrigation of western lands. John Wesley Powell's *Report on the Lands of the Arid Regions of the United States in 1878* had provided the nation's lawmakers with basic information and necessary awareness of the problem, while the drought of the mid-1880s provided them with the rationale for action. As a result, Congress authorized three major western irrigation surveys—in 1888, 1890, and 1891. Irrigation publicist William E. Smythe, began to gather adherents of irrigation into several Irrigation Congresses during the 1890s, and the entire cause gathered enough momentum to become a national issue by 1900.[21]

Outside of Utah, irrigation projects throughout the settled West began as small private undertakings of which the ditches and canals dug in Harney County during the 1870s and 1880s were typical. Most diversions, in Harney County as elsewhere, were built to irrigate forage crops. Only as western farmers became more ambitious, coincident with increased demands for cash crops and the return of good times in the mid-1890s did the need for collective action arise.

Private companies were the first to try, and they performed minor miracles in areas such as the Boise Valley. In general, however, these efforts, like the efforts of individuals, failed to solve the basic problem of aridity. As Powell and his adherents had suggested, the scope of the problem was too vast to be handled piecemeal through private investment. After 1900, most westerners agreed, the more foresighted among them recognizing that the twentieth century was going to demand more, not less, collective action in order to develop national resources. It was "in the twentieth century [that] Westerners . . . [looked] to Washington for irrigation and electric power."[22]

Much of this new reliance upon the central government stemmed from an exaggerated notion of what irrigation might be able to do for the arid West. Coupled with the chamber-of-commerce attitude typical of growing western settlements, this view led local newspapers like those in Harney County to talk of aridity as though it were a positive blessing and of government help as though it were a patriotic duty of the Washington establishment.[23] The dominant misconception, in southeastern Oregon at least, was the conviction fueled by irrigation propaganda that desert soil was as rich as, or richer than soil in the better-watered regions of the country. Some of the most responsible officials in the federal government promoted this notion. In 1901, Frederick Newell, the Chief Hydrographer of the United States, made a trip through southeastern Oregon with the Chief of the Bureau of Forestry Gifford Pinchot, during which he was quoted in the *Daily Oregonian* as saying: "agriculture brings in greater yield to the acre than sheep or cattle raising, and, in the end, a large portion of eastern Oregon must be given over to the farmers." Secretary of the Interior Ethan Allen Hitchcock lent the authority of his office to the idea that "desert land in America would support 50,000,000 people if it were irrigated." Small wonder, then, that Burns newspapermen felt they were voicing the best hopes of their subscribers by publishing articles such as the one entitled "The Poorest Land in the U.S. Can be Made to Pay a Profit" and describing southeastern Oregon's desert as "land . . . as fertile and productive when brought under the requisite condition of moisture as any in the world."[24]

By this logic, all that southeastern Oregon needed to assure its growth was water. Settlement, which after all was the *raison d'être* behind the entire irrigation scheme, would quickly follow. That, in fact, was the logic behind the official view in Washington; irrigation was to be an adjunct of homestead policy. Newell's remarks in 1902 clearly showed this bias: "The result of the irrigation scheme will be that small farms will replace large ones." Oregon's politicians took care to be identified with this general philosophy. The *Harney Items* even published regular reports measuring how closely the Oregon delegation conformed. The great, undoubted good to be accomplished in the long run was what the editors of the Burns *Times-Herald* called the "bright visions of happy homes, of prosperous, contented people, attracted . . . [to the West] to transform those vast regions . . . [into a] succession of countless smiling farms.''[25] Thus, irrigation gave a fillip to the old rural American dream, the Jeffersonian dream: a dream no western politician could safely oppose.

Locally, the specific sins that monopolists committed to prevent this dream from coming true were enumerated as often as printers set type. Yet only the newspaper editors themselves talked of truck gardens and fruit orchards. Letters written by settlers to the local papers tended to equate farming with the gradual replacement of native meadow grass by domesticated grasses like bluestem, timothy, and alfalfa.[26] Close to the heart of settlers' attitudes was resentment of the big men, and some of the more practical could see federal irrigation measures as a means of loosening the grip of the cattle barons on large chunks of potentially irrigable pasture land.[27]

The big operators were, as always, shrewd. With an eye to the future, some in eastern Oregon found ways to join the growing forces of irrigation while at the same time advancing their own interests. Bill Hanley was such a man, and the instrument he used was the ill-fated Carey Act of 1894. Pursuant to it, he established the Harney Valley Improvement Company and designed a system of dikes, ditches, and reservoirs to divert the flow of the Silvies and store it for the irrigation of nearly 100,000 acres of Harney Valley land. Within this general design, Hanley had two specific goals: to irrigate vast portions of heretofore unirrigated land on the peripheries of the Silvies drainage, and to drain marshlands at the mouth of the Silvies River in order to make them useful for farming.[28]

The chief danger to the project was that it conflicted with the interests of the P.L.S. Company, for the company stood to lose its winter pasturage if the marshlands at the mouth of the Silvies River were drained. On the other hand, Hanley had the support of Charles Altschul, the agent of the Willamette Valley and Cascade Mountain Wagon Road Company, who approved of the venture because it would increase the salability of the company's land. Hanley himself stood to make a profit on the contract and also to benefit from the enhanced value of several hundred acres of his own deeded land, which until that time had not been irrigable with water from the Silvies. Though there is no evidence to indicate he was insincere, it seems altogether possible that a man of Hanley's perspicacity would realize that even had the project failed to meet government specifications, or run afoul of a law suit by the P.L.S. Company, the Harney Valley Improvement Company would control all of the aforementioned land, except 20,000 acres belonging to the P.L.S. Company, until either the suit was decided or the work was completed or the state forfeited its grant. Hanley thus would effectively control valuable grazing privileges free of change for as long as litigation continued or completion of the project was delayed.

As it turned out, the career of Hanley's company was a tortured one from the start. The P.L.S. Company brought suit before the planned improvements fairly got under way but by this action suddenly became the villain of the piece. By contrast, Hanley became the noble deliverer whose progressive plans were being sacrificed to greed; but as the years went by with only cursory improvements to show for all of Hanley's efforts, and with the P.L.S. case still pending, Hanley's following in the community dwindled. In 1903, the great deliverer was being labeled the unscrupulous head of "the Carey land-grab concern."[29]

In the meantime a number of other companies, some very small, some large, formed to develop irrigation under the terms of the act. None in southeastern Oregon survived, and none built their proposed works. The most feasible project after the Silvies River scheme seemed to be one at Silver Creek, but the state engineer dropped that for lack of a contractual commitment and because there was some question about the sufficiency of federal lands within the proposed district.[30]

This pattern was duplicated elsewhere throughout the West and led to wholesale disillusionment with the Carey Act after 1900. Engineering was poor, surveys inadequate. The states exercised too little care in selecting applicants and too little supervision after selecting them. Indeed, the failure of the states to make progress under the Carey Act was in good measure responsible for that change of attitude already mentioned which led western citizens to believe that the federal government was the only agency capable of forwarding irrigation. The ultimate result was the passage on June 13, 1902, by a sizable margin in both houses of Congress, of the National Reclamation Act or Newlands Act, as it has come more commonly to be labeled.[31]

By its terms, proceeds from the sale of public lands were to be set aside in a reclamation fund that would be dispersed to build and maintain dams, reservoirs, and canals, under government management and control, for the purpose of reclaiming western lands and encouraging bona fide settlers thereon. Again the emphasis was on government aid to assure individual free enterprise and discourage monopoly, the promotion of long-standing middle-class American values through government assistance—a typically progressive aim, and one that accorded well with sentiment in Harney County.[32]

Plans for a project on Silver Creek were revived, and the county hired one John Johnson to make a new survey of the Silvies River. In June of 1903, Secretary of the Interior Hitchcock temporarily withdrew 622,000 acres of land in Oregon, including all public land in the Silvies drainage, in order to determine how much land could be irrigated and how much water would be needed. Funds for the project would be available the next summer. In the meantime, the Oregon Irrigation Association had already supported the Silvies River site as the best available in Oregon; and since Oregon's public land sales had already earned the state nearly $1,000,000 in reclamation funds, few in southeastern Oregon—or anywhere else in the state for that matter—doubted that the Silvies River would be the first Newlands project in the state.[33]

Within two years after the passage of the act, all of the dreams of irrigation in southeastern Oregon went the way of the dreams of a desert railroad. The survey of the Silver Creek drainage confirmed what had been suspected before: there was not enough federal land within the proposed district to warrant its development.[34] As for the Silvies River project, the federal engineer's report was blunt to the point of tactlessness: "at present time there is little demand for products other than those which can be used for stock feeding."[35] In other words, an irrigation project on the Silvies River would benefit mostly the large stockgrowers who owned most of the deeded land that would be affected by it.

In a stroke, settlers' hopes were dashed; townsmen saw their vision of commercial prosperity fade, and firstcomers found themselves thwarted in their hopes of curbing the range barons while acquiring some newly irrigated land for their own stock. The range barons themselves, epitomized by Hanley (who by this time had bought out Riley and Hardin and was running the P ranch as well as his original spread on the Silvies River), lost their gamble—though it was an admitted long shot—for unexpected aid from the federal government. The loss was shared by segments of every major socio-economic group in Harney County. However, it was not the kind of loss that bound hostile groups together in that friendship born of adversity; instead, it produced a spate of minor witch-hunts and a good deal of scapegoatism. If the newspapers were any indication, those to blame were, in roughly ascending order: the federal engineer and eastern influence in general; the apathy of powerful politicians in western Oregon; the pitiable plight of a section without railroads, population, industry or influence; the confused state of water rights in Oregon; and, at the top of the list, the self-serving manipulations of the large cattle barons who retarded progress by their very existence. As the *Items* hopefully put it, "with the decline of the cowboy period, the rest of the state and the nation will begin to realize that southeastern Oregon has other resources as well."[36]

The cause of equal opportunity through federally operated irrigation had seemingly been dealt a blow in southeastern Oregon. Unquestionably the arid regions deemed cultivable and endowed with the government's blessing under the Reclamation Act leapt ahead faster in the first years of the twentieth century than they otherwise might have. Yet the history of the Newlands Act was also a history of maturing western attitudes about the supposed panacea of irrigation. The would-be farmer learned a good deal, and so did the government. Some of these lessons were painful indeed, and Harney County was at least spared the agony of boom and bust caused by the administrative and scientific blunders accompanying, for example, the Truckee-Carson Irrigation Project in northwestern Nevada from 1903-1907.[37] What is more, the decision against the Silvies River site was not a final decision; the case for irrigation there was never fully closed. Harney County publicists could, with some truth, point to a new era of opportunity no farther away than the day of the railroad—thus fusing two glowing promises that were always on the horizon of a country sustained as much by promises as by real accomplishment.[38]

The Migratory Impulse

With or without good roads or federal irrigation, settlement proceeded at a fairly steady pace in southeastern Oregon. The migratory impulse itself was as important as the potential attractions of Harney County. Certain impelling as well as certain attracting forces constantly operated on migrating groups in the United States; the relative strength of each depended upon what social and economic conditions prevailed in the regions of the United States or overseas from which immigrants came and the degree to which such conditions differed in the place where immigrants were going. Whatever these conditions, they were influenced strongly by the effects of good or bad times: those who came during good times were generally far more numerous and better off, bringing capital with them, while those who came during hard times tended to be less numerous and poorer and usually came shorter distances. This latter group was distinguished by the number of laborers within it, while the former was notable for the number of farmers and professional men it included.[39]

There was a multitude of complexly intermeshed causes to account for people moving from older places to newer ones, from the country to the city, from older settled areas to the frontier. There is no attempt here to simplify the mass movements of the late nineteenth and early twentieth centuries any more than to make the southeastern Oregon experience stand for the experience of the West as a whole. These generalizations are advanced only to help add broader dimensions to specific cases in southeastern Oregon.

The mid-1890s were desperate years in the economic history of the United States, the kind of years that historians and demographers have associated with lower "horizontal" mobility. Nothing that happened in southeastern Oregon contradicts that fact. The national depression that began in 1893 retarded settlement for four years. In fact, the whole period from 1890 to about 1897, for all of the growth it brought to the Burns vicinity and the area around Malheur Lake, was for the country as a whole a period of negligible growth and difficult times in addition to being a period of relatively poor weather—the very conditions that underlay andexacerbated the difficulties between the settlers and Peter French. A small immigration did occur during those years, however, and it had the general attributes ascribed to groups that migrated during hard times.

From 1897 until 1907, settlement increased as the effects of the depression wore off and weather improved. Predictably, settlers during this period had the attributes of groups that migrated during good times. They formed the first wave of what later became the tremendous flood of settlers into Harney County between 1907 and 1918, during the so-called "homesteaders' era"—the flood that was, in turn, a part of the greater ocean that swirled around the last dry hillocks of vacant land in the American West and washed over the last empty outlying fringes of the last frontier before it retreated to more natural boundaries by 1920. In the flood and ebb of that great tide the land was forever changed, much of its lure and glamour gone, even in places like southeastern Oregon where the frontier lingered on.

The settlers of the precursive wave from 1897 to 1907, including some who came as early as 1893 and 1895, formed the last contingent of important groups in the development of Harney County's rural society. As subsequent experience showed, Harney County was not a place that could be considered within the natural boundaries of settlement. It was, instead, one of "the last dry hillocks," and consequently the "homesteaders' era" proved ephemeral. There were small surges of permanent settlement in the late 1920s and early 1930s, and again after the Second World War, but these were mostly in the towns, where their impact on rural society came to seem more a threat to stability than a boon. As might be suspected, those who stayed on from the wave of settlement between 1897 and 1907 had the hardest time getting started, persisting, and achieving social and economic prominence of all those who had stayed from earlier migrations; yet once the persevering among them succeeded in establishing themselves, they and their families were as influential and powerful in rural society as any who had come before. Theirs, then, was the last experience with a fresh beginning on Oregon's last frontier. It is an experience worth careful attention.

The Course of Settlement

In his study of public land law, Paul Wallace Gates offers a rhetorical description of the attitude of members of the United States Congress, especially Republicans, who were loath to recognize that the era of free lands for farms was essentially over after 1890: "What free homesteads had done for Kansas, Nebraska, and the Dakotas in the '70's and '80's might they not do for the Rocky Mountain Interior Basin and Coast States?"[40] These congressmen undoubtedly reflected the attitude of most Americans. After all, Congress was not the sole source of rural expansionism; most people considered national growth by the agency of independent farmers and businessmen a fundamental condition of American life.

Part of the American heritage of unlimited space was the popular notion that the right to cheap land was an inalienable right which could not be restricted any more than cheap or free land in America would ever really run out. This thinking proved the undoing of many an immigrant. A letter from a Sacramento hardware dealer to the Oregon State Land Office in Salem asking for agricultural and timber land "near the California line in the north" was dated October 19, 1898, long after most of the good land in that area was gone; yet it had the same ring of confident expectancy as an earlier report of one J. W. Ambrose of Illinois, who wrote the *Blue Mountain Eagle* that "many people from [Illinois] will come to Oregon in the spring," even though neither he nor those he wrote of knew exactly where they intended to go in Oregon or what they might find once they got there.[41] There was no question that people in the late nineteenth century felt, much as their forbears did, that they could exercise their birthright—and that whatever the intervening years since their fathers' times had brought, no person or thing, short of treason, could stand in their way. This attitude had been noteworthy among midwesterners, and from 1890 to 1897 midwesterners continued to dominate immigration into Harney County.

There was a total immigration into Harney County during the 1890s of approximately 1,070 people, nearly 40 percent less than that during the 1880s; and those who were born in the Midwest again accounted for over one third of the total. Unfortunately, the same shortcomings of the data for the 1870s and 1880s extend to those of the 1890s. Without original census schedules or documents showing the vital statistics of every individual by name, it is impossible to make more than very general kinds of comparisons with the incoming populations of the preceding decades. The sample from the county "mug book" is so small for newcomers of this decade as to be nearly useless. Even though that source of information dealt only with a small percentage of better-off settlers, it accounted for their backgrounds as no other source did; without it there is no way to tell even generally what percentage came directly from the Midwest and what percentage came after several detours through other states or territories. It can only be assumed that some trends set during the 1880s continued through the 1890s, meaning that immigrants tended more and more to come directly to eastern Oregon and Washington by rail. As in the 1880s, this would also indicate that those who came had at least enough money to afford the fare, though this in itself may not have meant much: railroad transportation seems to have attracted immigrants from more widely dispersed areas who were more cosmopolitan and, at the same time, both better off and worse off than immigrants who had come before.[42]

The Harney County tax rolls are incomplete for the years 1896-1900. Consequently, no adequate distinction can be made between settlers who came early in that decade and those who came late: i.e., those who were a part of the migration during hard times and those who came on the tide of rising prosperity. What is left is something like guesswork but, one may hope, better ordered and less open to chance since the four statistical sources available for analyzing settlement patterns before and just after the turn of the century include certain categories of information that complement each other.

One of the sources is the categorical data of the United States Census, which show characteristics of the total population, albeit anonymously. A second source is the personal data in the tax rolls, which, with the exception of the few years mentioned, annually show the names of taxpayers and tell something about the amount of property each owned relative to others as well as the general locale in which each taxpayer lived. The chief disadvantage of the tax rolls is that they include only taxpayers' names, thus excluding that percentage of the population which either did not own taxable property in the county or did not declare it. The third source is the General County Voter Registration Book, which shows the vital statistics of age and nativity by individual name for every male of voting age in the county— approximately 39 percent of the total population. Fourth is the county "mug book," which, as has been mentioned, includes too few personal histories of settlers who arrived during the 1890s to be of more than limited use. Still, a combination of this and the sources listed above, together with some well-qualified statements about them, allows for at least a fair impression of settlement patterns and social trends. There is even a reasonable basis from which comparisons can be drawn with patterns and trends of the 1870s and 1880s.

There are still some problems in linking hard times in the Midwest with the motives of those who came from there to Harney County during the period from 1890 to 1897. No letters or diaries have come to light, nor are there many Harney County residents today who trace their families back to these immigrants; those who do have, for one reason or another, been fruitless sources. Nonetheless, some leads can be gleaned from general histories of the era, and these can be used to suggest something about settlers' motives. For example, according to many writers, a good deal of the political radicalism already noted among midwestern immigrants was spawned in the states of Kansas and Nebraska where the miseries of a number of dry years culminated in the plague of grasshoppers that covered these states during the mid-1890s. In the small sample of the population represented in the "mug book," two of the five midwestern families who arrived in Harney County in the early 1890s came from these two states. What is more, the data on the ages of immigrants recorded in the County Voter Registration Book show that the average age of just the Kansas and Nebraska group was twenty-three. This group represented only 3 percent of the total number of immigrants born in the Midwest, but judging from their youth it is likely most of them came directly from those two states. The percentage of Missouri-born immigrants is large enough to indicate a considerable number of probable trans-Kansas and trans-Nebraska migrants, and this probability is increased by the fact that the average age of those born in Missouri was forty-four, making them twenty-one years older than those born in Kansas and Nebraska. The Kansas and Nebraska group came early in the 1890s and generally corresponded to the category of immigrants who came during hard times: three of the four Kansas-born immigrants were listed as laborers in the voter registration book, while the Missouri-born group showed the highest percentage of laborers among midwesterners with the exception of the groups from Indiana and Illinois.[43]

It is harder to say what accounted for the immigration of the midwesterners from states other than Kansas and Nebraska during those years. The special miseries of Kansans and Nebraskans were not generally felt, although the entire Midwest was wracked by the depression in commercial agriculture.[44] A partial answer, however, may lie somewhere behind the particular limitations of the data; for despite the tendency already alluded to for immigrants to come directly from the Midwest by rail, many of those born in the Midwest undoubtedly came from as near as California and the Willamette Valley. Those who came from the Willamette Valley in the 1880s were better off than those from anywhere else. For the 1890s the data show that despite the high percentage of laborers, the total of the midwestern-born included the highest percentage of all immigrants in non-agricultural pursuits. Furthermore, natives of the Midwest as a whole were dramatically better off than those categorized as midwestern during the 1880s. Since the depression of the 1890s stuck the Willamette Valley less hard than elsewhere, it seems likely that among the two doctors, the three engineers, the two merchants, the insurance broker, the contractor, and the two elective officials who were listed in the voter registration book as born in the Midwest, a good many, if not most of them, must have come from the Willamette Valley. There is no corroboration for this guess except that the society columns of the newspapers show that among these people many visited the Willamette Valley quite regularly suggesting that political and economic leadership remained in the hands of those who came over from the western side of the Cascades.[45]

Not surprisingly, almost exactly half of the midwestern-born immigrants congregated in or close to the three towns of Burns, Harney City, and Drewsey and in or near the growing settlement of "Narrows" between Harney and Malheur lakes. Whether the agriculturists among them called themselves farmers or stockmen (and most of them thought of themselves as farmers), they seemed to reflect a preference for the farm-community environment many of them may have recalled from their midwestern past. Eighty-six percent of the midwestern-born settled in the north end. Of the remaining 14 percent who settled south of the lakes, just under half chose Happy and Diamond valleys, where, though land was becoming dear, the chances for farming it were probably better than in any other region south of the lakes. Indeed, in all the places midwesterners tended to locate, they chose for the most part the last of the best land near the main streams. In doing so they were frequently in the company of Oregon-born immigrants, who had much in common with midwesterners. The two groups together numerically dominated settlement in all but one of the precincts north of the lakes during the 1890s.[46]

In the south end, the nativity of newcomers corresponded closely with that of immigrants who had come to that region during the 1880s: Californians were prominent east of Steens Mountain in the vicinity of the White Horse and Alvord ranches, where many of them were hired hands. In general, Californians included the highest percentage of laborers of any immigrant group outside of southwesterners. They also represented nearly 30 percent of all newcomers who came to the south end, by far the largest percentage of incoming groups in that area. Unlike the midwesterners, however, only 19 percent of the Californians were in occupations other than agriculture, and only one was a professional man. The older cultural distinctions between north and south seem to have been reinforced by immigration throughout the remainder of the nineteenth century. The high percentage of easterners in the south end tends also to reflect this former pattern: as in the 1880s, easterners were generally older, many having come west during gold rush days, and, though their total number was smaller, again most were trying their luck at mining in the Pueblo Mountains near the Nevada line.[47]

As repetitive as the above patterns seem to have been, others emerge that were strikingly different from those of the 1880s. For example, the rate of turnover in the county was much less than during the previous decade; fewer people came in and fewer went out, perhaps confirming the postulate that people do not move as much during hard times as in good, and revealing the fact that the county's rude pioneer beginnings were becoming a part of its past. But, in using the idea of population turnover to suggest degrees of persistence and stability in various parts of the county, comparisons can be drawn between specific areas that can, when the history of these areas is brought into play, indicate the role of social forces in promoting or discouraging such stability.

The two areas of Drewsey and Pine Creek on the one hand, and the area around Malheur Lake and the lower Blitzen, including the precincts of Diamond, Happy Valley, Crane Creek, and Lake on the other, best suit the purpose. The lake area, where the rate of turnover during the 1880s had been the highest in the county, lost only 34 percent of its 1890 population by 1900. Even more remarkably, this region gained a greater number of people than did any other area in the county except Burns.[49] By contrast Pine Creek, one of the areas of greatest stability between 1880 and 1890, lost 35 percent of its 1890 population and ended the decade with 50 fewer people than the 142 with which it started. Drewsey, though it actually gained in total numbers of people, experienced a loss of 69 percent of its 1890 population by 1900. In the case of both Drewsey and Pine Creek, over 10 percent of their 1900 population came from pioneer stock which had been there since the 1870s—a high percentage considering the fact that the county as a whole could claim only 6 percent of its pioneers of that decade, and only one other precinct, Harney City, could claim as high a percentage as theirs.[50]

The figures reveal a high degree of persistence among early families in those areas, but there are anomalies that demand a historical accounting. For example, Drewsey's high rate of turnover in the 1890s may seem odd—unless it is noted that the town had become a freighting center by that time, in addition to being the cow town it had always been. This change came early in the 1890s, bringing in its wake many more laborers and skilled workers than before and supplanting some older citizens who had been engaged in purely agricultural service pursuits.[51] Pine Creek's high net loss of population might be explained, at least in part, by P.L.S. Company policies during the 1890s. Always at pains to protect its interests, the company had bought a fair amount of Pine Creek land and had followed a course resolutely opposed to irrigation projects on Pine Creek. Undoubtedly this discouraged some settlers, whereas the tendencies of both the company and firstcomers to consolidate their holdings probably discouraged a good many more. The Pine Creek and Drewsey areas were becoming, by 1900, closed areas more and more tightly controlled by old families and the P.L.S. Company.

It was argued earlier that instability in the Malheur Lake and lower Blitzen region stemmed from the insecurity of property rights around the lake—an insecurity immensely aggravated by the threatening presence of Peter French, whose policies were potentially, and often very actively, a deterrent to permanent settlement. The seeming anomaly was that the settlers of this region suddenly became the most tenacious in the county during the 1890s, the very decade when their troubles with French were approaching a crisis. Yet the deed records, the purposes of French's policies and those of big men in general during the 1890s, demonstrate that big owners were buying up claims as never before. The very instability of this area, both in law and in fact, allowed for a multitude of settlers' claims, and these could later be sold off for a grubstake elsewhere. Early lake-bed settlers made their stake relatively quickly. Indeed, by the early 1900s a significant percentage of persevering firstcomers in the county had already won their foothold from selling their claims on the lush haylands of the lower Silvies and the Malheur lake bed to others; in that victory there was a lesson that was not lost on those who staked out the marshes and clung to them for dear life through the turbulent decade of the 1890s.[52]

In over thirty years of Harney County's history, the areas where the greatest degree of persistence occurred tended to be the areas where settlers had the best long-range opportunities. Those opportunities were a product of social and economic stability as well as good soil and an adequate supply of water: despite the high agricultural potential of the lake region, special circumstances there made the degree of persistence in that area comparatively low, whereas, despite the turnover of the 1890s in the Drewsey–Pine Creek area, the degree of persistence there was quite high. The same was true in Island precinct, Saddle Butte, and the vicinity around Harney City, all of which were socially and economically more stable in addition to being better suited to agriculture than many other places in the county.[53]

After 1897, the pace of settlement quickened and the impulses behind it changed. Sources of immigration remained generally the same as before except that conditions in Kansas and Nebraska were improving at the same time that more generally distributed dry weather was occurring throughout much of the rest of the Midwest. Concurrently, the semi-arid regions of the Pacific Northwest were enjoying one of their periodic wet spells, which made them appear more attractive at the precise moment when most of the Midwest was appearing less so. To this set of natural circumstances was added the discovery of the great gold bonanzas of the Yukon. Resulting cheaper money helped make prices rise so that more would-be immigrants were able to dispose of their properties and move west.[54] The last great gold rush then was linked to the beginning of the last great movement of agricultural peoples in America, and the Pacific Northwest became both the locus for and the gateway to new and attractive opportunities. A flurry of promotional literature billowed out of railroad land offices in the East and Midwest. One flyer boasted, ''there are pastures there that turn out 250 pound sheep and 2,200 pound cattle. There is no winter cold, no summer heat, no blizzards, no drought, and no crop failures.''[55]

Whether immigrants actually believed such things or not, in the spring of 1901 thousands of midwesterners were on the move toward the Pacific Northwest. A colony of Nebraskans petitioned for 50,000 acres of eastern Oregon land, which it intended to occupy that summer. Sixteen hundred pilgrims from several midwestern states passed through Spokane in the month of May on their way to new homes in central Washington. Later that month, 600 came through Huntington, Oregon, bound for whatever last frontiers might be left.[56]

For southeastern Oregon, the period from 1897 to 1907 was one of active speculation, quickening but not spectacular growth, and incessant rumors of a great land boom to come. A modest ranch in Wallowa County was reported to have sold for $10,500 in 1901. One George Thompson was reported to have sold his homestead for $5,000 in 1902. Yet the Grant and Harney county deed books show no significant increase in land prices from 1875 up to 1900. In fact, The Dalles Military Wagon Road Company, which had sold land for roughly $1.25 per acre in 1875, sold comparable land in 1900 for nearly the same price. If there was any real attraction to southeastern Oregon, it was not in the allurements described by railroad land-office flyers but in the low prices being asked for the land that was available. In all other respects, immigrants found southeastern Oregon the least attractive part of the state.[57]

In this new era of optimism, Harney County's supporters were convinced that it was only a matter of time before their region was filled up and booming like the rest. Circumstances soon proved them right. In the meantime, promoters of the region saw its population turn over without increasing remarkably and watched as promoters and speculators drifted in and drifted out again like fat trout eyeing the bait, too full of better food to take it.[58]

It was not the speculator that Harney County claimed it wanted. When the *Times-Herald* quoted approvingly the statement of Senator

Francis Warren of Wyoming, "What is the public domain for if not to be absorbed?" it meant that it should be absorbed by *bona fide* settlers, not by speculators or large corporate interests—unless, of course, it appeared that some redeeming economic or social good might follow from the introduction of some powerful interest into the local scheme of land ownership.[59] In this, the newspaper was merely recognizing what later historians have acknowledged: that speculation, especially by well-financed outside interests, could provide one of the key means by which developmental capital could be brought into a community. In that light, a community like Burns could ill afford to discourage it.[60]

Organized Speculation at the Turn of the Century

To speak of organized speculation in Harney County before the homestead era is to single out no more than one or two large landowners who, as much as any railroad land office, fed the rumors of the boom to come in the sale of Harney County lands. There were few if any smaller speculators, at least of the kind as easily identifiable as the locators of a decade later. Yet there were unmistakable signs of growth in Harney County. The general spatial pattern evolving throughout the county was one in which settlement on and near the lake lands was thinning perceptibly and spreading out from its original locus in ever widening circles. At the same time, formerly vacant areas in other parts of the county were filling up. The thinning process on the lower Silvies was wrought partially by gradual consolidation, one sign that squatting in that area was coming to an end. By 1900 the lands around Saddle Butte were being taken up, and the Crane Creek settlement was not growing much, only because old-timers were consolidating and newcomers were settling higher in the Crane Creek Mountains and farther up the south fork of the Malheur River. The good land was obviously nearly gone, and those who had held land off the market awaiting its appreciation thought this the ideal time to prepare for its sale.[61]

The most redoubtable speculator in Harney County was the Willamette Valley and Cascade Mountain Wagon Road Company. The patience of its owners, the French investment house of Lazard Freres, was like that of Job, to have suffered the attacks of settlers and state officials and the bumbling of its own executives, and still to have survived. But survive the company did, partially because its owners had ample financial resources and partially because of the business acumen of the company's talented agent, Charles Altschul. Altschul always maintained in the face of much contrary evidence that the land was potentially valuable, and the company backed his efforts to keep it intact and off the market despite the unpopularity that policy bred in two generations of Harney County citizens. By careful manipulations, Altschul managed to consolidate the company's holdings, selling off isolated parcels to local men such as William Buchanan and C. W. Jones who were well entrenched, expanding, and willing to pay.[62]

Through Altschul's good offices, ill feeling in the community toward the company was kept to a minimum throughout the 1890s. Rentals were made to those who requested them, and taxes were paid to the county on time albeit frequently under protest over the high rate. By 1903, however, pressures against the company began to grow as settlement increased. During one term of court alone, the company fought and won eight ejectment proceedings against local citizens, five of whom were established small owners who must have been turning their livestock loose onto company land in defiance of rental obligations.[63] Notwithstanding, Altschul kept the land off the market until after 1910, when he was vindicated in the eyes of his employers by the rush of homesteaders. Prices rose markedly, and the company was able to dispose of its entire holdings at a profit over a ten-year period.

Better known and less feared, if perhaps less respected for his speculations, was Bill Hanley, whose corporate entity was the aforementioned Harney Valley Improvement Company. Even his detractors admitted that Hanley was a staunch promoter of southeastern Oregon and seemed deeply interested in the area's welfare and future. After all, he had cast his lot with his neighbors as few large speculators did; but large speculator he was and closely associated with outside money as well.[64] In fact, Hanley's numerous speculations were never one-man ventures. Legal and financial support came primarily from Portland but secondarily from Salt Lake City.

When the Harney Valley Improvement Company was formed, the land it acquired was mostly Carey Act land. The rest included a small amount of swampland and a substantial parcel of Hanley's own land. When the company's irrigation schemes ran afoul of the P.L.S. Company, the investment properties were reshuffled in order to put the company in a better position to continue without benefit of the Carey Act land. Between 1903 and 1906, according to the Hanley Company records, the Harney Valley Improvement Company exchanged 16,000 acres of land with the Willamette Valley and Cascade Mountain Wagon Road Company.[65] In so doing Hanley was able to retain control of some of the better parts of the Silvies drainage and from this position became a strong force in promotion of the county during the homestead rush. With the profits he made during that rush, he was able to extend his interests into Malheur County.

In this and similar ways, the two best-entrenched, best-capitalized local speculators moved during the late 1890s and the first few years of the twentieth century to take advantage of what they calculated to be good times ahead. Others could profitably have followed their example. As an oldtimer in the county said: "When you find a good cuttin' horse, let him lead."

The Process of Consolidation

When the early twentieth century saw land developers stirring in the warm sun of growing prosperity, the preceding decade of the 1890s saw mostly the slow consolidation of holdings by firstcomers—a vital process in their adapting to the demands of an altered market and a changing technology. The general process on the Illinois and Iowa prairies during the mid-nineteenth century was not so different from what it was in Harney County during the 1890s: "the man who came west, bought a tract of the size that he thought necessary for his farming operations, and then tilled it for the rest of his life was rare indeed. The more common picture was one of several moves or repeated purchases and sales . . . and all this activity moved, to some extent, in tune with economic conditions—when times were good, more land changed hands."[66] There was also a difference between firstcomers and newcomers, as between those who could afford to buy land during hard times and those who could not.

The term "firstcomers" here includes both those who came during the 1880s and those who came during the 1870s—except for the big owners. During the 1890s a few in Harney County were either able to, or disposed to, buy parcels to add to land they already owned, but only a few—twenty-seven in all including the big owners, or a mere 4 percent of the total number of taxpayers listed in the tax rolls of 1900. Twenty-four of these were firstcomers from the 1870s and 1880s, while only three were newcomers from the 1890s. The four big owners, Riley and Hardin, French, the P.L.S. Company, and Bill Hanley, were organizing their last attempt to bring what they could of available agricultural and pasture land under their control. Of the total 198,601 acres purchased for consolidation, 187,885 acres were bought by these four—most of it just before and after the hard middle years of the decade when many settlers got the best price they could and moved on. During that period only 10,716 acres went into the consolidation of holdings of smaller men who had come between 1870 and 1890, but that meant an average of 466 acres each for the twenty-three who acquired more land during that period—a substantial amount when compared with most of their original holdings.[67]

Between 1900 and 1912 the records show that the smaller owners more than doubled their purchases even though the number of purchasers among them decreased. In the same period the number of government land claims more than tripled, including as before claims filed by firstcomers who had not purchased land outright but who used their claims to build already expanded holdings. By contrast, the acreage purchased by the large outfits fell to a paltry 15,418 acres during that same period.[68] The day when large owners could engross land by threats and subterfuge was long past; after 1900, it seemed that the day when they could do so through heavy capital outlays was also past.

Yet these statistical descriptions need qualification. In the case of the larger owners, much of what they bought during the 1890s was what they had used free of charge during the 1870s and 1880s. Forest Service acquisitions had taken the best of the mountain ranges, but these were still available for grazing after 1906 under a system of grazing fees. From 1900 to 1912, then, there was little need for large owners to buy more land. Also, according to interviewees, the land that was beginning to go to homeseekers was land the larger owners and firstcomers figured would not support new settlers and would ultimately revert by one means or another to those who had been there first. It is possible, however, that large owners and firstcomers were less convinced of that at the time.[69]

Those who purchased land during the good times after 1897 seem to have been much the same people who purchased it earlier during bad times.[70] While it is true that more land changed hands during good times, at least in Harney County, the exchange was between fewer owners. Newcomers were by 1910 virtually frozen out of the market in deeded land. Whether by design or not, firstcomers were nearly the only ones who could buy. Mortgage records help show why.

The amount of money lent within the county during the 1890s was $247,924, all but a small amount from private sources and most lent by Henry Miller to the French–Glenn partnership. The largest single amount lent to smaller owners of the 1870s and 1880s and other settlers was $27,100 from merchants McKinney and Sparrow; the next largest amount ($25,000) came from the state School Fund Commission. Miller himself lent over $9,000 to settlers. Of the sixteen lenders recorded in the mortgage records, seven were merchants, two were big owners, and the rest were firstcomers; there is no way of telling how many private transactions went unrecorded.

The motives behind merchants' lending need little explanation. It is enough to remember that Harney County settlers were as short on ready capital as were pioneer settlers anywhere else and that they were engaged in agricultural pursuits—which meant they needed credit in order to grow and harvest their commodities, including cattle, until these could be transformed into cash at selling time. Each merchant carried large amounts of credit on his books, but the largest amounts by far were reserved for establishing citizens. It is entirely likely that amounts of $2,000 or over lent to men like Jezreel Venator, Peter Andrews, J. R. Lamb, John Witzel, the Sitz brothers, Henry Welcome, and Peter Stenger went for cattle or land. Merchant capitalists could not afford to risk such sizable loans on strangers, especially during hard times.[72]

In the case of the big owners who lent money—Henry Miller and the Nevada cattle baron N. H. A. Mason, who lent modestly in Harney County during the 1890s—there were recorded foreclosures against many people whose names appear for the first time in county records in that context and do not appear again. For the most part, the two big owners rarely lent to firstcomers; they lent instead to a number of other small owners, most of them newcomers, in average amounts of from $175 to $200.

It is hard to avoid the conclusion that Miller and Mason preferred to lend to borrowers who were precariously situated and consequently more apt to default. Borrowers might actually have used these loans to commute a claim; in any event neither Miller nor Mason stood to lose much if the borrower did default. On the contrary, they stood to gain a richer prize than the interest: the foreclosed collateral, a piece of deeded land, or a preemption, or a homestead, desert land, or timber culture claim. The P.L.S. Company doubled its deeded holdings during those years, and at least a few parcels of land must have come to the company in this way. Undoubtedly for a few of the borrowers Miller's and Mason's loans provided a needed source of credit with which they were able to buy the necessities, hang on to their land, and survive.[73] It is, however, extremely doubtful that any of these small borrowers could ever have used their loans for the purchase of land. The only other major source of credit, the state School Commission Fund, was, by contemporary usage, mostly a land-purchase fund; yet during the 1890s the entire $25,000 lent by the commission in Harney County went to four substantial citizens in chunks of $2,000 or more, and in two of these cases it was obviously used for the purchase of land or cattle or both.[74]

In the next decade, the total amount of money lent from all sources in the county nearly quadrupled. By this time Burns had two new banks, but, like most banks during that time, they lent on personal rather than real property collateral; the loans of both together amounted to only $5,946. Private citizens like Sarah Marshall, Herman Ruh, and Chauncey Cummins lent nearly that much and often considerably more. By contrast, Henry Miller totally abandoned his policies of the 1890s, lending to only two persons: one of his hands, J. Miranda, in the amount of $200, and a Burns attorney, Cyrus Sweek, in the amount of $7,200. Neither of these loans appears to have involved mortgages on land.[75]

During the 1890s, and for that matter until the First World War, the lion's share of credit came from the State Land Board. Here again, the list of mortgagors reads like a roll call of firstcomers. Of the ninety-two loans made by the board in Harney County between 1900 and 1917, seventy-eight or 85 percent went to these established citizens, and only two of those loans ended in default.[76]

Clearly mortgage borrowing and lending was not only a respectable way of obtaining capital but an exclusive way of doing so, since, as far as the records show, it did not extend to the majority of citizens. Older families were able to develop reserves of capital that they could lend out in turn. Most often the borrowers were members of other old families. Sometimes they exchanged roles: borrowers in one decade became lenders in the next and vice versa. Families often borrowed money to lend to other members of their own family, who, in their turn, would lend to the members of the family from which they borrowed originally. By the end of the first decade of the twentieth century, something of a financial elite was beginning to emerge from among the persistent early settlers.[77]

Aside from the obvious fact that the men with money could buy land, the means by which this advantage could be used to consolidate holdings were as exclusive as the means by which credit was controlled. There were problems unique to each separate region in the county, but in every region, all else being equal, the early families with capital made out better than newcomers even if newcomers had capital too. As county tax rolls show, the early families were able to increase the amount of tillable land held in their names by 323 percent between 1900 and 1912. This increase came from tax-delinquent land as well as from direct sales. During the 1890s, the largest number of tax sales had been made to big owners, but after 1900 the auctioneer's gavel fell more regularly on the high bid of firstcomers though it came down hardly at all on a newcomer's bid.[78]

Furthermore, a process of intermarriage was under way among the early settlers that, though difficult to measure, was apparently helpful to consolidation. By 1912, 40 of the 124 families who traced their beginnings in the county back to the period between 1870 and 1890 had intermarried at least once; in 13 of these families, two or more members had intermarried. Assessment rolls show that seventeen of these families, or 14 percent of the total number of early settlers in the county for whom figures are available, owned between them 27 percent of the tillable land and 19 percent of the non-tillable land owned by all firstcomers. In addition, these seventeen families owned more land per tax unit than did any other group of settlers. Perhaps most significant of all, they increased their holdings two and one-half times from 1890 to 1912 compared with two times for the rest of the early families.[79]

Intermarriage together with land purchasing power gave firstcomers the flexibility they needed to build up large, integrated holdings. Yet, the basic ingredient of consolidation was still what it had been earlier—the availability of government land. Without it, money would undoubtedly have run out too soon for most would-be cattle kings. Even the best off of the early citizens filed claims on government land well into the second decade of the twentieth century. Continuing changes in land laws and the ongoing problems of enforcing them allowed, as before, for duplication and evasions, which all took advantage of whenever they could. For instance, one of the provisions of the amended Desert Land Act allowed both husband and wife to file claims, and this procedure was used with some regularity around the county. Of the twenty-eight desert filings around Riley in the spring of 1903, two went to established early citizens Anton and Sophia Egli and two each to the families of Carl and Logue Cecil.[80]

The Timber Culture Act had been another source of either land or capital or both until its repeal in 1891. But its passing was little mourned as long as the Timber and Stone Act was still in force. Indeed, this act worked out much better for Oregonians. It allowed 160 acres of timber land to pass to any *bona fide* applicant who could pay $2.50 per acre for it. In a state where timber interests lay anxiously in wait, such a claim could be looked upon as an investment worth at least from three to five times more than what it had cost. Some claimants filed application and sold the land for a profit in the same day without using any of their own money in the transaction. Newspaper notices of filed claims increased in number to such an extent by 1901 that the authors of the previously cited report of land values within the old Malheur Indian Reservation who tabulated the frequency of these claims guessed facetiously that the act "apparently intended a sawmill in Harney County every 160 acres." Their report asserted in addition that the Timber and Stone Act in particular was one of the most helpful instruments in "the amalgamation of early stock ranches."[81]

As for homestead claims, there were proportionately more along the lower Silvies River and around Malheur Lake than anywhere else in the county, once the Marshall case in 1902 had opened up the exposed lake bed for the first time to homesteading. Settlement thinned out slightly in this region during the 1890s partially as a result of consolidation: once the threat of contest was lessened after 1902, early settlers immediately filed preemptions to which they often added a homestead claim and, if they had the means, bought land from neighbors, large or small.[82]

The case of Peter Clemens shows what a little capital, a good credit position, and the advantage of early arrival could do for a man in that district. Clemens arrived some time during the early 1880s and spent a year or so doing seasonal work for Peter French. In 1885 or 1886, he squatted on a section of land a mile west of the East Fork of the Silvies River about four miles southeast of Burns. The land was Willamette Valley and Cascade Mountain Wagon Road Company land, which at the time had no access to water closer than the Silvies and no rights on the Silvies that would assure its getting any water in the foreseeable future. Prior rights were in the hands of one Porter, who held a homestead in the neighboring section nearest the Silvies, and a preemptioner named Owens, who lived on a quarter of that same section. The entire east half of the section was originally a piece of Devine's swampland holdings of the late 1870s.[83]

In the late 1880s, when Devine was reacting to the court decision that disallowed most of his swampland claims by buying up all the claims he had filed on previously, he again sold off some of the parcels that he evidently considered poorly located. The east half of section 33 was one of those parcels so alienated. Meanwhile, Clemens had gone into partnership with one Smith sometime during the late 1880s, and, though mortgage records do not show any exchange of money between the two, Clemens came into enough cash to be able to buy the 320 acres of swampland in section 33 at the exact time Devine was ready to sell it. In the same year, 1899, the Owens preemption was transferred to Smith.

In the early 1890s, Clemens took up a homestead claim on the northwest quarter of section 4 in the same township as the other parcels, just two miles east of Burns near one of the larger tributaries of the East Fork. Some time during that period he had dealings with the State Land Board, and in 1893 his name appears in the county deed records as the purchaser of the 640 acres of wagon road land in section 34 upon which he had been squatting for nearly ten years. In 1897, Clemens bought out one Varien, who had acquired a homestead next to Clemens' section 4, and in 1899 he bought a total of 320 acres, which must have included the Stephens and Harris homestead shown in the deed records to have been in that same section.

The only pieces of land transferred to Clemens for which there is apparently no record were the Porter homestead in section 33 and the Bugler homestead in section 4. Porter's holdings may have been acquired earlier by Smith; the transfer of Bugler's property is noted in the hearings record cited above as occurring in 1898, so that both pieces appear in the 1900 tax rolls under Clemens's name after Clemens had bought out Smith's share of the partnership sometime between 1898 and 1900.[84] By 1900 Clemens, whose holdings had been a mere 160 acres in 1890, owned three full sections of land in the choicest part of the county. He had also acquired what often came to be the equivalent of a badge of success in that region—a suit with the P.L.S. Company over his right to water from the Silvies, which he was by then diverting through a long two-section ditch that finally brought the old wagon-road section under irrigation. Clemens had progressed far enough by 1901 to be a respected member of the community. His purchase that year of the remainder of Devine's famous Durham herd even merited a congratulatory article in the *Harney Items*.

The degree to which the lot of newcomers was harder was plainly revealed in an article in the *Harney Items*. In its view, a newcomer with little capital, which is to say most of them, stood a chance if he was willing literally to live in a hillside dugout and put every dollar he could spare back into young cattle that he could then turn out on the surrounding range. Then, barring natural disasters or disease, he might be able to sell one or two three-year-old steers, assuming he had stayed long enough for them to mature, after which he could afford to take the time to build a house for himself and his family. The trick was, as always, to find a parcel of land that could be watered in some way so as to raise winter feed. After the turn of the century such parcels were the little fifteen- to forty-acre plots earlier pioneers had been unwilling to try. For the energetic there was extra money available from scalp bounties on coyotes, mountain lions, gray wolves, and cougars, and there was always the chance to contest a neighbor's claim if he either walked off it or failed in some other way to prove up.[85] Whatever the newcomer's choice, after 1900 he got the first taste of harsh realities of a land no longer able to support the hopes of yeoman immigrants.

A review of the available statistics taken from county tax rolls for over a twenty-two-year period helps to summarize graphically the fate of newcomers in the whole process of land consolidation up to 1912. The persistent settlers from before the turn of the century break down into four categories. The term "firstcomers" is used only for those who came during the 1870s. The term "secondcomers" is used to describe those who came during the 1880s and "newcomers" to describe those who came during the 1890s. Big owners form the fourth category. Between 1890 and 1900, first- and secondcomers increased their total taxable holdings—including both land acquired by government claim and land purchased outright—by 67 percent, while the big owners increased theirs by a remarkable 300 percent. Yet land acquired by all other taxpayers—495 in all, including all newcomers but excluding the Willamette Valley and Cascade Mountain Wagon Road Company—amounted to only 8 percent of all the taxable land in the county in 1900. When this is compared with the 5.8 percent owned by the first- and secondcomers and the 45 percent owned by the four big owners, the top-heavy nature of land ownership in the county becomes apparent.[86]

The statistics show an even greater relative ascendancy among the first families by 1912. The holdings of first- and secondcomers had increased since 1900 by 77 percent, a 10-percent-larger increase than during the 1890s. During that same period the holdings of big owners actually decreased by 12 percent, at the very time when the total amount of taxable land in the county increased by 62 percent. Of the entire county acreage, then, the first- and secondcomers, who now represented only 12.2 percent of the total number of tax units, owned 6.3 percent of the taxable property—an increase of only .5 percent since the 1890s. Big owners, in the meantime, now owned only 25 percent, a decrease of 15 percent since 1900. The holdings of both groups plus those of the road company accounted for less of the county's land than in 1900, but many more people were in the county by 1912 and more of those by proportion were speculators than twelve years earlier. As it was, 90 percent of the county's taxpayers owned only 46 percent of the county's taxable land. In terms of average holdings per unit, this meant that the early families now owned 521 acres per tax unit while the others, excluding big men and the road company, but including three new land companies two of which owned over 100,000 acres between them, owned 511 acres per tax unit.

Not surprisingly, the newcomer group was statistically the least well off of the three. Leaving out, for the moment, the large owners and referring just to firstcomers, secondcomers, and newcomers, in 1912, thirty-three taxpayers were firstcomers, representing only 22 percent of the total number of people in all three groups, but owning 24 percent of all the land: an average of 586 acres per tax unit. Secondcomers constituted the largest group of old-timers in 1912—ninety-one in all, or 61 percent of those in all three groups. Also not surprisingly, this group owned most of the land among the three; yet secondcomers owned only 507 acres per unit or an average of 79 acres per unit less than the firstcomers. Newcomers, on the other hand, numbered only twenty-six. The amount of land they owned was only 15 percent of the total, and the average size was only 446 acres per unit.

The pattern that emerges from these data confirms the hypothesis used in their selection: the persistent settlers of the 1870s were the best off outside of the big owners in terms of land ownership by 1912. Next to them, the group from the 1880s fared far better than the majority of taxpayers in 1912, but less well than the big owners and the firstcomers of the 1870s. The newcomers from the 1890s fared worse than any of the other three groups that came before them. If there is any single description that encapsulates what happened in Harney County, it is not so much Turner's or Curti's concept of frontier democracy as the old adage about the early bird and the worm.

The Emergence of the Modern Cattleman

In the fifteen years between Peter French's death in 1897 and the homesteaders' rush in 1912, an integrated cattleman's society with a fairly well-developed sense of its own identity grew up in Harney County to replace the older cattle baron—sodbuster society of the late nineteenth century—a society fraught with divisive and disintegrative tendencies. This social change was brought about largely by the growth of a strong, permanent core of established firstcomers, which constituted a powerful counterbalance to the influence of the larger owners. Though there was never a fusion between the groups, they achieved a rapprochement rooted in the multitude of common concerns that all cattlemen shared and based upon certain commonly held attitudes, habits, and customs that have become the distinguishing characteristics of the cattleman today.

Modern scholarship has emphasized the economic aspects of the transition period, essentially the permanent shift from open-range methods to stock-farming methods. Not so often emphasized are the effects of this shift upon social relationships within communities of cattle growers, and scarcely emphasized at all are its effects upon community relationships in areas where the big outfits of the open-range era survived.

Most scholars have acknowledged that order and stability came to the range country only after the rangelands had been fenced or otherwise controlled and after the cattle barons had come around to some form of stock farming. It was not that stock farming was unknown, but that few wanted to engage in it while the range was free and cattle prices were soaring.[1]

In Harney County, where the competition between range users was predominantly competition between large and small livestock growers, tensions were reduced in proportion to the amount of land each purchased or otherwise controlled and the extent to which successful regulation was imposed upon the remaining public range. In great part the change in the image of the big cattlemen came in the wake of their purchase of hay land and their acceptance of range regulation under the system of grazing fees instituted in the Blue Mountains in 1904.

But small owners were mostly farmers turned cattlemen who were also interested in promoting the industry for their own benefit, which came to mean promoting it in ways that made for more harmony with larger growers. Thus even in this very early period there can be seen the beginnings of that rapproachement between large and small owners which stemmed partly from their common interest in preserving the public rangeland exclusively for livestock grazing. Their probing for ways to get along reached into social relationships as well.

No one would claim that all was on its way to becoming sunshine and roses. The conflict of the 1890s was not easily dispelled, and many bitter legal and political fights ensued; yet the trend toward more peaceful accommodation began to appear after 1912. Its evolution was gradual, yet seemingly as inexorable as the transition of the industry itself. When cattlemen began to discover that the cattle business was a long-term investment with minimum dividends and with financial security deriving through the ownership of land as much as of cattle, then "the metamorphosis from an open range to a ranch economy became more accepted with each passing year."[2]

The social aspects of this process can be seen in the changing image of the cattle baron, the development of newer methods of cattle-raising, and the self-conscious response of both groups to outside policy-making agencies, particularly the federal government.

The Changing Image of the Cattle Baron

The big owners in Harney County, unlike their compatriots on the Great Plains, were persistent and successful; the death of Peter French did nothing to change that fact, or to alter in any fundamental way the economic structure of the county. By 1900, large-scale consolidation among the big owners had come to an end; but because they were constantly improving their methods of raising cattle and their marketing procedures, their economic dominance over the county continued uninterrupted. Only the names of the owners and managers changed. The giant machinery of the ranches, like great inertial wheels, ran on largely undisturbed.[3]

This changing of the guard was significant in the social aspects of the county, particularly in the case of Bill Hanley, who ascended to the management of the P Ranch after French's death. In fact, the emergence of Hanley effected one of the most important social changes in the county during the early twentieth century.

Any change in the image of the big men occurred in the face of a strongly ingrained popular resentment against them. The general impression abroad was that big owners were exploitative, monopolistic giants, and this impression was never dispelled; but the big cattlemen managed to graft onto their image in Harney County a certain benevolent paternalism of a kind quite consciously striven for by other big businessmen in America during this same period. The fact that the big owners were successful represented a heroic accomplishment; yet their success must be attributed in part to the pact that the older image of the big men had never been a completely tarnished one.[4]

The cattle barons had had, for instance, a legitimate reputation as breeders of superior cattle, and many a local small owner begrudgingly admitted the big owners' skill when it came to animal husbandry (though he was usually quick to add that one ought to expect that of wealthy cattle raisers). The cattle barons' very wealth and power commanded, as wealth and power always have in America, a certain amount of admiration and respect. When speaking of the big men, smaller owners used the deferential terms with which on pays the devil his due, particularly when they referred to the apparently easy access big owners had to credit—especially during hard times when local credit for smaller owners usually dried up.[5] Big owners might be thought of as exploiters in the abstract, but they were so far from being considered exploiters of the men they employed that there was actual status attached to being hired as a head wrangler or trail boss, or, especially, a foreman on the big spreads. There was something gratifying for the community in seeing one of their own kind "make good" by becoming the foreman of one of the big outfits. To be hired as a mere cowpuncher was, of course, less prestigious, though there was about the cowboy on the big spread a certain enviable elan much sought after and emulated by the youngsters of the community, not to mention scions of city-bred families in Portland and other communities.[6]

There was, in short, some basis during the transition period for the later development of a mode of life that knit together big men and small in a community of cattlemen tied together by the rituals of their occupation, and held fast thereby despite dissimilarities in their social, political, and economic values. This development did not mean a return to the symbiosis of earlier years; the rise of the independent firstcomers had pretty well demolished that relationship. It was, instead, a new sort of parochialism born of good times and nurtured by a sure knowledge on the part of each other that the other was there to stay. This knowledge had partially underlain the struggles of the 1890s and in some measure helped limit those struggles mostly to institutional forms of conflict.

The big owners no longer operated among their smaller neighbors in the roughshod manner of earlier years. To the contrary, they became much more civilized. In fact the political and social adjustments they made were prodigious, as Hanley's career and that of the P.L.S.

Company foreman, John Gilchrist, illustrate. Besides, the big boys of the early twentieth century were, economically at least, no longer on the defensive. Assessment records show that after the years of consolidation in the 1890s, each big owner had a substantial new investment in real estate to look out for. If that meant compromising attitudes and values associated with their early privileged position and moving closer, at least in appearance, to the value system of the yeoman rancher, then no one could gainsay the need for it; as with all good businessmen, they knew the value of peace.[7]

From 1900 to 1912, the period during which the large outfits worked to transform much of their newly acquired lands into irrigated pastures, dramatic shifts in ownership took place that brought Oregonians into control of most of the big spreads. Bill Hanley was the pivotal figure in the shift, and his story consequently bears telling.[8]

Young Hanley left his father's mule ranch in Jackson County when he was in his teens. After several years of being on his own he came with his brother Ed to Harney County to help their older brother, John, with his new spread just southeast of Burns. John owned comparatively little land, but what he owned was choice. Some time between 1880 and 1885 the two younger brothers assumed control of the ranch, building it up by 1890 to 1,200 acres of taxable land, most of which was agricultural land along the East Fork of the Silvies River. The following spring Hanley traveled back to Jackson County to buy cattle. Upon his return, he began putting together parcels of old homesteads, preemptions, and deeded lands to make contiguous blocks stretching the length of seven sections along the rich hay land rimming the East Fork of the river. By 1898, the Hanleys' Bell-A Ranch had been augmented by nearly 3,000 acres, and the Hanley herds had grown from 300 head to nearly 1,000. These assets put the Hanleys on the way to becoming big owners.

In 1898, Bill was ready to make the move that would build his own cattle empire in southeastern Oregon. He had already woven financial ties with H. L. Corbett of Portland and commission broker M. K. Parsons of Salt Lake City. Because he was personable and at the peak of his powers, he had little trouble cultivating powerful friends among influential politicians, cattlemen, and railroad magnates. One of these was F. C. Lusk, attorney for the French-Glenn Corporation, who, when French was murdered in 1897, asked Bill to manage the company's properties until a disposition of the land could be made. Almost as if Lusk's invitation began a series of subterranean shock waves, Hanley's ambition erupted like a volcano. In a single year he bought out his brother's interests in the Bell-A and took over control of the great P Ranch. When Harney County citizens awoke to it all, they saw thirty years of California control in the Blitzen Valley abruptly terminated and the place of the mighty French filled, for better or for worse, by an ambitious young extrovert who now controlled more of the county's land than any of the fabulous range barons before him—195,163 acres of owned land in all, or 31 percent of the county's total private land.[9]

But Hanley did not stop there. He reduced California control still further in 1903 when he bought out Riley and Hardin, thereby bringing under his control the OO with its 8,621 acres of well-watered lower Silver Creek land. What vestiges there were of out-of-state influence in the Blitzen Valley disappeared in 1907 when a corporation called the Blitzen Valley Land Company, headed by Corbett and supported by Hanley's close friend C. E. S. Wood, bought out French—Glenn interests.[10] From that time on the locus of big ownership in the county shifted from out of town to just next door. Hanley's policies thereafter were dictated not only by his new business obligations, but by his position as a member of the community—and not just the community of cattlemen, but the community "del Norte" upon which the town of Burns had always had such a powerful impact. Hanley thus became the first town-influenced cattle baron, which, in his own estimation, meant the first progressive, twentieth-century cattle baron in Harney County. In that stance he encouraged unlimited settlement, played the master irrigator, fought for a railroad, and, when the automobile came, led the battle for paved highways and improved county roads.[11]

Hanley's new dominion was, of course, never complete. Its boundaries confronted the P.L.S. Company at several points. Even before 1900, during the years of the Carey Act, Hanley's irrigation schemes plunged him into a series of lawsuits with the company. The P.L.S. Company had pushed its advantages wherever it could, using standard techniques for consolidating land and appropriating and controlling water. But these techniques seemed more and more contrary to the settlers' and smaller owners' sense of fair play. All P.L.S. diversions in the Harney and Silvies valleys were designed to flood-irrigate the natural hay and to provide stock water. In the Pine Creek area, the company resolutely opposed any other systematic use of the water, and for as long as the company held land in Harney Valley it was the implacable foe of schemes for the storage of water.[12]

In the Pine Creek and Drewsey areas the company's dominance was so complete and its policy so in accord with the firstcomers who were there that there was no overt bickering. But in Harney Valley the situation was such that the company became the victim of repeated harassments and petty rustling throughout the 1890s. Through the very height of these troubles, and perhaps partially because of them, the P.L.S. Company fundamentally altered its approach.

As early as 1892, the company seemed to have been reading the signs of change and gaining a rudimentary sense of public relations. For example, in its support of Harney City in the county-seat fight, the company built an imposing headquarters near the intended site of the Harney City courthouse. When the campaign fizzled, the company, after an appropriate period of mourning, moved the building to Burns. It was at this time that Miller hired the articulate, diplomatic John Gilchrist to manage his affairs in Harney County. With Gilchrist there began a decade in which the company tried in a multitude of ways to mend its fences with the community: by offering a good chain pump to the county for its proposed drinking well on the road across Windy Point, by providing lumber and tools free of charge for a bridge over Fritz Mace's new diversion ditch, by hiring a local man, Bill Harris, as foreman of the company's Mann Lake spread—policies that worked successfully to lessen the hostility between the community and the company.[13]

An apocryphal story that is a favorite among Harney County residents points up the ultimate success of Gilchrist's policy. In it Henry Miller, dressed in his rough clothes and out riding alone, chanced upon a homesteader cutting open one of the company's beeves. Miller dismounted and, expert butcher that he was, helped the man "gut out" the carcass. As Miller did so, he asked the homesteader what the steer's owners would say if they caught him. "Aw, hell!" the homesteader is supposed to have replied, "they stole so many theirselves they wouldn't miss this one." "Well, I'm Henry Miller," the butcher replied, "and if you won't tell on me, I won't tell on you."[14]

Changing Methods, 1890-1912

By 1900 there were in Harney County at last five of the six categories of agriculturists that Ernest Staples Osgood distinguishes in his study of the role of cattlemen in the agricultural history of the Northwest: the few remaining large companies that owned large blocks of land; a number of small cattle growers who close-herded their stock and partially used rangeland grazing; a group of irrigators in favorable spots; the frontier farmer or "granger" on the fringe of agricultural settlement; and sheep owners, large and small. The sixth category— the older agricultural communities in th more fertile valleys where "the moisture was sufficient to carry on farming with a minimum of irrigation"—was not represented in Harney County, but the fences on the public domain were coming down for the most part and enclosures around large chunks of hay land were going up instead. Few if any relied exclusively upon the open range. With the death of John Devine in 1901, the last of the colorful "rawhiders" of the old open-range era in Harney County was gone, and a new era was taking shape.[15]

In this new era, large owners generally kept up with changing methods, particularly Hanley, who was in the best-watered location with the best soil and had the financial resources to carry on experiments and improve the efficiency of his management. However, the big owners were no longer in the vanguard of innovation in Harney County as they had been before the turn of the century. Perhaps one of the reasons was that after 1900 big owners were no longer expanding; for whatever reason, they felt they already had what they needed in the way of pastureland and that no one was going seriously to threaten their keeping it.

Certainly it was apparent to nearly everyone in Harney County after 1900 that cattle-growing was not simply going to become "an aspect of general farming operations" as it had in the Columbia Basin. There, stockmen had been replaced by farmers who became stockmen on a moderate scale.[16] In Harney County farmers did not replace stockmen; instead would-be farmers became stockmen who then farmed on a moderate scale to support their herds. Thus, the gradual moving together of large and small owners at the beginning of the new century was not only a phase of burgeoning land ownership and government regulation; it was also a reflection of the evolution of methods among early persistent settlers who, in order to survive, had to become stockmen first and farmers second. It was this total process that began to produce the definable cattleman's subculture already spoken of, which incorporated few of the values of the early range barons but many of those of the would-be farmer who transposed them to fit the habits and demands of his adopted occupation.

The process by which all this came about was just beginning in the 1890s. Approximately two townships southeast of Burns in the so-called "Ryegrass District" were arable and actually supported small-scale farming operations. Also, the wetter climate of the 1890s attracted a number of newcomers to the higher ground adjacent to better-watered regions. Though not much can be told about them from the available records, these newcomers were evidently committed to farming and persistent enough at it so that, along with the more successful Ryegrass settlers, they managed to keep alive the debate over what Harney County would eventually become—farm or cattle country.[17]

Thus the impulse behind changed methods of livestock raising in Harney County after 1890 was not only to seek better markets but, in a way, to probe for better means of using sparse resources in order to find what precisely the limits of adaptability of the county really were. As in all periods before and after, however, when it came to improving methods of raising livestock, only a relative few were truly innovators; some made cautious adjustments, but a sizable number made no real changes at all. Though it has pitfalls, there is a way to tell generally how many tried to keep up with the times; by comparing expenditures made for farm machinery and implements, and by looking at the ratio between improved and unimproved land. These categories appear in the assessment rolls.

Several significant trends can be identified. The large owners, on the average, changed more of their land to hayland by 1912 than did any other group, though they lagged behind in that process in 1900. The group that emerged as most progressive in these terms was the firstcomer group of the 1870s, 67 percent of whose land was hayland in 1912. Settlers from the 1880s held a little over 50 percent of their land in hay, while those of the 1890s had actually decreased their relative amount of hayland by 1912. Predictably, the lowest percentage of hayland was in the hands of the newest settlers in 1912.[19]

As to expenditures for machinery and implements, the large owners increased their expenditures by the greatest amount. Firstcomers from the 1870s and 1880s were rather cautious in that respect. In the case of newcomers from the 1890s, the increase was mysteriously larger than any other group; yet this group was just starting relative to the others, and that fact is reflected in the average amount of expenditure per unit, which was as low as the rest.

In summary, the big owners somewhat outstripped firstcomers in the crucial matters of improving their carrying capacity and modernizing the farming aspects of their business, but the margin between them was slim. A much greater disparity appears between firstcomers and newcomers. Indeed, the newcomer group, which had experienced the greatest amount of attrition from the time it came to the county until 1912, came to own less hayland while it spent more for machinery and implements. Small acreages did not lend themselves efficiently to machinery. Thus the newcomers were faced with a high ratio of fixed costs to land that would work toward an even higher rate of attrition among these settlers in the next decade—a bleak prospect in an era of supposedly unprecedented opportunities for agriculturalists and, in many ways, a crueller case than that of the oncoming homesteader, who would never stay as long or venture as much. Overall, the figures point to firstcomers as the rising innovators of the new age.

Cattle Raising

The only general statement that can be made about methods of raising livestock is that initial feeding operations, especially among those cattle growers who had used the open range extensively, were carried on simply to guarantee survival of the brood herd; only as the market demanded better grades of beef were these operations focused more on programs to develop heavier cattle and better qualities of beef. It must, of course, be borne in mind that the more progressive cattle-raisers had done this all along. Even so, the common practice for nearly all cattlemen was to turn their herds out onto the range in early March when snow was melting and the range just beginning to "green up." The roundup for market would begin in September or October, but brood cows, bulls, and non-marketable stock might not come off the range until mid-December—well after the first snow had fallen and the ground had begun to freeze. At this stage in the evolution of feeding practices this method was comparatively enlightened. Today, after sixty years of cattle feeding and advances in standards of cattle care, it would again be called nothing but "rawhiding."[20]

Problems of balancing the factors or production, though common to all, were worked out differently in each section of the county (not to mention within each level of the hierarchy of land owners and, for that matter, on each individual ranch). Such adjustments can be seen as demonstrating developing habits of management that, in turn, took on some importance as indicators of changed social and economic allegiances and new status relationships.

There were roughly four categories of livestock owners in Harney County in 1900. First, there were the large owners who owned over 1,000 head of cattle and over 4,000 acres of land. While these big owners are clearly distinguishable, the other three categories have to be drawn with a judicious use of the incidental information available in the biographies of the county "mug book," in the stories told by old-timers, and in newspaper references to herd size and ownership.[21] From all of these sources there seems little doubt that anyone who owned within the wide range of 120 to 1,000 head of cattle and of 330 to 4,000 acres was well off in the sense that he could survive protracted amounts of poor weather, hold stock off the market until it could be sold profitably, sustain himself and his family at a comfortable level on just the proceeds from cattle sales, and borrow readily from the available sources of credit. This was true whether he was one of the two who owned 800 head and undoubtedly hired laborers to help or was one of the twenty-seven who owned between 120 and 200 head and who most likely operated his spread as a family stock farm.

Anyone owning between 25 and 120 head of cattle and between 160 and 330 acres of land was a small owner—a category that might, in the modern jargon of agricultural economics, be termed an "economic unit," meaning an operation of sufficient size to sustain a family entirely on sales from its production. This, in turn, meant that the acreage of pasture land had to be sufficient for the number of cattle carried; that the number of cattle had to be sufficiently large to include brood cows, weaner calves, and replacement heifers; and that the 20 percent of marketable stock would provide enough yearly income during normal years for a family of four to live solely off the unit. The crucial difference between this category and the well off was that this unit had less reserve potential against hard years. At the level of 25 head and 160 acres, all reserve potential was essentially gone.

Outfits that listed 25 or fewer cattle and 160 acres or less could be considered, again in modern terms, "marginal" or "submarginal" in that a family of four could not live off the proceeds of the spread alone, nor could the unit provide reserve feed for an emergency. As with the category above, there were, of course, alternatives to providing one's own livestock feed: buying hay was such an alternative and one that was practiced even during normal years by owners in all categories. The main problem for those in the marginal and submarginal category was that such purchases might often be five or ten times more costly since they had to be made during an emergency; the group that was most dependent upon them was the one least able to afford them.

There were, of course, other money-making opportunities for a stock-raiser in this category beyond what he could make from his cattle. As earlier in Harney County's history, one could work part time for the large owners, particularly during the peak of haying and roundup. After 1900, there were several well-off owners who needed seasonal help and could afford to pay for it. It was possible also to obtain a variety of work in the towns if one was close enough to these centers to take advantage of them. Despite such opportunities, it was from among those in this last category that most of the impermanent, transient citizens came, and it was into this category that most of the newcomers fitted; more to the point, mobility upward from it was more difficult than from the two intermediate categories.

An intriguing aspect of this categorization is that the north end of the county, where the best land was located, was also the area that harbored the greatest percentage of cattle growers in the small and marginal or submarginal categories. Over three quarters of all those whose residences were recorded in the north end in either the 1900 assessment rolls or the voter registration book were in these two categories. In the south end only a little over one half of the cattle growers were in these two categories, and only 16 percent of all those listed in that area were marginal or submarginal owners as compared with 25 percent from the north end.[22] What the data on population turnover show is confirmed here: the areas of the richest prize were the areas of greatest risk. More newcomers and homesteaders tried their luck in the north end than anywhere else in the county.

When it came to the seasonal handling of livestock around the county, Bill Hanley was, of course, in an enviable position compared with the rest. His Bell-A and OO spreads combined made, as one old-timer put it, "the best hay ranch in the country."[23] As early as 1901 Hanley was operating what amounted to a feeder operation, buying steers in the spring and selling them in the early winter. This made Hanley the envy of the less well off, not only because of the choice property he had accumulated, but because of the methods he was thereby able to use. Others owned large chunks of hayland in the valley and were able to do some of the things Hanley could do, only on a smaller scale; to the degree that they could, their status as cattle growers in the community was enhanced. If they were able through intensive use to turn their spread even partially into a feeder operation, they might merit the label "progressive cattleman," which was coming more and more to be associated with social prestige.[24]

Needless to say, feeder operations were not the standard operation throughout the county. The normal mode of cattle raising was what is now called the "cow-calf" operation—the classical stock-farm operation—employing a full herd, including about one bull to every forty cows and one replacement heifer to every four and five brood cows. The operation involved every age of marketable cow from weaner to four-year-old, depending upon how much feed could be produced and how long the owner wished to keep his calves before selling them.

The prototypical example of such an operation among the big spreads in Harney County was the great Whitehorse Ranch in the south end. On the Whitehorse, only cows, calves, and young heifers were fed hay during the winter, though that practice was itself a significant change from methods used on the ranch during the 1870s and 1880s. Steers, replacement heifers, and market heifers were allowed to graze on the surrounding range because "the pasture in the fields was so bountiful."[25] Not much care was taken with spring grass; cattle were turned out in March and early April to catch the young green shoots, a practice that would be considered poor range management today. When fall came, cattle were rounded up and calves branded, all out on the open range without benefit of corrals or partition fencing. The big spreads, aside from Hanley's, lagged behind in improving methods; the situation at the Whitehorse helps explain why. The great ranch controlled nearly all the resources within a radius of fifty miles, and, in contrast to the smaller spreads in neighboring Wildhorse Valley and Pueblo Valley (where by 1905 all cattle were winter-fed as a matter of course), the Whitehorse could afford to use its ranges and pasture more casually and still maintain a profitable operation.[26]

The owner, the manager, and even the foreman of the Whitehorse Ranch, possessed status because they represented power and wealth on a scale of values familiar in the national culture; but they had little status as measured by the values of the cattleman's subculture, which lay in the ranch's method of raising cattle. David Shirk, who lived in Catlow Valley, where natural conditions were harsher than in Whitehorse Valley, was typically contemptuous of such methods. He knew others who had been unwilling or unready to put up hay or buy it, and he could not equate their actions with anything short of stupidity—especially when the results of such negligence led cattle to starve or die. The prestige attached to methods used in a cow—calf operation related less to its size or the extent of its natural resources than to the way in which it preserved and maintained its living product, the beef cattle themselves. The small owner who managed to make a profit while keeping his cattle well fed and maintaining a high percentage of his calf crop enjoyed a status that combined both the contemporary American values of material gain and the subcultural values of the cattle industry, which emphasized a certain skill in the care of animals.[27]

Cattle Breeding

Although it might be difficult to prove such a hypothesis, it may well have been that cattle growers with more of a farming background adjusted more easily and quickly to the farming aspects of stock raising than did owners who had been miners or section hands or open-range cowboys, drovers, and stock raisers. The same ability to adapt might apply to cattlemen whose experience gave them some special knowledge of pastoral animal husbandry using sizable herds of animals, as contrasted with the farming system that grew out of transhumance and involved animal husbandry on a small scale with more intimate care of fewer animals. Whatever the reasons, the big owners in both ends of the county were rather far ahead when it came to cattle breeding.

Obviously, the big owners were financially better able to invest in purebred stock, and by 1900 they owned sufficient land to keep their pastures entirely to themselves. The necessity for buying out-of-state blooded stock was an obstacle all Oregon breeders had to overcome, but there never was a time when the big owners were not able to import blooded cattle. This again narrowed the opportunities for some of the smaller owners: they could not afford to buy such imported stock, while the large owners who became the only source of high-quality breeding stock in the vicinity did not hesitate to charge handsome stud fees.[28]

Yet the smaller and less well-off owners paid the fees when they needed to, for by 1900 better breeding was no longer an esoteric pastime for the rich, or the exclusive practice of larger owners. It was becoming the sine qua non of profits in a market fast shifting toward more particular consumers and more discriminating cattle buyers. Good-quality stock was bringing as much as $323 per head in the Chicago market in 1902. Those who were in the business for the money had to look to the quality of their beef.[29]

Owners like Hanley and Henry Miller had long bought pedigreed stock. Both were deep in the Hereford market by 1905, having bought certified bulls and purebred brood cows. John Devine long had a national reputation for his Durhams. By 1904, many of the smaller owners were able to compete with their giant counterparts by virtue of their own upgraded stock. Good breeding practices had always existed among certain of the smaller owners and might have among others had all of them been able to buy or rent bulls. The Cecils, Smyths, Garretts, the Martin brothers, Homer Mace, Jones and Poujade, J. P. Withers, and others had built enclosures, fed carefully, culled and bred with skill, so that they were attracting independent buyers to their home grounds after 1900—a sure sign of their growing economic independence and their heightened status in the community of cattlemen.[30]

The Labor Factor

The costs involved in upgrading native stock were treated at the time as an investment. Today the expenses associated with better breeding are generally thought of as fixed current costs like taxes, upkeep, and the depreciation of machinery. One cost, however, was and still is a heavy annual cost, but only for the big owners: that of labor. Indeed, the chief distinction between the methods used by large and small owners was that for most small owners the expenses of labor were absorbed within the family. Large owners could not absorb costs of labor in that way, no matter how large the family might be. The foreman, the trail boss, the wrangler, the cook, the cowhand himself were all functionaries of the large spread. No such specialization was ever a part of the family stock farm, though all the jobs for which these specialists were needed were common to every operation. The stock farmer himself and his family shared all these jobs and perforce mastered a variety of skills seldom learned by true ranch hands.[31]

While the big spreads adopted farming methods insofar as these methods helped improve feeding, the only new job description that resulted was "irrigator." For the rest of the work—mowing, raking, and putting up the hay and grain, or driving the teams or riding a plow—the other laborers were used, often to their displeasure. To laborers on the big outfits, the farming tasks were just so many distasteful chores to be done as quickly as possible so that the real work of the ranch could be gotton on with; for the family stock farmer the real work of stock raising included all phases in their proper season, none of them ranking above or below another.[32]

There were, however, some variations worth noting in the county. Cattle growers in the north end spent more time haying; some summers, two full cuttings were possible with still enough left over for pasture in the fall. In the south end range-riding occupied more time than in the north. It was simply a matter of balancing resources. Shirk tells in his diary of him and his family being "almost constantly in the saddle, doing our own work and thus lessening expenses." The only labor costs he incurred were for herders to "ride the outside ranges." From all reports this was a tough job, without corrals and with only the bare ground or grass to bed down on at night. It took a few dollars a day to hire a man to do this work, and the owner was lucky if he stayed on to do it again the next year. North-end cowboys might have preferred more of this kind of work. Laborers on the Island Ranch were farmers one-quarter of the year. By 1903 the P.L.S. Company was contracting such work out to locals who were glad to have it.[33]

Seasonal requirements still made for wide fluctuations in the labor force on the big spreads. There had always been a need for more laborers during roundups, a need that was satisfied in earlier days by settlers most of whom had just moved into the area. By 1900, however, this seasonal requirement was not as great as that for summer hay hands. Older settlers were better established and busy with their own work, and new settlers were only a partial answer to the labor problem. They might work during roundups, which could still be run jointly with other larger owners as late as 1910, but they were generally as busy as the old-timers during haying season—particularly those settlers who were trying to raise grains and cereal crops.[34]

In short, the problem for the larger owners of finding good hands for seasonal work became much tougher in the twentieth century. Even keeping good, reliable, year-round hands was becoming a problem. In the manner of the indentured servants of an earlier and different America, once they finished their stint they took off with their savings to try their luck somewhere else on their own. The reality of fewer opportunities, so apparent with hindsight, was evidently not as apparent to these men as were the obvious growing good times in the early 1900s. As a consequence roving cowhands from widely different areas who lived "where [they] could do a day's work" began to be the laborers hired by most big spreads.[35]

There was in all this a portent for the years to come. With each shift in the industry from extensive to intensive methods, the demands upon capital and resources became greater, making it more and more difficult for anyone to start from scratch. The opportunity for a sunburned cowhand to become a beaver-Stetsoned cattle baron become even slimmer than for a homesteader in Harney County to become a grain farmer. With the increasing competition of higher-paying jobs in urban areas, the cost of labor became a crucial factor. Large owners could either raise their wages to meet this competition or settle for inferior cowhands. Since the other factors of production were seemingly not as easy to manipulate, the big owners settled for transient labor, thereby encouraging the growth of the drifting proletariat of ranch workers typical of the business today. In a more general sense, the progress of management and investment has worked to limit opportunities for newcomers all along, until today such opportunities are literally gone the way of the vanished frontier.

The Modern Market

Changes in the national market worked against the limiting effects of investment and management patterns. Ever since the construction of the Oregon Short Line through Ontario in 1884, southeastern Oregon cattlemen had been lured in increasing numbers to the so-called "Chicago market." Even in 1889 and 1890, when prices on the San Francisco market collapsed, the Chicago market had remained steady. During the middle and late 1890s eastern markets drew ever more southeastern Oregon cattle, and eastern buyers flocked to the ranges of Grant, Lake, Malheur, and Harney counties—all as part of the strong resurgence of the cattle industry after the disasters of the late 1880s and early 1890s. Throughout the nation consumer demand rose until by 1905 per capita consumption of beef was greater than ever before in America's history.[36]

By that same year, however, the eastern market outlet for southeastern Oregon cattle was nearly overshadowed by the remarkable rise of the northwestern markets and the new vitality of the San Francisco market. The livestock agency for the O.R. and N. Company noted this change in 1901 and attributed it to the growth of America's new empire of the Pacific (of which Alaska was a vital part). Certainly the Seattle market was booming, and more cattle were being fattened at home and shipped either via Portland to Puget Sound or south to San Francisco than ever before.³⁷ Things were definitely looking up for Harney County cattle growers. A sellers market, then as now, does not discriminate between large and small owners as long as the quality of their product is comparable, and the greater market for the cattle of smaller owners represented a significant shift of emphasis for the society of cattle growers in Harney County. Prices climbed steadily from 1898 to 1905, although they did not vary much between eastern and northwestern or western markets.³⁸

For the cattlemen of southeastern Oregon, the greatest impact from changes in the market came not so much from rising prices or from the new market outlets in the Northwest, but from the expanded number of alternatives these changes represented. Development of newer techniques of cattle breeding, together with the introduction of stock farming on an almost universal scale, were as much responses to the demand for better meat as they were reactions to the calamities of the middle and late 1880s. Once these changes were set in motion they inevitably led to corresponding changes in market procedures: winter feeding meant cattle now might be ready for market in the spring, while better breeding meant cattle might be sold younger with less feeding costs to the producer for the weight they attained. These changes combined eventually to make the notion of a single fall-season market for fully matured cattle obsolete. As early as 1902 cattle growers in southeastern Oregon were selling yearlings instead of two- and three-year-olds, and selling them in the winter and spring as well as the fall.³⁹

Bill Hanley in particular enjoyed great flexibility in marketing by virtue of the superior resources at his command. Other large concerns without Hanley's good fortune simply perfected older methods by turning to shipments of larger volume once or twice a year and by using their better pastures more intensively.⁴⁰ For smaller owners, the period from 1897 to 1905 was one of emancipation from the cruel constraints of distance and oppressive competition. The pattern old-timer Ira Stubblefield had to put up with as a matter of course in 1888—driving his herd of marketable cattle all the way from Cow Creek near Harney City across the high desert and over the Cascades to a Willamette Valley market—was all but unthinkable thirteen years later. The longest drives were still to the Ontario railroad, but by 1900 smaller owners rarely drove their own cattle there alone; two or three owners would join their cattle in larger herds. Even more often, smaller owners sold to Hanley or his buyers. If this practice brings recollection of the situation during the late 1870s and 1880s when the monopoly of the big owners was so complete that smaller owners had to sell to them for whatever prices they could get, the similarity is superficial.⁴¹ The invasion of competing buyers from the East, the Northwest, and San Francisco changed the big owner-small owner marketing relationship forever.

The mechanics of this change appear in the successful pattern of transactions carried on among Bill Hanley, Alphena Venator, M. K. Parsons, and H. Y. Blackwell. Alphena Venator was a small owner and the son of doughty firstcomer Jezreel Venator, one of Harney County's five earliest settlers. M. K. Parsons was a wealthy Salt Lake City commission broker, who was one of Hanley's major buyers and one of his closest business associates. The buyer H. Y. Blackwell was representative for the Carstein Brothers of Seattle, Washington.[42]

With the increasing emphasis on the quality of market animals, some of the established smaller owners in the county like Venator, who had been careful with their resources and had achieved an adequate balance between land and cattle, could claim top price for their beef as often as the large owners. Their chief problems came from lack of volume, seasonal inflexibility, and the distances to shipping facilities. Hanley must have recognized that this situation could produce profits for anyone who could function as both local buyer and seller in the manner of earlier Southern cotton brokers or on the principle of the twentieth-century midwestern grain cooperatives. Hanley had the feed, which meant he could buy weaner calves from smaller owners and thereby trade his burden of maintaining a full cow-and-calf operation for keeping calves of proven quality that he could feed for quick gain and sell with minimum upkeep. It also meant he was left with more marketable cattle more often during the year than he would have had if he had stayed exclusively with a cow-calf operation. The practice in turn brought the small owners the seasonal flexibility most of them desired.

To provide a continuing outlet for these increasing numbers of marketable cattle, Hanley entered into an extended business relationship with M. K. Parsons. One need not go far in to Hanley's business records to see that the essential benefit Parsons derived from this arrangement was the guarantee it gave him of a large volume of reputable southeastern Oregon cattle to be delivered from a single shipping point on Parsons' demand at any time from late April until October or November. Through the careful construction of a system by which these commitments were made operative, Hanley and Parsons became the "principal cattle dealers in the entire region."[43]

Of the local producers, Hanley dealt with the Venators somewhat more than with others. Alphena Venator, then a young man, became Hanley's trail contractor—a job in which he had some personal stake, since each time he sold to Hanley he sold him almost all of his marketable cattle. In this way he profited not only from the sale of his own cattle but also from the contract to deliver Hanley's herds safely—a contract that seems to have paid well enough to attract Venator's interest from 1899 to 1903, although evidence of its precise terms has not come to light. In any case, Venator was, by 1905, as big a cattle producer as W. C. Cecil and George Smyth, two of the bigger small owners in the north end. A sure sign of his eminence was that he began dealing with financial institutions outside the state and was able on his own to tap a Salt Lake City livestock brokerage concern.[44]

The story is not complete without the dynamics by which success was achieved: the competitive tension between Parsons and H. Y. Blackwell, which was a mirror of the growth of competition among buyers throughout southeastern Oregon during this period. Blackwell was ubiquitous. Undoubtedly he would have liked dealing with one or two big spreads for the ease with which he could conduct his business as Parsons was able to conduct his, but, like a modern insurance salesman, he looked for the added security of many clients—more each year—if only to protect his interests against the kind of misfortune that might lay a single large client low and leave the buyer with one-third to one-half or more of his purchasing commitments unfulfilled.[45]

Thus Blackwell bought not only from Hanley but from Sisson in the south end—the only other client who could be classified as a large owner—and from numerous small owners, notably Henry Levens and Fritz and Homer Mace, whose pastures he leased during the spring and fall to feed the cattle he had already bought from others preparatory to driving them to market. Levens' fields actually became the site for north end cattle sales involving smaller owners. These sales were mostly fall sales at which other buyers besides Blackwell bid for local stock. Attendance was always good, with as many as half a dozen to a dozen cattle growers selling their stock there during any one week.[46]

The advance of the buyers early in the century thus confirmed the position of old-timers and firstcomers while it established a new rapprochement of big owners and small owners. There is, however, no evidence that buyers were inclined to deal in any special way with newcomers or others just starting in the business; the buyers' influence worked to encourage the raising of quality livestock, which put a premium on experience and good management. In that respect Harney County had something to be proud of after 1900. Even Canyon City's paper, the *Blue Mountain Eagle*, conceded in 1901:

> The numbers of the great herds speak volumes for the magnitude of Harney County as a breeding ground for cattle, and the fact that the foremost dealers of the country are active in their efforts to secure the stock from this country is proof of the quality of beef it furnishes to the world.[47]

Sheep on the Range

Harney County became for the firs time a major sheep range as well as a cattle range between 1895 and 1905. The increase in Harney County sheep during the 1880s was minor compared with the overwhelming flood of sheep into the county twenty years later. Nothing before equaled it, and nothing has equaled it since, either for its size or for its short duration. Tax rolls are reputedly the worst sources of accurate information about the number of sheep in any western county at any given time almost until 1940, because most sheep in the early days were just "passing through"—the charges of transient herders who owned no property, who ranged their animals hundreds of miles over free range and were never in one county long enough to be assessed. Still, on the tax rolls of Harney County the assessor recorded an almost incredible increase of 565,530 sheep from 1896 to 1907—an increase of almost 1,000 percent.[48] The one major circumstance which might be said to account for this was the shift in livestock production from the Columbia Basin to semi-arid regions of Washington and southeastern Oregon, a shift that had been going on in the last quarter of the nineteenth century and was still going on after 1900 as the population along the great river continued to increase. In the face of this influx, sheepmen, like wild game before a forest fire, moved toward the last free ranges of southeastern Oregon, which by that time were located predominantly in Harney County.[49]

In Harney County, however, large and small cattlemen had already fought their major battles in the war over rangeland jurisdiction; by 1900 each side had pretty well carved out the terms of a settlement by which they could live in peace or at least contend without violence. Parties to that peace were the twenty or so resident sheepraisers in the county who had been among the earliest settlers and who were, almost to a man, people of property with a stake in Harney County society.[50]

Though assessment rolls show the number of sheep in the county increasing after 1896, the number of sheepmen recorded in the rolls who might have been transients was still quite small even in 1900. Little mention was made in the local papers of a "transient sheep problem" or of anything that might be interpreted as one. The topic did occasionally come up, but mostly in reference to the "cattle and sheep wars" in Crook and Morrow counties. In other words, there was not an excessive amount of concern in Harney County before 1900 over prospects of a range war ever happening in the county. By the time the transient sheepmen finally did arrive the range users no longer relied exclusively upon the free range to feed their livestock. The story of how this affected relationships between cattlemen and sheepmen in Harney County may help unravel some of the misconceptions surrounding the subject of western "cattle and sheep wars" in historical literature to the present day.

What was true of cattle prices from 1896 on was equally true of sheep and wool prices during that same period: both climbed to new highs almost yearly. Despite some setbacks, all signs seemed to point to a continued growth in the sheep market after 1900. A large-scale wool auction was held for the first time in Shaniko in the summer of 1901. Freighters and sheep shearers were profiting as never before. Buyers who came to Harney County came directly from Swift and Company to purchase Crane Creek stock, which they bought almost as fast as it could be driven to the sheep pens at Harper.[51]

At the same time, major developments or, more accurately, extensions of earlier developments were radically changing the techniques of marketing. In 1901, S. A. Carson, a Wyoming sheep buyer, signaled the end of sheep trailing from Oregon and in the West generally when he noted that market transactions with Rocky Mountain outlets were beginning to be made in the fall rather than the spring of the year. The system had been to purchase in the spring and afterwards to trail the sheep from Oregon and Washington in bands as large as six or seven thousand across Idaho and Wyoming and Colorado for fall delivery. But the growing number of resident range users in those states intervened in ways that soon reduced trailing to practically nothing. In 1901, Idaho and Wyoming set embargoes on transient sheep and revamped taxing procedures in order to crack down on evasion and delinquency. Even older sheepmen who had since settled down in those states joined with those who wished trailing discontinued. Thenceforth Oregon's transient sheepmen were, for all practical purposes, restricted to ranges in the Cascades, "mining claims" in the Blue Mountains, semi-desert lands in the Owyhee Basin, Catlow and Warner valleys, and the unappropriated lands high up on Steens Mountain.[52]

Pressures began to build in Harney County after 1900. Rising prices, coming during a time of decreasing rangelands elsewhere, attracted vast herds to the county and led local papers to voice their fears of coming friction between range users. The situation in neighboring counties was much worse. In July, Crook County cattlemen formally resolved to drive sheepmen out. At the same time Governor George E. Chamberlain issued a resolution encouraging strict enforcement of existing laws in all the livestock-growing counties, though he conceded that they could at any moment be broken because of "differences [between cattle and sheepmen] as to their respective rights to the range." There was no denying the fact that contention in Crook, Morrow, and even Grant counties had grown into a range war of major proportions.[53] Yet, with the fires burning all around and transient sheepmen arriving in droves, Harney County livestock growers remained unscathed.

Old-time sheepherder Bill Davies, a Welsh immigrant who came to Harney County in 1900, helps reveal why.[54] Davies came to work for the Jenkins Brothers, established sheepmen themselves and, like Davies, of Welsh descent. Davies' herding responsibilities took him to summer pastures on Steens Mountain and to winter grounds in Barren Valley—both terminals of what southeastern Oregon sheepmen called in that day the "eastern circle." The Jenkins brothers owned strategically located forty-acre plots in both places, thus assuring their stock of some water and grass almost all year. Transients like "Buffalo Buck" and "Water Sack Ed," who herded more sheep than many of the established local sheepmen, owned no land and had to haul their water in skin sacks or barrels, which they refilled at each stream they passed. These men had to take their chances both summer and winter and on a first-come, first-serve basis at every bedding or lambing ground on the eastern circle.

As long as the weather was mild, the climate moist, and the grass plentiful, and the number of bands of sheep were moderately few, cursing and arguments would generally comprise whatever altercations occurred. But as the number of sheep rose, arguments became more common, frequently embellished with fistfights and even an occasional pistol-whipping. At worst, however, Steens Mountain and Barren Valley were never the stages for even a minor skirmish between cattlemen and sheepmen, much less a major war between the two. The fighting was between transient sheepmen over the chunks of free range that were left because the cattlemen and resident sheepmen had already acquired most of the pastureland and water rights they needed.[56]

The framework for conflict in Harney County was thus built from hostilities between would-be homemakers and would-be exploiters, not between cattle and sheep interests *per se*. To be a sheepman was no sin as long as one owned land, paid taxes, and otherwise identified himself with the community. The Jenkins brothers ran sheep exclusively, as did the colorful "Irish King," Jim Paul, but they both were established residents of the community. When their names and the names of other local resident sheepmen appeared in the Burns newspaper, as they often did, they appeared as "prominent sheepmen" or "successful sheepraisers," or even "sheep barons." This was not mere condescension on the part of local editors. Indeed, E. H. King, a "respected sheepman" of Happy Valley, complained in the *Harney Items* in September, 1903, "there are over 200,000 head of sheep in the Steen [sic] Mountain country, a large part of which is outside stock. The range is pretty badly crowded and there will soon be no feed unless something is done to relieve the situation." All established, non-transient sheep owners in Harney County, like their brothers in Idaho who helped put a stop to trailing, opposed transient sheepherding.[57]

Of course, the real complaint against transients was that they imposed disorder upon the range and risked the security of established livestock owners. Arguments based on the supposed biological incompatibility between cattle and sheep were false arguments used to cover the argument from self-interest with a gloss of pseudo-scientific authority.[58] Established cattle- and sheepmen themselves gave the lie to it. Henry Miller had raised sheep along with cattle on his Nevada ranches for years. Assessment rolls in Harney County for 1912 show that nearly one-half of all those who owned sheep ran a few cattle as well—sometimes no more than five head, but sometimes as many as forty or fifty head. Abner Robbins of Drewsey ran 1,200 sheep and 525 head of cattle as early as 1900. In a letter to a banking investment house in Seattle, Bill Hanley said of the P Ranch: "By adding a sheep department to the present cattle and horse business, it could be made to pay a great deal larger dividend. . . ."[59]

So, far from being incompatible range users, cattle and sheep actually offered complementary advantages to anyone willing to run both or to alternate between the two animals over a period of years. Cattle eat grasses and use them better than sheep, whereas sheep eat weeds or forbs and use them better than cattle. Sheep also migrate better, moving greater distances without so-called "shrinkage" or fatigue and foraging better during the winter snow. In semi-arid lands sheep can actually graze on a desert range in the winter and use snow for stock water where cattle would parch, starve, and freeze under the same conditions. Still, the deciding factor is and has always been the skill and the particular preference of the owner, a preference often decisively influenced by relative prices on the livestock market.[60]

Government Policy: Direction and Response

In Washington's Nile Valley, "sheep raising and cattle feeding on home lots . . . became [after 1908] a valley practice." This practice followed the enforced tearing down of fences on the public domain, the establishment of forest grazing regulations, and the culmination of a process of consolidation and fencing of private land similar to that which was going on in Harney County. Thus, the imposition of outside controls in crucial areas of range usage where individuals could not or would not agree helped reduce the threat of overgrazing—which was, after all, the basic issue.[61]

Government policy was crucial to the orderly use of the range and thus critical to peace between rangeusers. For all the times the *Harney Items* expressed its fear of overgrazing, it showed equal concern that the government would either fail to move or if it moved would do so in the wrong direction. When the federal fence order was finally enforced in 1903 under the eye of special agents from the U. S. Department of Interior, the *Items* warned, "trouble may possibly occur after the public lands are restored. . . . This might lead to clashes between sheep and cattle growers in eastern Oregon."[62] Thus the question of public policy and the local response to it is a significant part of the story.

Federal land laws and the degree to which they were enforceable have been discussed previously in the context of the promise of equal opportunity as it heightened the expectations of immigrants and thus became a condition favoring settlement. In fact, however, equal opportunity became less and less a condition of settlement despite the rationale of government policy. Opportunities decreased not just because of Harney County's sparse natural resources and the failure of government agencies to act, but because of the active opposition of the county's elite groups.

As in countless other areas of American life, special interests or privileged groups have always risen up to modify, curtail, or thwart the promise of equal opportunity. In the process factions have been formed, led by elite representatives of the special interests so dictated, and these factions have acquired the necessary power to have much their own way until a sufficiently large constituency can blunt their power through political counterforces. To whatever extent these counterforces have succeeded—whether through the agency of hastily organized opposing factions, or through a massive political response to apparent injustices—they have never entirely achieved the goals originally intended, which, in a society of factions, must always be ideal rather than realizable goals.

The Harney County experience with public policy encapsulates this process, which is the heart of the American political process. Aside from irrigation and forest regulations, the provisions that most directly affected Harney County's citizens were the requirement to remove all fences on the public domain and range regulation to balance the availability of resources with their usage. The purpose of the first was to guarantee equal access to public lands; that of the second, to provide a fair means for all livestock producers to utilize open public rangelands. Being policies well suited to the furtherance of equal opportunity in southeastern Oregon, both of them drew opposition from the more powerful vested interests in the county.

Opposition crystallized around the federal government's efforts to enforce no-fencing directives. The Department of the Interior put agents in the field in southeastern Oregon to "ride herd" on range users. To no one's surprise, the vested interests in Harney County supported fencing as a means of controlling the range for their own benefit. The difference now was that these interests included the well-established, better-off firstcomers who had formerly disparaged fencing as a monopolist's trick but had come to advocate it as a means of controlling their own "pasture out back" or areas in their vicinity where shipping corrals might be set up.[63] As with the range barons before, them, so now with the established early settlers: fences protected the accustomed rights of the better-off members of the community against the depredations of less desirable citizens, especially transients. The issue shows in yet another way how big owners and small owners were beginning to join forces. Nonetheless, fences continued to come down wherever inspectors were patient enough to see to their removal.

The issue of grazing provides an added dimension. Throughout the West, the period from roughly 1900 to 1906 was one of extensive overgrazing largely because of the lack of regulation of public lands. The ostensible discontinuance of fencing in Harney County forced stockgrowers there to confront the question of just how the range should be regulated in their area and how that regulation could be worked out for their benefit.

All influential opinion in the county could be divided three ways: newspaper opinion, which favored homesteading; the opinion of the big cattle outfits and firstcomers, which favored leasing the public domain; and the opinion of smaller owners, which leaned toward federal grazing regulations. Among these smaller owners there was a considerable division of opinion over what measures should be introduced to control grazing and what agency should institute these measures, but only transient sheepmen and a few holdovers from the old order favored no leasing or regulation whatsoever. Thus the issue of an equitable policy of range regulation drew a response almost exactly along class and status lines. More importantly, it tested the mettle of the influential stockgrowers in Harney County and exposed the Harney County Stockgrowers Association for what it was: an organization to protect the vested interests of the firstcomers and large owners, of which the most important, aside from curbing rustlers, was being free from any and all outside interference. Collective action to protect individual freedom had, as always, its peculiar pitfalls and inconsistencies.

Local livestock associations were common throughout the state, but they were organized on a rather limited and superficial basis when

compared with similar groups in other industries in the Pacific Northwest. The history of the association in Harney County was, from all
reports, typical. *Ad hoc* organizations in the 1870s and 1880s gave way
to a more formal organization in the 1890s. The Harney County
Stockgrowers Association came into being some time late in that
decade.[64] Its most pressing problem was rustling, a problem for every
stock raiser rather than just for the few large owners. Advertisements
undersigned by the association offering as much as $100 and sometimes
more for information leading to the arrest of rustlers appeared in both
Burns newspapers.

This does not mean that there were not other problems that were
equally pressing, but if these were discussed in more than a casual way
at the association's regular semi-annual meetings it is not apparent
either from contemporary interviews or from newspaper reports of
the time. As far as can be told, none of the multitude of other common concerns that stockgrowers of that period shared, such as cattle
diseases, predator control, or marketing and grazing problems, ever
came up for serious discussion, much less common action. Indeed, the
idea of taking common action where individual action might serve was
generally deplored.[65]

That is remarkable, considering the membership of the organization. In 1901 there were forty listed members—about 10 percent of
all livestock owners in the county—and of them, thirty-one were from
among the pioneer stock of the 1870-1890 period. No sheepmen
belonged, which could be misleading unless it is borne in mind that
most prominent Harney County sheepmen already belonged to the
state Wool Association and were members of the Heppner or Shaniko
wool markets. Hanley and the P.L.S. Company carried memberships,
but the evolution of the cattle industry in Harney County had produced
a group of leaders mostly from among the firstcomers, who, together
with the large owners, formed the local elite that conceived of the
stockgrowers' association as an instrument of its own policy. Certain
townsmen were active members—mostly politicians and professional
men rather than businessmen.[66] For all outward appearances, then, the
Harney County Stockgrowers Association was a model of homogeneity and likemindedness.

The answer to why the association did not exercise greater collective power in broader spheres lay partly in the fact that collective action was really not necessary. For example, there was nothing the
association could do about controlling predators that an individual
could not do himself. Yet the other part of the answer—the most important part for this discussion—was that, from its very beginning, the
association was dedicated to a philosophy of individual rights that has
since become the central tenet of the modern cattleman's code of

behavior; it shapes his role in American society as well as his relationship with the federal government. Thus, its manifestations during this period are significant.

These manifestations can be brought into sharper focus by reviewing the argument over range leasing. Nearly every stockgrower, large and small, agreed that something had to be done about overgrazing. But so controversial were the alternative proposals then advanced that the local association could not come up with a proposal agreeable to all, and the local debate then became swallowed up in the national debate.[67] A brief summary of that dispute will help explain the leasing idea and the problems the local associations had in dealing with it.

An inspector for the U.S. Department of Agriculture, Frederick Coville, was an official spokesman for range leasing. According to him, the advantages of a system whereby range users would be made to pay the government a sum to lease appropriate portions of the range would include assurance of dependable pasture and forage, incentives for stockraisers to conserve grass, the tendency to encourage better breeding on regulated pastures, a clear counter to rustling, and the comparative ease of supplemental feeding. All of these advantages would mean greater predictability and stability for the stock-raising industry.

Despite Coville's arguments, not many of his colleagues in the Department of Agriculture agreed with him. His most forceful opponent was Joseph Nimmo, then noted for his report to the House of Representatives on the range-cattle industry. Nimmo's main point in this dispute was that the rights of homesteaders would be sacrificed. "It will be much more promotive of the public interests," Nimmo is quoted as saying, "if the lands now held by the government shall be dedicated to the rearing of men rather than cattle."[68] In a time of progressive reform against those whom President Roosevelt called "malefactors of great wealth," Coville appeared to be arguing the cattle barons' case.

Modern scholars may be as contemptuous of the "big cattleman's" arguments as was Nimmo; but in semi-arid regions like Harney County where, through bitter experience, settlers learned that farming had to be joined with stock-raising if a would-be farmer were to survive, a leasing arrangement could mean range protection—a way out of a potentially dangerous situation wherein the enemy might not so much be the big owner who could afford to pay as it might be the transient exploiter who could not.[69] Despite the potential advantage of leasing for the firstcomers and large owners, their organization, the Harney County Stockgrowers Association, could not find its voice. Issues of regulation as opposed to leasing as opposed to free access to the public domain plunged local citizens into disagreements that were themselves immersed in a welter of patriotic utterances about the vital connections among homesteading, irrigation, and the national survival. At the very time that federal reclamation was beginning elsewhere in earnest, the cattlemen in the county appeared to be advocating cessation of the homestead policy that was so closely associated with it.

Townsmen were particularly organized and vehement. The *Burns Times-Herald*, now under the vigorous new editorship of twenty-seven-year-old Julian Byrd, led a devastating attack against the local "range lords" and their associates. With a righteous indignation reminiscent of the old *Items*, Byrd cried:

> We are sheeped to death, and we are cattled to death, and we are cay-used to death. In short, the custom of permitting free range to all stock-men has given them a feeling of proprietorship until they have come to demand it as a right. . . . The solution is just this—ownership of the range upon which a man pastures his livestock. Leasing, would certain-ly be of benefit to the big cattle concerns but who else would it help? [Advocates] fail to consider the damage it would do to the advancement of a sparsely settled country in the way of increasing population and the location of public lands for homes."[70]

In editorial after editorial Byrd evoked the sanctioned en-trepreneurial vision of a prosperous, well-settled hinterland. Anyone advancing a common-sense appraisal of the developing troubles on the grasslands above town had hard going?

> Soon we will have an aristocracy of range lords and cattle kings, domineering and selfish, ruling our mountains and plains. We must not give the opportunity for controlling vast areas of land to one man, which might makes homes for large and thriving communities. It is not American.[71]

Caught then in a barrage of Jacksonian rhetoric, cowed into retreat from a position that would identify local stock-growers with the hated monopolists of old, the Harney County Stock-growers Association abandoned the field to the men who, from a popular point of view, were least likely to win the day—the big owners, John Gilchrist of P.L.S. Company and F. C. Lusk, newly elected president of the French-Glenn Company.

Gilchrist reasoned patiently with his opponents, nearly at the cost of over a decade of carefully constructed good will with his neighbors—and all to no avail. Late that year, the Harney County Stockgrowers Association broke its silence to vote unanimously against leasing the public domain, and the following year the American Cattle Growers' Association leasing bill was defeated in Congress. After that the future of the range lay in the development of federal regulation.

Byrd's guns were smoking, but the streets of the town were clear and the local folks could walk them once again in peace. The big coun-try boys who had somehow caused all the trouble knew they had better lay low for a while, and lay low they did until after the many futile tries at homesteading during the next decade vindicated them, at least in their own eyes. Only later, when federal action was designed to encourage and protect a multitude of range uses in addition to that of grazing, and when both state and federal policy began to seem more protective of natural resources than of the cattleman's exclusive use of them, did the association rise at last as one to protect the individual rights of its members.[72]

A Portrait: The Setting for Values, Attitudes, and Status

Julian Byrd's stance was inappropriate for Harney County in 1903. The vista before local stockmen after 1900 was a broad and sunlit one. The depression of 1893 was a decade in the past. Despite threats of overgrazing, the livestock market was active and prices that had risen steadily for six years were continuing to rise. Against the hopes of townsmen, Harney County had become, in the words of one townsman, a "livestock empire" instead of the "succession of countless smiling farms." envisioned by the *Harney Items.* If townsmen doubted that was true, there was always the official report of the federal engineers that "there is little demand for products other than those which can be used for stock feeding. . . . "[73]

But townsmen and their values and attitudes had impact in the cattleman's society. Something of what has been called "rurbanization"— the bringing of country and town together—had subtly taken place during the 1890s and the early 1900s. Certain profound influences accompanied changes from more self-sufficient to more commercial techniques of farming, influences that worked to filter out and select those who could adapt and that produced in the process a more commercially oriented agriculturist who was at the same time more of a speculator dependent upon contact with urban centers.[74]

In Harney County these processes produced attitudes of self-confidence and feelings of success among those who had proved their adaptability. That meant more than adaptation to changing techniques of agriculture; it meant adaptation to the rugged, harsh southeastern Oregon country that seemed somehow to winnow out the best in people and hone them to a finer edge than was possible in the soft environment of the cities.[75] This was the stuff of which the emergent "rugged individualism" was made, and it showed up in every popular utterance and every personal account of that day. When a young man wrote Bill Hanley asking for work, Hanley's advice was what any Burns businessman or cattle-grower would automatically give: "[This] is strictly a make good business and a man's fate in this country depends upon his ability to deliver."[76]

The concomitant of such a philosophy, however, was failure of cooperative effort even though the tenets of good management by which a cattle grower succeeded demanded cooperativeness—a trait to be prized and the reason good foremen drew such handsome pay. A family operation too demanded teamwork, so that the values of individualism and cooperation were never considered absolutes if they were considered a philosophical terms at all. Both were desirable, and a man's character depended largely on the artistry with which he could balance their separate demands.[77]

There was, however, a wider circle of relationships in which stereotyping and prejudice took over. Here the differences between the functions of townsmen and those of agriculturists entered in. For example, a lawyer was basically not to be trusted. Few cattlemen knew what might be involved in a lawyer's profession; so to explain his function the cattlegrower generally stereotyped him. The same was true of a cattleman's opinion of schoolteachers ("educated fools"), doctors ("quacks" or "sawbones"), and especially bankers ("no cow can give a good calf that sucks herself"). Of course these labels or epithets were rarely if ever spoken in earnest directly to those they described; such behavior would be the least artistic way to express one's individualism. Instead these attitudes were circulated largely through the cattleman's subculture while generally only being suspected by the townspeople who were targets of them.[78]

Yet stereotyping was, often as not, in fun, and room for it was made within the community as it is in all communities where social patterns are interdependent, continuing, and intimate. Society's members had to be able to have their biases, commit their acts of anger and frustration, even break the law, but be able still to have an avenue by which they could save face and go on being members of the community. "Stubb" Currey, and old-time rancher and cowhand tells the story of Izadore Poujade, who caught a neighbor with two of Poujade's bulls that the neighbor had turned out among his own cows. Poujade casually rode over, dismounted, and lit up a Bull Durham wrapped in Rizla. He and the neighbor talked of the heat, remarked about the dry year, inquired after members of each other's families, then bid each other goodbye on the pretext of how much "d—d work" had yet to be done. As Poujade rode away, the neighbor drove the two bulls back out of his pasture. He had been allowed to save face, but that did not mean he was freed from retribution. He had to live with the story, which was told and retold on him, of how he bought "the first polled stock he ever had in his life" just one week later.[79]

If there were any real attitudes of contempt for others, they were reserved for outsiders. Of course different kinds of people constituted outsiders to townsmen and to cattlemen. For cattlemen, a settler or "nester" was an outsider worthy of contempt or pity, while for a townsman he was the hope of the future and was welcomed with open arms.[80] On the other hand, there were the kinds of outsiders neither cattleman nor townsman could look upon as other than inferiors: those outside the white race, particularly Indians and Chinese who worked as menials and who were thought of as not only outside the parochial sphere of values and traditions but outside those of the nation as well.[81]

The same attitudes applied to certain outsiders whose skin might not be a different color but whose cultural habits were strange or distasteful. This meant a person of differing ethnic background; perhaps even one with whom a cowman or townsman might have been in conflict or, worse yet, bested in the bargain, such as the "repulsive Jew" Hanley wrote of who won a disagreement with him over the question of America's Chinese exclusion policy. All such people, including the "Huns, Italians," and others of the "lowest and the poorest and the most vicious of all nations" were considered so many pollutants of the pure native strain.[82]

Yet in the cattleman's subculture, if not in town, a separate set of criteria operated to soften and even eliminate prejudice and xenophobia. The demanding requirements of a cattleman's life elevated a whole set of rituals to the level of initiatory rites. If a man could ride ten to fourteen hours a day during roundup and neither whimper over his own lot nor treat his horses badly; if he could ride a "rank bronc" to a frazzle or, after he had "reached for the saddle horn and come up with a handful of grass," get back up on him and try it again; if he was loyal to his boss and honest with his friends—that is, a good buckaroo and a good bunkie; if he could count the cattle in a herd without using his fingers; if he did not faint at the sight of blood or turn away from castrations and dehornings; if he could stand pain, spit on a hot day, drink out of a muddy creek, kill a rattlesnake with his boot, throw a loop, roll a "butt," tell a cancer eye from a sunburn, reach into a cow and turn her calf from breach, carry a stray on his saddle, fall asleep on a rock, wash in a cold bucket, curse like a sea captain, drink like a sailor, tell stories a mile high, outsmart his competitors and outlast his detractors: then he could live among the men of that country as a full equal regardless of his former training or the color of his skin or the origins of his birth.[83]

There was one outside influence that often seemed more foreign and contemptible to the cattleman than any other: the interfering government agent. It was not that the cattleman was unpatriotic. To the contrary, the Fourth of July rodeo represented a confluence of pride in America and pride in the cattleman's way of life, and nothing at that stage in the nation's development indicated that the two were anything but synonymous. Indeed, the cattleman viewed his values as truly American values too little attended to by other segments of society. When a special agent of the Department of the Interior reported Bill Hanley for illegally fencing the public domain, Hanley directed his anger more toward the "nasty-minded" special agent whom he accused of blackmailing him than toward the federal government itself.[84]

In Hanley's eyes at least, the government was the symbolic protector of individual freedoms—the Jeffersonian structure so familiar to rural America if so recently defiled by corporate businesses in the East. All cattlemen may not have made the same distinction between the federal government and its agents, but, as with most western progressives and Republicans of that day, Harney County cattlemen began to look upon federal regulation generally as a way of preserving their own sacred liberty while curbing its excesses elsewhere. As long as federal action tended to preserve the open range for original users it met with approval. That the open range was in fact so preserved kept Harney County cattlemen voting Republican for decades. Only with the advent of the Taylor Grazing Act in 1934 did they change—and then because the Democratic administration under Franklin Roosevelt had sanctified, through that act, the cattleman's prior right to the range.[85]

If the cattleman was ethnocentric, provincial, individualistic, and egalitarian, these traits generally paralleled the values of white Anglo-Saxon, middle-class Americans—values that helped assign status in accordance with occupation and material wealth and limited these assignments to whites. Harney County at the turn of the century evidenced a status structure reflective of these values. A clear line was drawn between races, which meant that the Indians who were the most numerous racial minority were locked into patterns of segregation, discrimination, and economic dependence. They lived in a separate area located under a hill east of Burns, and the only whites who regularly associated with them were ministers and teachers. They were dependent for income upon the menial tasks of ranching, and the only chance for them to achieve another status was in the masculine value system of the cattleman's subculture working on a ranch.[86] Members of other racial minorities were so few as to be insignificant except for Basques, who kept to themselves mostly in the Jordan Valley and from there herded sheep in and out of Harney County. While they represented potential overgrazing of the ranges of Harney County, they earned the respect of other sheepmen, and even cattlemen, who admired their ability with animals—an ability that ranked them high on the stockmen's scale of values.[87]

As to considerations of status among whites, not much had changed between 1890 and 1912. The hierarchy, at least from the cattleman's point of view, still included the large owners, local business leaders, and professional men grouped at the top; the well-off stock raisers, farmers, and small entrepreneurs next; and workers, homesteaders, and service personnel last. The major difference was that introduced by Bill Hanley, Harney County's first resident owner, manager, and cattle king. His patterns of behavior were, of course, urbanized to the extent that most of his business contacts and some of his closer friends were in cities like Portland and Salt Lake City. He traveled extensively outside the region, registering frequently at the Waldorf-Astoria in New York, the Mark Hopkins in San Francisco, and the Palmer House in Chicago. In all such places he combined both business and pleasure while pursuing far-flung enterprises. Yet the functions he took on with greatest gusto and clearly enjoyed the most were promoting southeastern Oregon and entertaining the great and the near great at his spacious house on the Bell-A Ranch.[88]

These two functions were often combined. James Hill of the Great Northern and his son were Hanley's guests. Cattle buyers, senators, and financiers from both inside and outside the state passed pleasant evenings in the Hanley home, where their only duty, and a pleasant one from all reports, was to listen while Hanley regaled them with stories of the country—its past, its prospects, its opportunities—or took them on guided tours, which invariably included visits with town leaders such as Nathan Brown, the former merchant turned banker, or Attorney J. W. Biggs of the Burns Commercial Club.[89]

If Hanley consciously took on a role it was that of homespun aristocrat, and to play it he took to conspicuous consumption, displaying custom-made, leather-covered solid oak furniture in the living room of the Bell-A and equipping the house with the latest in electrical lights and indoor plumbing. In 1910 he purchased an automobile in Portland, and when he was not riding around in it he was showing off his expensive horse-drawn carriage, which sported the finest span of halter-broken grays in the county.[90]

Quite naturally, Hanley's flamboyant part-Mark Twain, part-Buffalo Bill, part-Jimmy Walker pose, while it merely bemused some, drew contempt as well as envy from other local citizens. Indeed, memories of Hanley are ambivalent. As old homesteader Bill Hirsch remarked: "He was big and could be very helpful. He helped develop the country. He hired homesteaders. But he was sort of a blowhard and I have heard several times of him not being too careful with a settler's milk cows when he drove his herds to market."[91]

For all of the contradictions of his public image, Hanley was indisputably Harney County's most famous figure and its leading public man. What is more, he could lay claim to the coveted title of "self-made man," and the power of that image made him a model of success for others to emulate. Firstcomers whose histories in the county in many cases antedated Hanley's but whose fortunes had not been nearly so great testified to their rising state by buying or building town houses. "Rye" Smyth, of Diamond, bought a town lot in 1901. Antone Egli, of Wagontire, and E. H. King built winter town houses the next year. Carroll Cecil was another, and to his old ranch house on Silver Creek he added a centralized water system and indoor plumbing. Often such town houses served the cattleman's family so that children might go to high school, but even then the kinds of houses these families built were of such quality as to suggest that they were reaching beyond the values of their subculture to establish their positions in the larger social sphere. To whatever extent they did, it was in the direction of the town and toward its attractions—an indication of the importance of urban influences that were seen as at once more sophisticated, varied, and enriching than the rounds of rural life. Not that there was a severe pull between the two; it was just that a good cowman who could buy a town house was that much more of a man for having kept up with his town brothers without playing their game.[92]

There was another influence at work. Women in the cattleman's family had much to do with moving to town. The values of the cattleman's subculture were, after all, masculine, and the degree to which women fitted them was the degree to which they could perform masculine tasks. The ultimate compliment for a cowman's daughter was "she rides like a man." Many a minor tragedy was enacted when the woman's temperament could not be made to adjust to the male world around her. For daughters of early families, intermarriage and cultural indoctrination smoothed clashes; but a few hearts were broken while other women simply fled or in rare but significant moments of despair died by their own hands.[93]

At the bottom of the social scale were the cowhands, of whom something has already been said, and homesteaders, whose story belongs appropriately to a later period; some remarks, however, can be made about them here. They related to each other much like lower-class groups identified by sociologists, although, by measures other than occupation or material wealth, they might have stood on higher social levels. For example, some were transplanted professionals—teachers mostly, but some lawyers, and even doctors as well—while others were young people simply out for a lark. The majority, however, were middle-class agriculturists who were, for all the varied reasons already discussed, looking for a new start. Associations among them were on a common level of deprivation. They congregated together, left their doors open to each other, endured loneliness and hardship, but withal they left accounts of a certain joy in their mutual dependence and their shared difficulties not unlike that remembered by participants in resettlement programs who lived under similar conditions during the depths of the depression in the 1930s.[94]

Rube Long's entertaining reminiscence of homestead life in eastern Oregon is a treasure trove of rich anecdotes about the homestead experience. One thing that relegated all who shared this experience to a lower rung on the social ladder was the fact that they were newcomers and, as such, fitted into a kind of outsider community. The homesteader of the 1912-1918 period, like the later agricultural worker in California, was looked upon as a member of a dependent class—a position much different for him from the symbiotic relationship between big cattlemen and settlers during the 1870s. The homesteader could move upward, but only if he proved up, stayed, and prospered on at least a moderate scale—which took about six to eight years, a length of time that few if any could endure on the waterless periphera of the good land. This rush was, in every particular, "a day late and a dollar short." A Rube Long said of it: "The homesteader had no chance. A homestead [was] supposed to be farmland—but the desert [wasn't] farmland."[95]

Thus the attitude most cattlemen had toward homesteaders was one of smug complacency, and the social relationship between the two was that of "cowboy" and "dude." With a tolerance born of success, the cattlemen turned a paternal eye toward these seemingly helpless interlopers and throughout most of the fruitless years of the homestead experience lived next to them in peace. When the homesteader ultimately failed he left only two permanent legacies: the expanded holdings of the cattlemen and, for better or worse, the fixed notion that Harney County could never become anything but a cowman's country.[96]

No matter; southeastern Oregonians in 1912 had much to be pleased about and even a few things to feel smug about. The economy might not have been as diversified as that of the rest of the state, but the modern wonders and mechanical miracles of the new century were not beyond the grasp of the better established cattle-country citizens. There were, for instance, only 150 automobiles in the entire state in 1905, but Archie McGowan of Burns had one of them. There was also a telegraph line that flashed news directly to the newspaper, so that citizens could read it within a day or two of its happening. As early as 1898 nineteen telephone units were installed in Burns, but so many more people evidently wanted to talk that in 1901 another company was set up connecting together residents from all over Harney Valley with people in other parts of the state and reducing the isolation of valley residents significantly thereby. For all of its heroic efforts, however, Burns could not lift itself out of its surroundings into the hinterlands of Peoria, or Sacramento, or Boise. Saloon-keepers had

become businessmen, and merchants had become bankers, but Burns
was still a small rural service town in 1912, and it showed it.[97]

There was some cause to think that the county might not always
be a cattle county. The evidence appeared strictly in the north end,
and specifically in Harney Valley, out of which came nearly the
county's total production of grains in 1900. Some areas like Lawen
and the Narrows were fertile and moist enough to attract tight clusters
of people, and an indication of their number and their optimistic
outlook was that some one or more of them in each place started a
store.[98] Thus there was a semblance of economic diversity; and when
lumbering became something more than a process of cutting down trees
and sawing them in portable mills and developed instead into a lively
production from two shingle mills and five permanent lumber mills,
the "boosters" could confidently trumpet the news that the county's
frontier days were long past and immigrants could expect to find social
amenities not far different from those they had left behind. As anyone
could see, the community had already evolved a specialized economy,
a well-defined social order, and an exuberant community spirit that
identified good things with the twentieth-century spirit of progress.[99]
Harney County comprised a stable, prospering body of citizens that
combined the homogeneity of a white, rural, middle-class population
with the heterogeneity of country and town life, cultural and subcultural traditions, and some commercial and agricultural diversity.
The limits of Harney County's resources had very nearly been explored,
and with their clearer definition the memories of the frontier period
began to fade further and further into the past.

One exception remained. Only on Steens Mountain was there still
a good deal of unclaimed or unregulated public property and a near
bonanza of both minerals and grass. In consequence the mountain produced the nearest thing to a state of nature in southeastern Oregon—
an intermingling of Basque and Irish sheepherders scouring for free
range, rawboned cowboys herding cattle from the P Ranch,
homesteaders hugging isolated segments of the mountain slope, twelve-
mule teams hauling borax out of Borax Lake, and gold prospectors pick-
axing the rocky slopes of Long Hollow.[100]

It was a motley frontier community that grew up on the mountain: an anachronism of tent roofs, open latrines, and bawdy houses,
all of which lasted as long as the bonanza opportunities remained,
which was nearly throughout the 1920s. Frontier scrapes as well as
frontier justice for the offenders were common fare on the Steens; and
yet this volatile little community never seriously erupted. Indeed, its
citizens seemed to sense the limits of their frontier freedom almost
as if they might have known that their experience on that particular
mountain would never be duplicated again on any other mountain

anywhere in the West. Theirs was a last "yahoo" of the kind first yelled in 1849 in San Francisco and again in the stockade of Fort Harney and the saloons of Egan. Growth and good times might mean increased stability and orderliness almost everywhere else in the county, but on the mountain it was pleasurably different. When one of the Steens' favorite daughters, Trixie Russell, went to Burns to answer charges of selling liquor without a license, her customers rallied to her side and the charge was dropped for "lack of evidence." Back up on "Whore House Flat" at Trixie's Place, Trixie threw the wildest three-day party anyone in those parts could remember, for on Steens Mountain lost innocence was innocence all the same.[101]

E P I L O G U E

Trails into the Sunset

Harney County has remained predominantly a cattle country from the early 1900s. Other and different changes have taken place, but broad-brimmed Stetsons are still the headgear in Burns, and the saloons are still the Saturday-night hangouts for men with pale foreheads and ruddy faces. Burns itself is still only a minor regional capital, short on resources and long on local color; yet the complex process of adjustment between Burns and Harney County and between Harney County and the nation continues—the interaction of "personal and impersonal factors" out of which social history develops.

Four themes emerge out of the county's history as it has been told in foregoing chapters, and these themes help organize county life even today. First: the older families of pioneer stock have enjoyed a virtual monopoly of political power and social prestige in the community that has been based, in part at least, on their long residence in Harney County. The process of intermarriage has worked to perpetuate and strengthen their position to the present day. Second: despite the overt appearances of harmony fostered by local newspapers and some community leaders throughout Harney County's history, political factionalism and social antagonism among residents of Burns and the surrounding country have been a normal, not an exceptional, part of the county's social development. Third: economic opportunity in the cattle industry and thus vertical social mobility have been severely limited since the turn of the century by sparsity of local resources, lack of economic diversification, and recently, tight cost—price ratios in the national markets. Fourth: gains in the population of Harney County have lagged much behind gains of the whole state. Consequently, Harney County society has been less cosmopolitan and less influenced by fresh ideas and new or different attitudes. This has been particularly true of rural residents who have grown more out of touch and more provincial with each passing year. Last: Harney County society has always been influenced by outside pressures and national trends but never more profoundly than in recent times. Modern advances in communications, transportation, and technology, coupled with the accelerated growth of population, have produced the most pervasive influences of all, dwarfing by comparison the effects of the bad winters and range wars of Harney County's more heroic era.

These themes can be traced since the time the study left off. A brief review of the county's history for six decades after 1912 will illustrate. During the decade that followed the homestead era, Harney County cattlemen underwent the strains of the agricultural depression of the 1920s. Cattle prices slid from $13.27 to $7.28 in three years. In the presidency of Calvin Coolidge, though important legislation was passed, the federal government was no more inclined to guide agriculturists through hard times than it had been during the era of Benjamin Harrison. Adjustments were by trial and error, costly to range users and destructive to the rangelands. The increase in sheep raising illustrates the point. Lambs and wool supported the highest prices on the livestock market in the 1920s. Cattlemen had hay to sell to a growing number of transient sheepherders, but the market was uncertain and insubstantial.[1] A glance at the vast areas of public domain in the south end around Steens Mountain convinced many cattlemen that they could profit by grazing sheep of their own, at least until the return of good times. Thus the cattleman extended his credit, hired a sheepherder, bought as many sheep as he could afford, and helped contribute thereby to a new period of ruthless overgrazing.[2] In 1928 Steens Mountain was roaring again; pocked with dummy homesteads and blanketed with sheep, wild horses, and cattle, it was a Darwinian jungle in which only the sheep conclusively demonstrated their fitness to survive. Overgrazing, drought, depression, and range regulations too long postponed all combined to bring on a crisis reminiscent of the 1890s.[3]

When the waters of Malheur Lake receded during the rainless years of 1932 and 1933, the last of the homeseekers plowed the newly exposed land and seeded it to wheat. By early autumn they stood with rifles to protect the grain from herds of starving cattle. Thus violence nearly marred the thirty-year-long record of peaceful accommodation between cattlemen and homeseekers. The Department of the Interior, after a belated government hearing in 1935, ousted the grain farmers but gave them enough compensation to set them up as the last of the "self-made" cattlemen in Harney County.[4]

Despite the turmoil of this period and the deservedly prominent place it receives in the histories of the locale, even more fundamental forces were working in the late 1920s and early 1930s to change the nature of the cattle business. One was the passage of the Taylor Grazing Act in 1934 confirmed the ascendancy of the cattleman. By its terms, preference was given in the issuance of grazing permits on the public land to those who were "landowners engaged in the livestock business, *bona fide* settlers and owners of water or water rights."[5] What is more, those who had established a "customary" range through long usage were granted continuing use of it as grazing permittees. In addition, an advisory board of local cattlemen was appointed to assist a chief grazier in the implementation of federal policy.

The grazier was accountable to the newly established Bureau of Land Management, but his position was weak from the start. With no staff, no personnel to police the range, and none but local advisers to assist him, he inevitably deferred to the wishes of the powerful cattlemen's advisory board. The logic of *laissez faire* had never suited cattlemen as neatly as its rhetoric. Their political party allegiance changed accordingly. Always conservative on the state and local issues, the majority of Harney County cattlemen shifted their votes to the Democratic Party in the national campaigns.[6] With the government on the cattleman's side, homesteaders and transient sheepmen were removed from competition for the range. The cattleman's society was becoming even more than before a closed society.

Where the Taylor Grazing Act afforded the cattleman a considerable measure of economic security, the third wave of settlers into Harney County precipitated a new and unsettling rural-urban split. In 1924 Burns became, after several false starts, a railhead. The primitive state of her economy up to the moment was dramatized by the fact that the railroad had to bring in on flatcars the lumber mill it was designed to serve. In 1928 the Hines Mill was dedicated, and by 1933 Burns had doubled its population.[7]

Workers from neighboring states who had helped with construction were replaced by mill hands drawn from the nation's growing army of unemployed. Local sheepmen, freshly excised from their herds, were joined by dust-bowl farmers driven from their desolated farms in Oklahoma. In the transition, the old once-a-week, Saturday night saloon town became an all-week-long, every-night barroom town. The town marshal willingly gave up his job to a four-man police department, which, to the consternation of the town council, often failed to make the fine distinction between the peccadillos of cattlemen and the misdemeanors of working stiffs.[8]

By 1935 Burns was more integrated into the national economy and way of life. A wage-laborer and business- and professional man's society had been superimposed onto the older agricultural, entrepreneurial society. Political factions formed around these separate elements, dividing the loyalties of the town between the older supporters of the cattleman-controlled county court and the newer community of interests centering on the Hines Mill. The urban division reflected the larger town-country split. The cattleman retained his power in the county court, but in order to do so he had to cater more assiduously to the needs of his town supporters. Less of the county budget went for roads in this period, and a good deal more went for the building and maintenance of public schools.[9]

Simultaneously, a Bend-Burns-Boise transportation nexus developed with the advent of the truck and the automobile, emphasizing both the increasing economic and political independence of Burns from the surrounding countryside and the declining influence of Burns's tributary hinterland. By the Second World War the urban newcomers had breached the fortress of county government when a doctor with neither pioneer ancestors nor relatives in the cattle business won one of the three county commissioners' seats. The War accelerated these trends and foreshadowed new ones. From 1940 to 1960 Burns grew by only 3.6 percent. A modern suburb in the town of Hines grew by over 300 percent during the same period.[10] Yet social mobility in both towns increased with the growing number of job opportunities. At the same time trends in the national economy made the cattleman's society more of a closed society than ever.

From the Second World War until 1970 land values in Harney County increased 465 percent.[11] In the south end of the county there appeared reincarnations of the cattle barons of long ago, this time in the shapes of a wealthy lumberman from Idaho, an executive of the Signal Oil Company from California, and a large corporation from San Francisco. But unlike the older cattle barons who engrossed the land by fair means and foul, these modern capitalists, like Hanley before them, bought it; and rather than use it to turn a profit, they pressed it into double service as a tax write-off and a retreat from executive cares and the pressures of city life.[12]

Other outside influences have been at work in the north end. The old notion that Harney County land would never be good for anything but cattle has been challenged by newcomers, mostly from the urban middleclass, who view it as a refuge from smog-drenched cities on the West Coast. They are generally as self-conscious as the old home-steader, but their ability to imitate the habits of cattlemen is not one of the conditions of survival. Indeed, they may constitute the next important wave of settlement. Together with retired persons and a growing number of tourists and sportsmen, they represent, on a local level, nationwide trends that have forced the federal government to reassess public-land policy. In 1958, when the Bureau of Land Management cut grazing allotments throughout the district by one third, it began to dawn on the cattleman that "multiple use" might come to apply to grazing lands as well as to other federally regulated segments of the public domain.[13]

Coincident with the increase in land values up through the mid-1970s was the marked rise in the cost of ranch machinery and equipment. In proportion, the price of cattle went down. In order to make ends meet the cattleman was forced to intensify his operation. Some failed to make the adjustment. Each year the size of ranches increased while the number of ranches decreased. Elder sons were increasingly torn between the ranch, with its long-term investment and deferred profits, and a job in town with its amenities and its advantages of fewer hours and quicker returns.[14]

Pressed from all sides, the cattleman has turned belatedly to cooperative methods of stockraising and marketing—methods never seriously undertaken by the older Harney County Stockgrowers Association. The chief obstacle was always the feeling that cooperatives of any kind would force the cattleman seriously to modify, or give up entirely, one of his most sacred shibboleths: the Jacksonian myth of the self-made man, a myth confirmed in the history of his own ancestors. Self-help has been at the core of his value system.[15] He still believes in its efficacy. To give it up might be to deprive the business of its special social quality—its appeal as a way of life.

Yet there is some evidence to show that the cattleman in Harney County came to think of himself as an independent figure more like the cattle baron of the 1890s as he appears in legend than the midwestern farmer from whom the modern cattleman came. In fact, the modern cattleman seems to have fashioned an image of himself not unlike the television cattleman of the "Bonanza" genre, an image reinforced by newcomers today who fully expect to see him play such a role. In Harney County, the cattleman, isolated and generally out of touch, may like to visit urban centers but seems to feel that cities and government agencies are blights on the American landscape. The cattleman's commitment to the business as a way of life may have led him to feel betrayed by a government committed to the interests of an urbanized, business-oriented, ethnically and racially complex society, in which the cattleman occupies only an insignificant part. This is not to say that crop farmers and businessmen elsewhere do not share a similar sentiment, but only to suggest that many of the apparent paradoxes in the cattleman's behavior toward the federal government might be better explained through an inquiry into its origin. Believing he is the last great hope of true American values, the cattleman, above all others, feels compelled to survive if he can.

NOTES

CHAPTER ONE

1. D. W. Meinig, "American Wests: Preface to a Geographical Interpretation," *Annals of the Association of American Geographers* 62 (June 1972): 159-184.
2. For a discussion of the breeds of Spanish descent see Charles Wayland Towne and Edward Norris Wentworth, *Cattle and Men* (Norman: University of Oklahoma Press, 1955), 238-240. The story of the dispersion of these cattle in America can be traced in Robert Glass Cleland, *The Cattle on a Thousand Hills: Southern California, 1850-1880* (San Marino, California: The Huntington Library, 1951), 7, 17-23, 43-45, 51, 102. Accounts of cattle introduced into the Willamette Valley appear in C. S. Kingston, "The Introduction of Cattle into the Pacific Northwest," *Washington Historical Quarterly* 14 (July 1923): 163-165, 181. On cattle breeds see Appendix 2, p. 364.
3. See Paul W. Gates, "Cattle Kings in the Prairies," *Mississippi Valley Historical Review* 35 (December 1948): 389-397, and Towne and Wentworth, *Cattle and Men*, 220, 221, 280, 281.
4. Russell, Majors and Waddell had 75,000 oxen at the height of their freighting trade. Towne and Wentworth, *Cattle and Men*, 193; Ernest Staples Osgood, *The Day of the Cattleman* (third ed,; Chicago and London: The University of Chicago Press, 1964), 16, 17, 22.
5. J. Orin Oliphant, "The Cattle Herds and Ranches of the Oregon Country, 1860-1890," *Agricultural History* 21 (October 1947): 220.
6. J. Frank Dobie, "The First Cattle in Texas and the Southwest Progenitors of the Longhorns," *Southwest Historical Quarterly* 42 (January 1939): 3-29.
7. Several accounts treat with this early Texas trade, notably Harry Sinclair Drago, *Great American Cattle Trails* (New York: Dodd, Mead, and Co., 1965), 83-86.
8. The Virginia City and later the South Pass strikes were of importance; Osgood, *Day of the Cattleman*, 22. Western Montana ranches were well established after the Alder Gulch strike in 1863; Drago, *Cattle Trails*, 23, 235-237. Beef was used to help pacify reservation Indians when it was available; E. E. Dale, *The Range Cattle Industry* (Norman: University of Oklahoma Press, 1930), 78, 80.
9. Figures are taken from Dale's compilation of statistics in the *Department of Agriculture Monthly Reports*, 1867. See Dale, *Range Cattle Industry*, 30, 31.
10. The Texas market was threefold from the beginning: Osgood, *Day of the Cattleman*, 89; Drago, *Cattle Trails*, 79, 202, 206, 230.
11. See Dobie, "First Cattle," 3.
12. J. Orin Oliphant, "The Eastward Movement of Cattle from the Oregon Country," *Agricultural History* 20 (January 1946): 19. For accounts of the gold strikes see George F. Brimlow, *Harney County, Oregon and its Range Land* (Portland: Binfords and Mort, 1951), 28-30. Accounts of the early cattle business near the Idaho mines appear in Martin F. Schmitt (ed.), *The Cattle Drives of David Shirk: From Texas to the Idaho Mines, 1871 and 1873* (Portland: The Champoeg Press, 1956), ii, iii, 32-34.

13. See Schmitt, *David Shirk*, iv, 45-50; Brimlow, *Harney County*, 44, 57-63, 75. For an indication of the extent to which consolidation of capital influenced southeastern Oregon, see Lewis A. McArthur, "Devine Monument Dedication," *Oregon Historical Quarterly* 29 (September 1928); 236. The Montana legislature reflected the interests of western Montanans when it exempted Oregon cattle from taxation for the first year: Osgood, *Day of the Cattleman*, 55, 56, 138.

14. For an early account, see Brimlow, *Harney County*, 57-59. The physiographic and climatic information below was taken from the following sources: State of Oregon, State Water Resources Board, *Hearing Record in the Matter of a Water Resource Program for the Malheur Lake Basin*, Burns, Oregon (January 19, 1966), 17-19, Exhibit 3, pp. 1, 2, Exhibit 11, pp. 1, 2, and U.S. Bureau of the Census, *Tenth Census of the United States: 1880, Population*, I:xii, Plate 25, 26; Gary H. Searle and Harvey O. Bennett, "The Whitehorse Ranch in Southeastern Oregon" (mimeographed), 4, 5; field trip with Harney County Extension Agent, June 23, 1968. See also Map No. 1.

15. On Devine see Oliphant, *On the Cattle Ranges of the Oregon Country* (Seattle: University of Washington Press, 1968), 88-90.

16. Rankin Crow, *Rankin Crow and the Oregon Country*, as told to Colleen Olp (Ironside, Oregon: by the author, 1950), 20, 21; Brimlow, *Harney County*, 57-62.

17. The way through the foothills mentioned above is now called Long Hollow Road. The difficulties it presented for travelers in the early days are alluded to in Brimlow, *Harney County*, 68, 69. The quote above appears in Schmitt, *David Shirk*, 128.

18. John Catlow, for whom the valley was named, ran cattle there a year earlier but never entered a claim in the valley. See Brimlow, *Harney County*, 61.

19. See A. A. Bardwell, D. C. Eggleston, and M. A. Palmer, "Appraisal of Land and Resources of the Malheur Indian Reservation" (mimeographed), 53, and General Land Office Survey Field Notes, Map No. 3.

20. For description, see particularly, *Water Resources Program, Board*, 17-19 and Exhibits No. 4 and 11, and Dale C. Eggleston, "Harney County, Oregon: Some Aspects of Sequent Occupancy and Land Use" (master's thesis, University of Oregon, 1970), 21-25.

21. John Scharff, interview with the author, Malheur Wildlife Refuge Headquarters, July 8, 1968. This valley is a graben, whereas the valleys of tributary streams as well as Catlow and Alvord Basins are of syniclinic origin. See Eggleston, "Harney County," 25.

22. *Water Resources Program*, 6, 7, and Exhibit No. 5. A visitor in 1873 told of the rich potential of the valley. See Oliphant, *Cattle Ranges*, 96.

23. E. R. Jackman, John Scharff, and Charles Conkling, *Steens Mountain in Oregon's High Desert Country* (Caldwell, Idaho: The Caxton Printers, 1968) 1, 2, 10, 136; Brimlow, *Harney County*, 55.

24. The commander of the Pacific Department of the U.S. Army, General John Wood, issued orders in 1856 forbidding settlement in this region. The army was simply not in a position to protect settlers. Brimlow, *Harney County*, 16, 23; F. Phil Brogan, *East of the Cascades* (Portland: Binfords and Mort, 1965), 83. The great-granddaughter of one of these immigrants tells of her great-grandfather's vow to "come back to this country before I die." Marjorie Shull, Burns, interview with the author, August 14, 1969.

25. Shull interview. See also *The History of Baker, Grant, Malheur, and Harney Counties* (Chicago: Western Historical Publishing Co., 1902), p. 684.
26. *The History of Baker, Grant*, 635.
27. For a description of the physiography of this area, see Eggleston, "Harney County," 44-47.
28. Marcus Haines, Haines Ranch, Interview with the author, September 10, 1968; Eggleston, "Harney County," 45; Map No. 3, p. 427.
29. Bardwell, *et al*, "Appraisal of Land," 12.
30. *Tenth Census, Agriculture*, Vol. III, "The Gordon Report," 125; Bill Hanley and Tom Allen, Reminiscences, July 22, 1922, typescript, William Hanley Collection, Oregon Historical Society Library, Portland, 5, 6 (hereafter Hanley Collection).
31. Margaret J. LoPiccolo, "Some Aspects of the Range Cattle Industry of Harney County, Oregon: 1870-1900" (master's thesis, University of Oregon, 1962), 20; Reminiscences: Hanley and Allen, 1, 4; Brimlow, *Harney County*, 63, 134. Hanley was always restrained and diplomatic: Hanley to C. E. S. Wood, April 17, 1918, Hanley Collection.
32. *Water Resource Program*, Exhibit No. 1.
33. *Ibid*. Water Resources Board, Exhibit No. 1. For a description of C. E. S. Wood's early view of the region, see Edwin A. Bingham, "C. E. S. Wood: An Era and a Realm, Part I, Three Vignettes" (typescript), p. 7. Accounts of the early settlers' enthusiasm appears in Bardwell, *et al*, "Appraisal of Land," 12, 13. See also *Blue Mountain Eagle*, (Canyon City), April 22, 1904.
34. Dale Eggleston calls it "the north-south transition zone between the Great Basin section of mountainous ranges and basins and the Blue Mountains section of forested mountains and plateaus": "Harney County," 1. It was originally part of the zone of cultural contact between plateau Indians and coastal tribes: Dorothy O. Johansen, and Charles Gates, *Empire of the Columbia* (New York; Harper and Bros, 1957), 5-22. Oliphant designates the Blue Mountains as the division between Columbia intermontane province and the basin and range province: *Cattle Ranges*, 75.

CHAPTER TWO

1. John Higham, *Strangers in the Land: Patterns of American Nativism, 1860-1925* (New York: Atheneum, 1965), 14-34.
2. Thomas C. Cochran and William Miller, *The Age of Enterprise: A Social History of Industrial America* (New York: The Macmillan Company, 1942), 131.
3. The best single work on mining in western America is Rodman W. Paul, *Mining Frontiers of the Far West 1848-1880* (New York: Holt, Rinehart and Winston, 1963).
4. Two classic treatments of the range cattle industry in the nineteenth century show this relationship in detail. See E. E. Dale, *The Range Cattle Industry* (Norman: University of Oklahoma Press, 1962), 30-42, and Ernest Staples Osgood, *The Day of the Cattleman* (Minneapolis: The University of Minnesota Press, 1929), 89-91.
5. The impact of American industrialism on the agricultural frontier is discussed in Walter Prescott Webb, *The Great Plains* (New York: Grosset and

Dunlap, 1931), 271-280, 295-318, 333-374. See also Gilbert S. Fite, *The Farmer's Frontier* (New York: Holt, Rinehart and Winston, 1966), 29-32, 52, 131.

6. See the discussion in Paul Wallace Gates, *History of Public Land Law Development* (Washington, D.C.: U.S. Government Printing Office, 1968), p. 391.

7. Anne Shannon Monroe (ed.), *Feelin' Fine* (Garden City: Doubleday, Doran and Co., Inc., 1931), p. 63.

8. Paul, *Mining Frontiers*, 135.

9. Good accounts of these movements are Herman Oliver, *Gold and Cattle Country* (Portland: Binfords and Mort, 1962), 20; George F. Brimlow, *Harney County, Oregon and Its Range Land* (Portland: Binfords and Mort, 1951), 28-30, 51; and Phil F. Brogan, *East of the Cascades* (Portland: Binfords and Mort, 1964), 48, 49.

10. The Idaho strike nearly coincided with the strikes in the Nez Perce Mountains, Canyon City, and the Powder River country in Oregon. Idaho territory was organized in 1862, the same year Baker County in Oregon was organized. Grant and Union counties were organized just two years later. Brimlow, *Harney County*, 28-30.

11. W. Turrentine Jackson, *Wagon Roads West: A Study of Federal Road Surveys and Construction in the Trans-Mississippi West, 1846-1869* (New Haven: Yale University Press, 1965), 319.

12. Thumbnail histories of each appear in Jerry A. O'Callaghan, *The Disposition of the Public Domain in Oregon* (Washington, D.C.: U.S. Government Printing Office, 1960), 50-55.

13. Brogan, *East of the Cascades*, 92; Brimlow, *Harney County*, 50.

14. Brogan, *East of the Cascades*, 54-60, 66; O'Callaghan, "Disposition," 52, Brimlow, *Harney County*, 26-28, 36. A concise description of the fort and of the roads it protected is in: U.S. Army, Military Division of the Pacific, *Outline Descriptions of the Military Posts in the Military Division of the Pacific*, 1870, 42, 43.

15. In the census of 1870, Canyon City was a town of only 423 people. U.S. Bureau of the Census, *Tenth Census of the United States: 1880, Population*, I: 75.

16. Brimlow, *Harney County*, 45, 46, 49, 50, 136. Fort Harney was among the more inaccessible and remote forts in the Division of the Pacific, but it carried a complement of 150 to 200 men in three full companies which, made it the tenth largest fort among the twenty-four in the division: *Outline Description*, 42-44, also U.S. Army, Department of the Columbia, Assistant Adjutant General's Office, *Roster of Troops Serving in the Department of the Columbia*, 1877, 4, and U.S. Army, Department of the Columbia, *General Orders*, 1869. Calculations of population figures for Harney Valley are difficult since precincts were much larger and there were fewer of them in 1870 than there were ten years later. By adding the total populations living in the several smaller precincts in 1880, which had been carved from three larger ones embracing the northern parts of the county in 1870, then calculating the percentage of people living in the valley in 1880 and using that same percentage in 1870, I estimated a total population living in Harney Valley in 1870 at 110 people. In this early period when the percentage of those persisting was high and the land they had settled on among the best, it can be supposed that the distribution remained about the same.

17. Giles French, *Cattle Country of Peter French* (Portland: Binfords and Mort, Publishers, 1965), 66, 67, 94, Brimlow, *Harney County*, 36-39; Robert Glass Cleland, *The Cattle on a Thousand Hills: Southern California: 1850-1880* (San Marino: The Huntington Library, 1951), 130-137.

18. A discussion of these patterns of migration appears in Fite, *Farmer's Frontier*, particularly 153, 154. See also Dorothy O. Johansen, *Empire of the Columbia: A History of the Pacific Northwest* (New York: Harper and Row, 1967), 371-378.

19. The process is described with skill in J. Orin Oliphant, *On the Cattle Ranges of the Oregon Country* (Seattle: University of Washington Press, 1968), 76, 77.

20. See Gate's description of the general Western patterns of farmer encroachment: *Public Land Law*, 466-473. The best available study of the early cattle industry in southeastern Oregon is a master's thesis dealing with the big owners in the region. This focus leads to occasional distortions. Many small cattle owners came in at the same time, thus making matters of range and water rights and political control of the region extremely complex. Although the big owners were in the ascendency a good deal of the time, as will be discussed further on, it is not possible to claim that they "ruled the region for the next 30 years." Margaret Lo Piccolo, "Some Aspects of the Range Cattle Industry of Harney County, Oregon, 1870-1900" (master's thesis, University of Oregon, 1962), 24.

21. Settlers preferred to buy the best available land rather than claim unclaimed land that was not good. Demand being what it was, small owners could invest, wait a few years, and sell out to larger owners for a small profit. Johansen, *Empire*, 234. Gates mentions that Willamette Valley land in the 1870's and 1880's was being "snapped up in great volume by men of means": *Public Land Law*, 443. See also Oliphant, *Cattle Ranges*, 77.

22. The greatest increase in the number of farms east of the Cascades occurred in Umatilla and Walla Walla counties, but eddies of the Willamette Valley overflow reached present-day Harney County during the 1870's. *Tenth Census, Population*, 75-76. Also, *Tenth Census of the United States, Population, Schedule I*, 1-9. See also Gretta Gossett, "Stock Grazing in Washington's Nile Valley: Receding Ranges in the Cascades," *Pacific Northwest Quarterly* (July 1964): 119-127.

23. *Tenth Census, Schedule I, ibid.* Routes taken by these settlers from the Middle West to the Willamette Valley and from there to southeastern Oregon are traced in Oliphant, *Cattle Ranges*, 107, 108, and A. A. Bardwell, D. C. Eggleston, and M. A. Palmer, "Appraisal of Land and Resources of the Malheur Indian Reservation," (Burns, (mimeographed) Oregon, 1958), 52, 53. Also Tables 1, 2, 3, pp. 383, 384, 386.

24. Such "riverine" settlement was described in the tenth census as a characteristic of the pioneer stage of settlement in the semi-arid and arid regions of the country. *Tenth Census, Population*, p. xx.

25. The original schedule of the tenth census reveals, to some extent, the mobility and restlessness of early pioneers. *Tenth Census, Population, Schedule I*, pp. 1-9. Material taken from the county "mug book" shows a much more detailed tracing of a narrow sample of early pioneers, revealing an average of 3.7 moves for all California immigrants into the area. See *History of Baker, Grant, Malheur, and Harney Counties* (Chicago: Western Historical Publishing Co., 1902), 659-715. The information in the following two paragraphs comes from an analysis of data from the

original schedules of the U.S. *Tenth Census* cited above. See Tables 3, 7, 11, pp. 386, 390, 397.

26. For an account of the drive see Martin F. Schmitt (ed.), *The Cattle Drives of David Shirk: From Texas to the Idaho Mines, 1871 and 1873* (Portland: The Champoeg Press, 1956), 45-50.

27. Brimlow, *Harney County*, 61.

28. The best study on the big business aspects of the range cattle industry in the nineteenth century is Gene M. Gressley, *Bankers and Cattlemen* (New York: Alfred A. Knopf, 1966).

29. The following census portrait is drawn from data in the original schedules of the *Tenth Census, Population, Schedule* I, 1-9; Table 2, *ibid.*

30. See the introductory comments by the Director of the Bureau of the Census, defining frontier characteristics. *Tenth Census, Population*, xvi-xx, xxxiv, xxxv; Table 2, *ibid.*

31. John Messing, "Public Lands, Politics, and Progressives: The Oregon Land Fraud Trials, 1903-1910," *Pacific Historical Review*, 35 (February 1966), 36.

32. *Burns Times Herald*, Diamond Jubilee edition, January 31, 1963.

33. For a good account see Dale C. Eggleston, "Harney County, Oregon: Some Aspects of the Sequent Occupancy and Land Use" (master's thesis, University of Oregon, 1970), 73.

34. Edward F. Treadwell and John L. Rand, *Brief in Support of Claims of Pacific Livestock Company*, Before the State Water Board of Oregon. Burns, Oregon, January 24, 1923, Harney County Court House, Burns, 77, 78.

35. Frank McLeod came in 1873. Tom Whiting came one year later. Each helped the other through the first years; yet neither was able to strike out independently until 1876. Lila E. Langdon, "A History of Education in Harney County, Oregon, 1875-1940" (master's thesis, Eastern Oregon College, 1959), 5, 6. Brimlow cites the same case; *Harney County*, 59, 62. This whole pattern corresponds closely to Osgood's description; see *Day of the Cattleman*, 42, 48, 49.

36. Treadwell and Rand, *Briefs*, 85.

37. This was accomplished simply by acquiring a piece of land adjacent to a stream. In the early days claimants were few. Consequently, none of the litigation which marred Harney County's later history arose during the 1870s; nor was anyone unduly concerned in that lawyerless land over doctrinal distinctions between riparian rights and those of prior appropriation. Later, these early claims came to be classified "vested rights" or rights exempt from the permits required by state law after 1909. The best and most exhaustive sources on the establishment of early water rights are: Hearing Before the State Engineer of the State of Oregon, "In the Matter of the Determination of the Relative Rights to the Use of the Waters of Donner and Blitzen River, a Tributary of Malheur Lake," Vols. 1-18 Harney County Court House, particularly 14: 9-21, and Hearing Before the State Engineer of the State of Oregon, "In the Matter of the Determination of the Relative Rights to the Use of the Waters of the Silvies River, a Tributary of Malheur Lake," Vols. 1-37, Harney County Court House, Burns.

38. Monroe, *Feelin Fine*, 37.

39. Early assessment records were not reliable sources for the number of cattle actually owned by the big men. See the discussion in Lo Piccolo, "Range Cattle Industry," 29, 113-115. Perhaps the best estimates were by the

"hands" who rode for the big owners. James Brandon was a Whitehorse Ranch hand for 15 years and estimated an average of 25,000 head of cattle and between 2,500 and 3,000 heads of horses on the Todhunter and Devine spread during those days. Treadwell and Rand, p. 94. Ike Foster's relationships with his employers, his cowhands, and the local settlers with whom he was on good terms are described in the reminiscences of Tom Allen and Bill Hanley. Tom Allen and Bill Hanley, reminiscences, August, 1922, typescript, Hanley Papers, Oregon Historical Society Library, Portland, 5-10.

40. French was first to pioneer the Omaha trade. Others followed suit as cattle surpluses increased. Oregon cattle were considered a higher grade of cattle and consequently brought a good price in Omaha. Gressley, *Bankers and Cattlemen*, 147,148. Oliphant, *Cattle Ranges*, 78, 97, 138, 139. Lo Piccolo mentions French's sale to N. R. Davis of Cheyenne of 12,000 cattle in 1879: "Range Cattle Industry," 89.

41. One of the more obvious rules was to keep the cattle close to running water and away from Indians. One also needed to take the cattle out of the valleys in the spring when poisonous, new-blooming larkspur might be grazed. Schmitt, *David Shirk*, 33, 34. Words of Spanish origin were used and had to be a part of every drover's vocabulary. See W. G. "Uncle Billy" Thompson, reminiscences, Typescript, Harney County Library, Burns, 1, 2.

42. Rankin Crow, *Rankin Crow and the Oregon Country*, as told to Colleen Olp (Ironside, Oregon: by the author, 1970), 27. Shirk's diary is the major source for this discussion: Schmitt, *David Shirk*, 126-128.

43. Harry Goulden, Jr., interview with the author, September 16, 1969. Goulden's father had been a OO hand during this period and had participated intimately in the society of which Shirk and French were a part. Other general accounts appear in Allen and Hanley, reminiscences, 1-4, and Brimlow, Harney County, 207, 208.

44. Both Crow's and Witzell's early careers are described in Crow, *Rankin Crow*, 20-27. The early pay records of the P.L.S. Company show over half the hands hired during peak seasons to be local settlers. P.L.S. Company Pay Records, Harney County Museum, Burns.

45. Crow, *Rankin Crow*, 20-27. The ideal of social democracy was, of course, uppermost. Shirk speaks with the smugness of the self-made man when he says, "There was no class, but all were common people, the foreman working with his men and not sitting around putting on airs. . . ." Schmitt, *David Shirk*, 106, 115, 116.

46. Few during the 1870s got beyond these crude beginnings. Most relied instead upon natural flooding and upon native grass for feed. Information on community populations was taken from historical information contained in: Brief of the State of Oregon, "The United States vs. the State of Oregon," in the Supreme Court of the United States, October term, 1934, Harney County Court House, 113, 114.

47. The following description is taken from information in Treadwell and Rand, *Brief*, 92; Bardwell, *et al.*, "Appraisal of Land," 55-58; Brief of the State of Oregon, 114, 115.

48. An interview with I. N. Davis cited in Bardwell, *et al.*, "Appraisal of Land," Eggleston, *et al.*, "Appraisal of Land," 62-63, is typical. He "landed [his] . . . first buckarooing job with Abner Robbins" in the late 1870's. Fort Harney was also a source of hay contracts for settlers. *Outline Description of Military Posts*, 44.

49. Bardwell, *et al*; "Appraisal of Land," 28, 54, 64.
50. In Homer Mace's words, "I had no objection to [my downstream neighbors] using the water that I turned out provided it did not interfere with me." Treadwell and Rand, *Brief*, 79.
51. Allen and Hanley, reminiscences, 1.
52. Brimlow, *Harney County*, 136.
53. Ilda Mae Hayes, interview with the author, July 23, 1969, Burns, Oregon. Hayes is the daughter of Scott Hayes, one of the earliest settlers in Harney Valley. Her mother recalled and passed on stories told her by her aunt of the dances at Fort Harney. See also Brimlow, *Harney County*, 136.
54. Langdon, "Education," 14, 15; Brimlow, *Harney County*, p. 66. This was generally true of other areas in the West where large, absentee-owned outfits were located. For obvious reasons none was particularly interested in promoting community stability or growth. See Gressley, *Bankers and Cattlemen*, 74, 87, 88. French is reported to have contributed to the Methodist Church. French, *Cattle Country*, 111.
55. Schmitt, *David Shirk*, 126.
56. *Ibid.*, 124; Brimlow, *Harney County*, 92, 93, 162. See Oliphant's brief discussion of Indian status in the early days of the cattle business: *Cattle Ranges*, 289, 301.
57. *Outline Description of Military Posts*, 44. This was the largest reservation in Oregon in terms of actual acreage and contained "an abundance of choice grazing land." Oliphant, *Cattle Ranges*, 290-291.
58. Oliphant, *Cattle Ranges*, 309.
59. Bardwell, *et al.*, "Appraisal of Land," 57, 58.
60. For Rinehart's troubles see Brimlow, *Harney County*, 129, 130 and Oliphant, *Cattle Ranges*, 137.
61. Oliphant has been criticized for his elevation of federal policy, which suggests that the government erred in giving the Indians too much in the first place. Nonetheless, Oliphant's account is well documented and informative. *Cattle Ranges*, 295-316.
62. Lo Piccolo cites estimated losses throughout eastern Oregon at approximately $300,000. The greatest losses were in horses; the number of cattle was not seriously reduced. "Range Cattle Industry," 105.
63. Bardwell, *et al.*, "Appraisal of Land," 63.
64. George E. Carter, "The Cattle Industry of Eastern Oregon, 1880-1890," *Oregon Historical Quarterly* 67 (June 1966): 150. For a balanced general comment see Oliphant, *Cattle Ranges*, 132.
65. See Oliphant for the effects of the two winters: *Cattle Ranges*, 276-281. The deleterious effects of overgrazing are described in Lo Piccolo, but according to the "Gordon Report" southeastern Oregon suffered less than other rangeland areas. Lo Piccolo, "Range Cattle Industry," 77; *Tenth Census, Agriculture*, 3: 128, 129. On consolidation after 1881, see Bardwell, *et al.*, "Appraisal of Land," 64, 66, 67, and Lo Piccolo, "Range Cattle Industry," 65, 66. Most of the best water rights on the former Malheur Reservation went to the big cattlemen. Eggleston, "Harney County," 75.
66. The population in the Harney County region increased from between 850 and 900 people in 1880 to 2,559 people in 1890. *Tenth Census, Population*, 75, 76; *Twelfth Census, Population*, 240, 264. Gates terms this surge of immigration westward in the late 1870s and 1880s "the third great rush to acquire a stake in the public lands,": *Public Land Law*, 417. See Table 1, p.

67. Johansen, *Empire*, 346, 347.
68. Gressley, *Bankers and Cattlemen* 97-99; Osgood, *Day of the Cattleman*, 194-202; Lo Piccolo, "Range Cattle Industry," 98, 99. Smaller men like Shirk recognized the need for change. "Yet we were now beginning to realize that if we were to remain in the livestock business, we must secure title to land and prepare feed for our stock during the winter months": Schmitt, *David Shirk*, 125, 126.
69. For a general description of land laws and their operation during the 1870s and 1880s see Gates, *Land Law*, 399-401, 421-462, 467.
70. Edward F. Treadwell, *The Cattle-King*; A Dramatized Biography (revised edition; Fresno: Valley Publishers, 1966), 59-61, 65-71, 73, 78-80, 85, 120-126; Brimlow, *Harney County*, 75, 148, 176; Lo Piccolo, "Range Cattle Industry"; 20-23; French, *Cattle Country*, An illustration of Miller's use of hired hands to claim homesteads in Agency Valley which later reverted to the partnership appears in a newspaper account of a case, *Gentry* vs. P.S.L. Co., *Harney Items*, (Burns), November 15, 1902.
71. Lo Piccolo, "Range Cattle Industry," 22.
72. For Devine's early career in Harney Valley see Treadwell and Rand, *Brief*, 91; Brimlow, *Harney County*, 60, and *History of Baker, Grant*, 635. The incident of fraud is reported in the American Guide series, *Oregon: End of the Trail*, cited in Brimlow, *Harney County*, 173.
73. Bardwell, *et al.*, "Appraisal of Land," 66, 67; Treadwell and Rand, *Brief*, 67, 113. Both these sources mention acreage and land prices. The total price is mentioned in Treadwell and Rand, p. 113. This was reportedly the first fenced land in the valley. See Lo Piccolo, pp. 55, 56, for a good, concise review of the origins of the Oregon act. See Maps No. 4 and 5, pp. 428, 429.
74. See testimony of Scott Hayes in Treadwell and Rand, *Brief*, 118-120; Treadwell, *Cattle-King*, 140-142. To most settlers this manipulation was on a par with hiring dummy entrymen to file on a homestead; however, as in the case of dummy homesteads, it is likely that settlers who were hired did not complain, just as it is likely there would have been fewer complaints among the 15 settlers had the swampland been offered to them for sale first.
75. Treadwell, *Cattle-King*, 145, 146; J. Orin Oliphant, "The Cattle Herds and Ranches of the Oregon Country, 1860-1890," *Agricultural History* 21 (October 1947); 223.
76. Joe Fine, interview with the author, November 30, 1969, Burns, Oregon (Fine was manager of Roaring Springs Ranch, originally part of French's great domain): Johnny Crow (grandson of James Rankin Crow and son of David Crow, both intimates of French), interview with author, July 25, 1968, Sod House, Oregon. French was the only manager among the big men who borrowed money on his personal signature from the bank in the growing town of Burns. Lo Piccolo, "Range Cattle Industry," 50. A romanticized, fictional biography of French builds to a climax around French's close association with the Diamond, Happy, and Harney Valley people with whom he is in constant contact and by whom he eventually dies. Elizabeth Lambert Wood, *Pete French: Cattle King* (Portland: Binfords and Mort, Publishers, 1951), particularly 171, 179, 192, 201, 209, 211-230.
77. Oliphant, *Cattle Ranges*, pp. 207, 208.
78. Schmitt, *David Shirk*, 132.

79. *Ibid.*, p. 131.

80. Shirk claimed French was using a ". . . corp of gunfighters." *Ibid.*, 131-140.

81. Brimlow, *Harney County*, 167; Lo Piccolo, "Range Cattle Industry," 54; Harney County, Record of Deeds, Book A, 116, 127, 224, 448.

82. County assessment records show Brown with only 160 acres from 1885 to 1890. He was delinquent in his taxes on this property for six years, yet by 1890 the gross value of his holdings had risen from $320 to $1,700, and the number of sheep he ran was reputed to be over 3,000 head, although he claimed only 500 on the 1890 tax rolls: Brimlow, *Harney County*, 133; Harney County Tax Rolls, 1890, 4; Grant County Tax Rolls, Delinquent Taxes: 1885-1890, Grant County Court House, John Day, 7, 16, 28. The most common label applied to Brown among the oldtimers today is that he was "colorful" or "quite a character." These people give him credit for his shrewdness and speak of him as a local man who made good on his own initiative. On the subject of his having shot Johnny Overstreet, the role ascribed to Brown is clearly that of the hard-working member of the range community defending his rights against outside monopolists. Juan Vallejo, Interviews with the author by Fields, Oregon, June 22, 1968; Orin Day, Sod House, Oregon, June 23, 1968; *Interview with* Jim McEwen, Riverside, Oregon, July 1, 1968. See also Brimlow, *Harney County*, p. 170.

83. It is not easy to identify firstcomers, but by using original surveys and deed records it is possible to distinguish most of them. In the U.S. census alone 26 percent of the total number of people appearing in the 1880 census persisted through the 1880s until 1890—a total of 109 out of 419 people mostly along the Malheur River. *Tenth Census, Population, Schedule 1*, 1-9; Harney County Tax Rolls, 1890; Original Surveys, 1873, 1879; Harney County Record of Deeds, Book A.

84. For example, Alphena Vanator bought out "Doc" Kiger on the south fork of the Malheur River. Kiger had been the victim of pressure from French at an earlier date and was a hold-out during the land-buying spree of Miller and Lux. Brimlow, *Harney County*, 61; Eggleston, "Harney County," 83.

85. John Mahon, an energetic firstcomer, instituted several contests against neighbors near the present town of Crane. As a recent owner of the Whitehorse Ranch put it: "Mahon and those boys had to look out for themselves. Nobody else was going to do it for them." Paul Stewart, interview with the author, Whitehorse Ranch, June 23, 1968.

86. *Tenth Census*, Agriculture, Schedule 2, 2-4; Harney County Tax Rolls, 1890, 5, 6, 19, 30, 34.

87. Bardwell, *et al.*, "Appraisal of Land," Table 11-A, 71, 72. Lo Piccolo suggests that the scarcity of water in Harney County helped the big men to control the range. Conversely, it was more difficult for Miller and Lux to maintain exclusive control of the Malheur River region where water was more plentiful than it was for the south end barons to do the same in their regions where its scarcity led to monopolization. Lo Piccolo, "Range Cattle Industry," 3.

88. An account of the difficulties encountered by settlers near Malheur Lake when they attempted to promote a road from Rockford to Narrows is in *History of Baker, Grant* 688. See also Harney County Road Petition, October 30, 1889, (Harney County Clerk's Office), signed by fourteen prominent settlers in the Narrows, lower Blitzen and Diamond areas. The list included five firstcomers but not French.

89. *History of Baker, Grant*, 643.

90. Paul, *Mining Frontiers*, 77, 97, 125, 151.

91. Robert R. Dykstra, *The Cattle Towns* (New York: Alfred A. Knopf, 1968), 76.

92. For concise and accurate general descriptions of the national cattle markets before the turn of the century see *ibid.*, 75, 76, and Marion Clawson, *The Western Range Livestock Industry* (New York: McGraw-Hill Book Co., 1950), 163-178. The function of the commission agent is explained in Gressley, *Bankers and Cattlemen*, 187-195. For a definition of marketing terms, see Appendix 4. The following discussion is a synthesis of information in the sources cited above and from countless interviews with cattlemen and oldtimers in Harney County.

93. Oliphant, *Cattle Ranges*, 138, 139, 161. Osgood describes the advantages and disadvantages of "pilgrim" cattle for stocking the northern ranges: *Day of the Cattleman*, 92-94. French claims these Oregon cattle were called "American" cattle. See French, *Cattle Country*, 55. Oliphant's revelations about the influence of Oregon stockers on the range cattle industry has acted as a healthy corrective to most of the literature in the field. But note the excellent study by Harry Drago done in 1920 which shows the exact patterns Oliphant later explored: Harry Sinclair Drago, *Great American Cattle Trails* (Norman: University of Oklahoma Press, 1920), 241-247.

94. Oliphant, *Cattle Ranges*, 183, 184.

95. "The Union Pacific, serving the southeastern counties, was far more important to the eastern Oregon cattle industry [than the Northern Pacific]." Carter, "Cattle Industry."

96. J. Orin Oliphant, "Cattle Trade," 77, and Oliphant, "The Eastward Movement of Cattle from the Oregon Country," *Agricultural History* 20 (January 1946): 33, 34.

97. *Tenth Census, Agriculture*, 82, 83, 167; *Eleventh Census, Agriculture*, 174, 175, 263, 303; Grant County, Assessment Rolls, 1885; Harney County, Tax Rolls, 1890.

98. Lo Piccolo, "Range Cattle Industry," 84; Oliphant, *Cattle Ranges*, 197.

99. The *Eastern Oregon Herald* evidently pleaded for more out-of-state buyers in 1889: Lo Piccolo, "Range Cattle Industry," 83. By the mid-1880's, the big men, particularly Miller and Lux, had established "accustomed" ranges on the choicest parts of the former Malheur Reservation range land. Bardwell, *et al.*, "Appraisal of Land," 57.

100. Johansen, Empire, 344, 345. Oregon's population more than doubled between 1880 and 1890 (174, 768 to 313,767 people). Eggleston, "Harney County," 75.

101. Johansen's famous anecdote holds that Western migrants were forced to choose between two alternate routes at Pacific Springs. These were marked by a "heap of glittering quartz on the California fork and a sign saying to Oregon" on the other fork. Those who could read went to Oregon." *Empire*, 153-154. In an unpublished memorandum Earl Pomeroy quotes from John M. Murphy, *Ramblings in Northwestern America: 1879*, relative to this subject: [people of the Pacific Northwest] "rarely yield to excitement, and indulge in no speculations that do not give an emphatic indication of success." Earl Pomeroy, "Has the Pacific Coast an Identifiable Culture?: A Memorandum on Backgrounds" (mimeographed), p. 6.

102. *Tenth Census, Population*, 75, 76, 303; *Twelfth Census, Population*, 125, 325, 326. Information on the following seven pages is taken from the *Eleventh Census, Population*, the Harney County tax rolls for 1890, and the *History of Baker, Grant*, except where noted.

103. This and the following demographic data have been compiled by analyzing the biographical sketches in the *History of Baker, Grant*, and comparing them with tabulated census data. Despite the generally unreliable, incomplete and non-representative nature of these sketches, demographic patterns can be adduced. See the discussion concerning this source in Allan G. Bogue, *From Prairie to Corn Belt: Farming on the Illinois and Iowa Prairies in the Nineteenth Century* (Chicago: Quadrangle Books, 1968), 22. See also John T. Ganoe, "The Pacific Far West One Generation After the Frontier," *Pacific Historical Review* 9 (June 1940): 205-217, and Pomeroy, "Identifiable Culture," 18.

104. Calculating from the number of children born to families along the way and using the local official history of the three southeastern Oregon counties, rough estimates can be made of the number of moves made by each group. Californians moved an average of 3.7 times upon reaching the Harney country. By contrast Midwesterners had moved 3.5 times and those from the Willamette Valley 3.4 times.

105. *History of Baker, Grant*, 663-668, 673, 681, 685, 687, 688, 694, 702, 708, 710, 714.

106. As early as 1889, the flood of county road petitions circulated in newly formed Harney County shows a predominance of midwesterners among the signers. Road Petitions, October 30, 1889, November 20, 1889, November 28, 1889, Harney County Clerk's Office.

107. By using information from the original government surveys and field notes, which show a number of squatters who do not appear on the tax rolls of the county, and combining that with information from the tax rolls which show the location and name of all owners of taxable units within the county, one can reconstruct reasonably accurate patterns of settlement during the 1880s. See Tables 6, 7, 8, pp. 389-391.

108. Tables 2, 7, 8, pp. 384, 390, 391. Map No. 2. The Crows were Californians who maintained connections with northern California for vital services—particularly hospital facilities at time of childbirth: Crow, *Rankin Crow*, 34. Oddly enough, there is no evidence that other than Californians selected such lands. The Californians mentioned are recorded in Harney County Tax Rolls, 1880, Grant County Tax Rolls, 1880, and *Tenth Census*, 1880.

109. Charles Cronin's testimony in the P.L.S. case was: "There was sort of a community settled on sections 4, 19, 2 and 11. They were all friendly." Treadwell and Rand, *Brief*, 76. See also the list of names and type of claim filed in this area. Within an area encompassed by two townships was every legal claim available under the laws of the day-preemption, homestead, swamp, timber culture, and desert-and approximately 60 squatters as well. See Treadwell and Rand, *Brief*, 72, 73, 76, 91. Those relatively few who stayed tended to stay a long time; (Philadelphia: University of Pennsylvania Press, 1961). The parents of the present Harney County surveyor homesteaded in this area: Clarence Young, interview with the author, Burns, Oregon, July 18, 1968.

110. Historian Allan Bogue attributes persistence to several factors, but most importantly to ethnic origins, the maturity of decision making, and the

area chosen. Here, the area chosen seems to have been of great importance. At least there was no distinctive ethnic group associated with early
settlement in the Malheur drainage. Bogue, *Prairie to Cornbelt*, 27;
Eleventh Census, Population 334-335.

111. *Tenth Census, Agriculture, Schedule 2*, 1-4; Harney County Tax Rolls,
1890. Tom Allen's remarks were, "I know that . . . in the Warm Springs
Valley that this settlement commenced and had taken in practically the
whole valley that was settled over that swamp land that Foster had."
Allen and Hanley, reminiscences, p. 4; *History of Baker, Grant*, 674-677,
682, 683, 688-690. Tables 6-8, 389-391, Map No. 5, p. 429.

112. OO foreman Ike Foster allowed settlers to cut as much hay as they liked
from the OO hayfield in the upper Silver Creek Valley. Allen and Hanley,
reminiscences, 5; *Twelfth Census, Population*, 325, 326.

113. Among the names of the sixty-three settlers and squatters who came to
the lower Silvies from 1880 to 1889, forty-eight names appear on the
county tax rolls of 1890. The following examples are illustrative: O.
Bardelfield joined one Beatty on the Malheur River northwest of Drewsey.
A. T. Clark went to Diamond Valley. Frank Jordan bought property on
Crane Creek. W. Morrison left for Soldier Creek. F. Mace moved to Burns
and showed 283 acres in 1890. A. Robbins appeared on the Middle Fork
of the Malheur River with 1,440 acres. James Smith went to the Upper
Silvies. One F. Gibson went to Coffee Pot Creek. All had chosen loca-
tions with good soil and drainage and near or on stable streams. Map
No. 3, p. 427; Harney County Tax Rolls, 1890; Treadwell and Rand, *Brief*,
72, 73, 91. Eggleston describes some of this process as well: "Harney
County," 82.

114. The Bardwell, Eggleston, and Palmer study calculated the average value
of the land in the area of the Malheur Reservation at $3 per acre during
the 1880's. Reservation land was, in general, the best land in the county,
but, on the basis of county assessment figures one can estimate a value
of $2 per acre as an average figure for all land in the county. Taking assess-
ment records of gross value for newcomers—a value well below market
value—30 percent were in a position to buy a parcel of land comprising
at least 250 acres for $500 leaving a $500 gross value after the purchase
was made. Bardwell, *et al.*, "Appraisal of Land," 66, 67; Harney County
Record of Deeds, Book A; Harney County Tax Rolls, 1890. See Eggleston,
"Harney County," 81.

115. Langdon, "Education," 13.

116. Except where noted, the story on the next two pages was compiled from
Treadwell and Rand, *Brief*, 61-65, 92, 93, 96.

117. *History of Baker, Grant* 699; Harney County Tax Rolls, 1890, 18.

118. On formation of the Harney Valley Dam and Ditch Company, see *History
of Baker, Grant*, 662; Harney County Tax Rolls, 1890, 14.

119. Similar stories—of I. Poujade, Homer Mace, and John Craddock—appear
in Treadwell and Rand, *Brief*, 20, 61, 63, 93. Symbol of this tenuous
harmony was the "major domo" or foreman of the large outfits. Daily
contacts between settlers and cattle barons were made through him and
his character and bearing influenced the degree to which each group ac-
commodated to the other. To a man, these foremen were highly respected
and were paid well for their services. Oliphant, *Cattle Ranges*, 211, 212.
Most of them were Spanish vaqueros, who, together with other Spanish
"hands," gave the south end a distinctively Spanish flavor: Lo Piccolo,

"Range Cattle Industry," 82. They were as famous in their way as the great men themselves and they live on today in the romantic rather than the exploitative tradition of the early cattle business in Harney County, as shown in interviews by the author with, among others, Johnny Crow, Voltage, Oregon, July 14, 1968; John Scharff, Director of the Malheur Wildlife Refuge, July 9, 1968; Jim McEwen, Riverside, Oregon, June 23, 1968; and Walter McEwen, Sod House, Oregon, September 1, 1968. These men were intimately acquainted with the great foremen.

120. In 1890, the number of sheep on the assessment rolls equaled the number of cattle and, in terms of grazing, represented about one-fifth of the impact that cattle had on the ranges. The percentage of sheepmen, however, was only 3 percent, or 18 out of a total of 604 taxable units. Harney County Tax Rolls, 1890. For a review of the business in eastern Oregon in the 1880's, see Peter A. Shroyer, "Oregon Sheep, Wool and Woolens Industries," *Oregon Historical Quarterly*, 67 (June 1966): 139-159. Joe Fine, the last of the great foremen alive today, got his start with sheep. Joe Fine, interview with the author, Burns, Oregon, November 30, 1969.

121. The nineteen sheep raisers accounted for $68,503 gross valuation; with oldtimers Stanclift, Cummins, and Cote added, their gross valuation amounted to $74,704. Harney County Tax Rolls, 1890.

122. Harney County Tax Rolls, 1968, 2004, 5003, 5026, 8501, 8502, 9011, 9012; *History of Baker, Grant*, 663, 668, 669, 674-711. Shirk started with sheep: Schmitt, *David Shirk* 42-44. The "cattle and sheep war" stereotype has a definite scenario. Cattle were first. Sheepmen came in and encroached on the range. Sheep grazed off the grass too close to the ground, cut up the sod with their hooves and left an unpleasant odor so that the range was ruined for cattle. In order to protect their interests, cattlemen fought back, often with bloody consequences. Some of this has a basis in fact. Where cattlemen came first, sheepmen caused antagonisms, and violence was often the result. However, writers who claim the range could not support both were simply perpetuating the cowman's propaganda. Much of that kind of mythology has been dispelled, but modern students of southeastern Oregon have continued to assume that the rest of the scenario was true. Brimlow mentions clashes between cattlemen and sheepmen during the 1880s with no citations to support his claim: *Harney County*, 142. Eggleston's study does the same and again without proof: "Harney County," 81.

123. Interview with the author by Tom Bailey, horse wrangler and son of pioneers Tom and Sarah Bailey, Burns, Oregon, July 21, 1968, and "Red" Leavitt, broncbuster and cowhand, Sod House, Oregon, July 16, 1968; *Harney Items*, March 19, 1897.

124. Harney County Tax Rolls, 1890.

125. See Brief of the State of Oregon, 3-5. One continuing source of income was the rabbit bounty offered by the state: "no one need go without legal tender if he's enterprising enough." *Harney Items*, February 16, 1887.

126. Eggleston, "Harney County," 80, 81. Uncharacteristically the *Harney Items* carried a note of pessimism in 1887: "the few dry seasons past . . . [have] discouraged a large number of people in this valley." March 19, 1887.

127. The emphasis in most of these is on particularly persevering and successful pioneers, and there is a tendency to eulogize early settlers. The

prose descriptions of hardship and primitive conditions, the general assumption that the cattlemen may have been romantic figures, but the settlers were right, permeates most accounts of eastern Oregon's early history. A classic of the genre is A. S. Mercer, *The Banditti of the Plains: or The Cattleman's Invasion of Wyoming in 1892 (The Crowning Infamy of the Ages)* (Norman: University of Oklahoma Press, 1954). See Brogan, *East of the Cascades*, 88, 89; Brimlow, *Harney County*, 60, 61, 67, 68, 146. Herman Oliver's book is a testament to the gospel of hard work: *Gold and Cattle Country*, E. R. Jackman, ed. (Portland: Binfords and Mort, 1962). With a liberal portion of frontier humor, Rube Long's book is the same: E. R. Jackman and R. A. Long, *The Oregon Desert* (Caldwell, Idaho: The Caxton Printers, Ltd., 1967). See also Langdon, "Education," 4-7.

128. Ernest Staples Osgood, one of the foremost authorities on the range cattle industry during the nineteenth century, describes the way the cattle kings adapted to changing conditions in the 1880s largely in terms of land purchase and consolidation—i.e., range control. Ernest S. Osgood, "The Cattleman in the Agricultural History of the Northwest," *Agricultural History*, 3 (July 1929): 126. French's experiments are described in Lo Piccolo, "Range Cattle Industry," 98.

129. Lo Piccolo suggests that the bad winter on the Great Plains helped move the southeastern Oregon cattlemen more decisively toward putting up hay. "Range Cattle Industry," 78-80. See also Schmitt, *David Shirk*, 125, 126. If the names from the original schedules of the tenth census are added to the names on the original survey maps, and compared with names on the 1890 tax rolls, 84 percent of those earlier names will be found on the 1890 rolls. *Tenth Census, Agriculture, Schedule 2*, 1-9; Harney County Tax Rolls, 1890; Tables 19, 20, pp. 409, 410. There was, however, a general decline in the number of cattle between 1880 and 1890, and the percentage of smaller owners who owned less than twenty-five cattle increased markedly. Table 21, p. 411.

130. Lo Piccolo, "Range Cattle Industry," 73.

131. *Ibid.*, 74, 75.

132. The southeastern Oregon partnerships were by no means trouble free. Devine had a profligate streak already mentioned, and Todhunter was evidently a suspicious man by nature. Colonel Hardin was not as familiar as Riley with the OO, and foreman Foster found it necessary to make his recommendations and requests to Riley instead. The only intention here is to point out that, on the whole, the southeastern Oregon partnerships were remarkably stable compared with other partnerships and cattle companies. As to the premium put upon good management, Cochran and Miller state it well, "In the chain of productive activities which create out of the raw materials of the soil the finished commodity for the ultimate consumer, that group which is least efficiently organized always gets the smallest share of the profit." Cochrane and Miller, *The Age of Enterprise*, 220. Gressley, *Bankers and Cattlemen*, 115-140.

CHAPTER TWO

1. Two early articles on the so-called "transition period" are especially noteworthy: Ernest S. Osgood, "The Cattleman in the Agricultural History of the Northwest," *Agricultural History* 3 (July 1929): 125, 126, and Edward Everett Dale, "The Cow Country in Transition," *Mississippi Valley Historical Review* 24 (June 1937): 18, 19. The most concise modern work on the range cattle business from the standpoint of developing methods is Marion Clawson, *The Western Range Livestock Industry* (New York: McGraw-Hill Book Company, 1950). See also Gene Gressley, *Bankers and Cattlemen* (New York: Alfred A. Knopf, 1966), 109.

2. The cattle "boom" of the 1880s and its relation to the national economy are treated well in such general works as Harold U. Faulkner, *Politics, Reform and Expansion*, (New York: Harper and Brothers, 1959), 4, 52-54, and Fred A. Shannon, *The Farmer's Last Frontier: Agriculture, 1860-1897* (New York: Holt, Rinehart and Winston, 1945), 95, 192, 236, 237. There is a particularly good discussion in Thomas C. Cochran and William Miller, *The Age of Enterprise: A Social History of Industrial America* (New York: The Macmillan Company, 1942), 211-219.

3. Osgood, "Cattleman," 126. For the special problems confronted by large, absentee-owned corporations see Gressley, *Bankers and Cattlemen*, 159, 160.

4. For a short, but incisive discussion of the era of rising prices see Cochran and Miller, *Age of Enterprise*, 222-225. See also Paul W. Gates, *History of Public Land Law Development* (Washington, D.C: U.S. Government Printing Office, 1968), 466.

5. Shannon, *Last Frontier*, 218, 219.

6. From the time of the first Public Land Commission report in 1879 until Theodore Roosevelt appointed a commission in 1902 to investigate the status of America's public lands, no national policy was ever formulated to regulate grazing on the public domain; yet the 1880s and 1890s were the decades during which the western frontier was obliterated by unprecedented numbers of people and the clash of opposing interests over grazing rights was transformed into a matter of great public concern. In 1890 the U.S. Supreme Court actually upheld a lower-court ruling based upon archaic English precedents unsuited to western conditions that an implied license existed for anyone to use the public domain as common pasture. The General Revision Act of a year later left this decision intact. By 1902, when recommendations for grazing regulation were made, the great war between settlers and range livestock users was essentially over. See Gates, *Public Land Law*, 428, 429, 466-468, 484, 485, 491; George F. Brimlow, *Harney County, Oregon, and Its Range Land* (Portland: Binfords and Mort, 1951), 55, 56; and Clawson, *Livestock Industry*, 141-144.

7. Dorothy Johansen holds that the transitional period transformed the lumber and fishing industries in the Northwest as well as the cattle business by "the advent of new populations and new capital." Johansen, *Empire of the Columbia: A History of The Pacific Northwest* (New York: Harper and Row, 1967), 408.

8. For a discussion of these changes in Oregon and Washington see *ibid.*, 409, 410.

9. Cochran and Miller, *Age of Enterprise*, 171, 190, 213. The very remoteness of most American farmers from centers of population made them woefully ignorant of marketing developments nationally and throughout the

world—a crucial disadvantage when combined with their other problems. See *ibid.*, 216.

10. Johansen, *Empire*, 320.

11. See Margaret Lo Piccolo, "Some Aspects of the Range Cattle Industry in Harney County, Oregon, 1870-1900," (master's thesis, University of Oregon, 1962), 110-112.

12. Table 21, p. 411. Lo Piccolo's use of census and assessment figures is supplemented by information of French-Glenn Company files which expectedly show some variations. Lo Piccolo, "Range Cattle Industry," 16. The pattern of the high plains after a hard winter like the winter of 1885-1886 was that the big owners, most of whom were absentee owners who had invested heavily in cattle, tended to fail: Gressley, *Bankers and Cattlemen*, 105, 109. In southeastern Oregon the pattern was just the reverse. Big owners survived while small owners tended to fail. Lo Piccolo cites convincing reasons: southeastern Oregon partnerships were unusually sound; California markets were open for export; California hay was available; and southeastern Oregon cattle kings were more experienced than the Eastern or foreign absentee owner and his manager on the high plains. Both the partners living in California and the partners living on the ranches in southeastern Oregon were closer to the business and more aware of problems than their eastern counterparts. The control of California and Nevada resources belonged exclusively to the big owner—small men could neither drive their herds south without a guaranteed outlet nor afford to buy California hay at the prices charged on the open market. Lo Piccolo, "Range Cattle Industry," 115, 116. J. Orin Oliphant alludes to the success with which the southeastern cattle barons survived bad winters and hard times: *On the Cattle Ranges of the Oregon Country* (Seattle: University of Washington Press, 1968, 188-199. See also *Tenth Census, Agriculture*, xiv, 82, 83, 130, 167, 316, 317; *Eleventh Census, Agriculture*, 44, 174, 175, 263, 303; Harney County Tax Rolls, 1890, Harney County Courthouse, Burns.

13. Gressley, Bankers and Cattlemen, 238.

14. Table 1, p. 383; *Tenth Census, Population, Schedule 1; Twelfth Census, Population, Volume I*, 325, 326.

15. A highly colored, intensely hostile account of the manipulations of the Willamette Valley and Cascade Mountain Wagon Road Company appears in *History of Baker, Grant, Malheur, and Harney Counties* (Chicago: Western Historical Publishing Co., 1902), 642-645. For an objective report see Jerry A. O'Callaghan, *The Disposition of the Public Domain in Oregon* (Washington, D.C.: U.S. Government Printing Office, 1960), 52-54. As late as 1900 the company's owners were still buying up land. *Blue Mountain Eagle*, (Canyon City) November 30, 1900.

16. *Eastern Oregon Herald* (Burns), February 6, 1890. Among the considerable number of letters directed to the state surveyor general testifying on the quality of the land desired was one from one of the contracting surveyors, B. J. Pengra, who, of course, was in an ideal position to survey and claim swamp land for himself. B. J. Pengra to Benjamin Simpson, State Surveyor General, Portland, Oregon, January 4, 1876, in the files of the State Land Office, Federal Records Center, Seattle, Washington.

17. "Gordon Report," *Tenth Census, Agriculture, Volume 3*, 126. See Clawson, 261, and Brimlow, *Harney County*, 174.

18. See the section below on Fraud and the Courts. The complete story is in the Report of the Special Master, "The United States vs. The State of Oregon," in the Supreme Court of the United States, October Term, 1934, copy in Harney County Library, Burns, but the summary of the state's case is more concise and less cumbersome: Brief of the State of Oregon, "The United States vs. The State of Oregon," in the Supreme Court of the United States, October Term, 1934, copy in Harney County Court House.

19. Brief of the State of Oregon, 29, 75, 87-90, 95-100, 103. Clarence Young, former Harney County water master, who helped survey the county's water rights preparatory to their adjudication under the state law of 1909, says: "They had to do something. These farmers were all shooting one another." Clarence Young, interview with the author, Harney County Court House, July 18, 1968.

20. Wright emphasizes religion and continuity with the past, but this pattern appears often enough to make it a subsidiary theme. Louis B. Wright, *Culture on the Moving Frontier* (Bloomington: Indiana University Press, 1955), 19, 42, 45, 56, 66, 67, 76, 84-97, 118, 131-132 and the last two chapters: "Instruments of Civilization," 168-241.

21. Richard G. Wade, *The Urban Frontier: The Rise of Western Cities, 1790-1830* (Cambridge, Mass.: Harvard University Press, 1959); Lewis Atherton, *Main Street on the Middle Border* (Bloomington: Indiana University Press, 1954); Robert Dykstra, *The Cattle Towns* (New York: Alfred A. Knopf, 1968). For example, cattle towns retained a degree of boisterousness not common to the development of Wright's frontier farm communities.

22. Dykstra, *Cattle Towns*, 1.

23. Burns had a newspaper, *The Harney Items*, by 1884. This unmistakable mark of civilization was printed in the back room of a bawdy house. Not until two years later did the girls move across the street to consolidate their resources with a saloon that thereafter called itself the "Pleasure Center." Brimlow, *Harney County*, 188.

24. *Ibid.*, 169, 187. Newspaper advertisements by the major stores in Burns were all geared to appeal to a settler's market. See *Harney Items*, March 19, 1887.

25. Harney County Tax Rolls, 1895, 1900; Table 18, p. 408. County population increased from 2,559 to 2,598 in that decade, while Burns grew from 547 to 719 during the same period: *Twelfth Census, Population, Volume 1*, 264, 325, 326. Throughout the United States the total value of agricultural land, improvements, and equipment increased at a much lower rate—from $13,773,000,000 to $17,365,000,000 between 1880 and 1890, or an increase of only 26 percent as compared with the Harney County increase, which was 49 percent. Bureau of the Census, *Historical Statistics of the United States, 1789-1945* (Washington, D.C.: U.S. Government Printing Office, 1949), 9.

26. In the absence of original census schedules for 1900, the Harney County tax rolls and the voter registration book used together show names of newcomers and their occupations. Neither of these sources constitutes a full census; but in the tax rolls the names and properties of all gainfully employed males are recorded with the exception of some squatters, while in the voter registration book all males over 21 years of age and their occupations are recorded. The percentage of new names on the 1900 tax

rolls compared with the names on the 1890 rolls is 55 percent. The percentage of new names on the voter registration book compared with 1890 tax rolls is 54 percent. In Burns alone the percentage of newcomers was 62 percent. Newcomers constituted 58 percent of the farmers in this precinct. General County Voter Registration Book, 1900; Harney County Tax Rolls, 1890 and 1900; Tables 9, 13, pp. 392, 403.

27. General County Voter Registration Book, 1900. By 1900, 45.2 percent of Burns's population was involved in nonagricultural pursuits. See Table 9, p. 392.

28. See Table 9, p. 392.

29. The number of occupations in the town of Burns rose from 22 in 1890 to 51 in 1900. See Tables 9, 14, pp. 392, 404. Together with occupations already in existence at the time, Burns provided a greater percentage of services than did Dykstra's frontier cattle towns at comparable stages of their growth. Table 14, p. 404; Dykstra, *Cattle Towns*, 107-109; Harney County Voter Registration Book, 1900.

30. Bill Hanley to A. Stirling, Burns, Oregon, February 14, 1902, and to Lewellyn F. Barker, Baltimore, Maryland, February 3, 1902, Hanley Papers, Oregon Historical Society, Portland; Anne Shannon Monroe (ed.), *Feelin' Fine* (Garden City, New York: Doubleday, Doran and Co., 1931), 235-240, 249, 250, 267-272, 291; Giles French, *Cattle Country of Peter French* (Portland: Binfords and Mort, Publishers 1965, pp. 148-150. For thoughtful questions about Peter French as he is pictured in Giles French's book, see Priscilla Knuth's review in the *Oregon Historical Quarterly* 66 (March 1965): 67-68. Devine came to town more often during the late 1880s, when the pressure of settlement was mounting. His visits, however, were political and were heralded scornfully in the *Harney Items* as visits from "King John, the great monopolist": *Harney Items*, March 19, 1897.

31. Brimlow, *Harney County*, 168, 169. Nathan Brown granted credit and loaned money liberally, yet, evidently, selected his debtors with sufficient care to be able to start Burns's first bank after the turn of the century. Al Brown, grandson of Nathan Brown, interview with the author, Burns, Oregon, July 22, 1968.

32. Membership Lists, Burns Lodge of Ancient, Free and Accepted Masons (in the files of the fraternity) and Burns Lodge No. 71 of Independent Order of Odd Fellows (in the files of the fraternity); "History of the Burns First Baptist Church" (Ladies Guild), (mimeographed), 2; Reverend Charles Perkins, Rector, St. Andrews Episcopal Church, 1954-1960, with the author, November 15, 1969; *Harney Items*, February 16, 1887.

33. See Lila E. Langdon, "A History of Education in Harney County, Oregon, 1875-1940" (master's thesis, Eastern Oregon College, 1959), 7-9, 37-39; Brimlow, *Harney County*, 135.

34. In 1903 this became a column entitled "Fact for Farmers": *Harney Items*, February 16, 1887, and April 11, 1903; *Eastern Oregon Herald*, March 6, 1889. For information about the *Harney Times* and *Burns News*, see Brimlow, *Harney County*, 201.

35. In his zeal the editor of the *Harney Items* published the most outrageous *non sequitur*, "Locals have ordered fruit trees and vines from Payette, Washington [actually Idaho]; yet climate and soil are no different here. We are located on the same latitude." *Harney Items*, February 16, 1887. Social occasions became so frequent that in 1887 a local brewer, Paul Locher, built a town hall for such occasions. Brimlow, *Harney County*, 187.

36. *History of Baker, Grant*, 636.

37. A post office was first established there early in 1885, just a year and a half after an executive order restored the reservation to the public domain. A. A. Bardwell, D. C. Eggleston, and M. A. Palmer, "Appraisal of Land and Resources of the Malheur Indian Reservation" (Burns, Oregon, 1958), 11, 12. See also Oliphant, *Cattle Ranges*, 304.

38. *Blue Mountain Eagle*, March 1, 1901; Brimlow, *Harney County*, 161-165; *Harney Items*, November 22, 1901 (quotation). I. Milton Davis, one of the original settlers in Drewsey in 1883, is reported to have remarked: "In pioneer days Drewsey was almost an exclusive cow town." Brimlow, *Harney County*, 163. See also the configuration of Drewsey's population in 1900, compared with Burns's. Table 14, p. 404. Among Dykstra's cattle towns, the configuration of Dodge City is closest to that of Drewsey, though Drewsey was much smaller and more primitive.

39. Harney County Tax Rolls, 1900. Harney City's growth rate during the decade from 1890 to 1900 had actually been greater than Burns's. Where Burns grew by a rate of 31 percent, Harney City leapt from 82 people to 240 people, a growth rate of 192 percent. *Twelfth Census, Population, Volume 1*, 325, 326. Compare Harney City's occupational configuration with that of Burns, Table 14, p. 404. Also Harney City's non-agricultural population was only 19.6 percent compared with Burns's 45.2 percent. See Table 9, p. 392.

40. *Harney Times*, July 29, 1888.

41. Oliphant's discussion of this point, however, is especially illuminating: *Cattle Ranges*, 322-343.

42. As Oliphant remarks, the traditional stance of the federal government ("the absentee landlord of all stockmen") was merely to restrict fencing of the public domain and this restriction had never been rigidly enforced. Reformers notwithstanding, cattlemen simply followed tradition. *Ibid*, 221.

43. Lake County and Baker County did not have stockman's associations until 1881: *Ibid.*, 246, 247.

44. For information on legislation supporting cattlemen, including the legislation against railroads mentioned above, see Brimlow, *Harney County*, 72, 174, and Oliphant, *Cattle Ranges*, 223-229, 235, 239-243. An article explaining the state brand recording statute appears in the *Eastern Oregon Herald*, May 31, 1893. Quarantine legislation had been passed during the 1870s.

45. Robert E. Burton, "A History of the Democratic Party in Oregon, 1900-1956" (Ph.D. dissertation, University of Oregon, 1969), 29-32. See also Brimlow, *Harney County*, 174. For a discussion of the Granger and Farmer's Alliance movements in Oregon see Johansen, *Empire*, 346, 347.

46. Cited in Lo Piccolo, "Range Cattle Industry," 58.

47. *Ibid*, 55-60.

48. There is an extensive literature on the Oregon land frauds that inspired this sentiment. One of the most unusual as well as the most detailed works in an expose by one of the participants: S. A. D. Puter and Horace Stevens, *Looters of the Public Domain* (Portland: The Portland Publishing House, 1908). Scandalous behavior was not a monopoly of big men. See an article admonishing settlers to "obey the law" in filing in timber and stone entries: *Blue Mountain Eagle*, April 22, 1904.

49. A typical local newspaper article ran, "if a man who two short years ago openly said, the settlers can go to h . . . " and that same fellow comes to you now and pretends to be the settler's friend, you need not believe a word of it" and continued by pleading with settlers to ". . . close ranks against the grinding monopolists who are behind the land frauds which have lately given our honest settlers so much trouble and grief." *Harney Items*, March 19, 1887.

50. Walter Goldschmidt, *As You Sow* (New York: Harcourt, Brace and Company, 1947), 163-164.

51. The discussion is taken from James S. Coleman, *Community Conflict* (New York: The Free Press, 1957), 2-26. For a terse assessment of this theory see William G. Robbins, "The Far Western Frontier: Economic Opportunity and Social Democracy in Early Roseburg, Oregon" (Ph.D. dissertation, University of Oregon, 1969), 83.

52. Dykstra, *Cattle Towns*, 151, 159. The situation in pioneer Roseburg, Oregon, was nearly identical. The county seat fight acted as a "unifying force" within the town community. Robbins, "Roseburg," 86.

53. Brimlow, *Harney County*, 195.

54. Record of Requisitions from the Circuit Court, Harney County Clerk's Office.

55. Burn's population was 264 in 1890 compared with Harney City's 240; the other towns—Drewsey and Riley—were far behind: *Twelfth Census, Population*, pp. 325, 326. When the *Harney Press* published a squib complimenting the *Harney Items* on its new five-page format, the *Items* returned the courtesy by wishing the *Press* success but added coyly, "not county seatically." *Harney Items*, March 19, 1887. By January 1889, almost any news, routine or otherwise, was placed in the context of the growing need for a county division. When the Grant County school superintendent ordered teachers to travel to Canyon City for certificate examinations, the editor of the *Eastern Oregon Herald* took the opportunity to warn those in power that " . . . if the county bill fails, teachers 150 miles distant ought to be allowed to continue without a certificate." *Eastern Oregon Herald*, January 31, 1889.

56. *Harney Items*, February 16, 1887. Also *History of Baker, Grant*, 637.

57. The occupational make-up of this delegation indicates the extent to which town and country elements around Burns had allied by 1888: 3 farmers, 2 stockraisers, 2 merchants, 2 attorneys, 1 druggist, 1 blacksmith, 1 flour and sawmill man, the town recorder, and the town clerk. General County Voter Registration Book, 1900; *Eastern Oregon Herald*, November 8, 1888.

58. For complaints about the expense of traveling to court in Canyon City see *Harney Items*, March 19, 1887. Details of the formation of the county appear in *Eastern Oregon Herald*, March 7, 1889.

59. Lo Piccolo, "Range Cattle Industry," 116-117.

60. The land-office manipulation is described in Brimlow, *Harney County*, 193. Johnson himself was said to have thought the summary evictions were "bad business." Lo Piccolo, "Range Cattle Industry," 118; Brimlow, *Harney County*, 175.

61. In their zeal, haystack burners sometimes burned stacks belonging to farmers and settlers. Newspaper reports were indignant when that happened: "hay burners . . . will get caught in their nefarious work one of these nights and reach the end of their rope, as it were." *Eastern Oregon*

Herald, February 20, 1890. Against an accusation by the Portland *Daily Oregonian* that the 101 Society was composed of "landgrabbers and claim jumpers who . . . kill corporation cattle and defy everybody," the *Eastern Oregon Herald* replied: "Many accusations cited against said organization are false. Settlers are still fighting landowners who obtained swampland fraudulently." October 4, 1893.

62. See Martin F. Schmitt (ed.), *The Cattle Drives of David Shirk; From Texas to the Idaho Mines, 1871 and 1873* (Portland: The Champoeg Press, 1956), 137; Lo Piccolo, "Range Cattle Industry," 123; Brimlow, *Harney County*, 185, 186.

63. Schmitt, *David Shirk*, 137. See also *Harney Items*, October 31, 1889.

64. *Ibid*. Lo Piccolo suggests the *Items* exploited and perhaps exaggerated the split between big corporations and settlers mostly at Devine's expense.

65. For effects in the Harney region, read the grisly account of cattle and sheep dying in the frozen snow in the *Burns Times*, March 6, 1890. Some of the survivors' new resentment was instilled by French's callous remonstrance against a road that settlers had requested for easier communication between the settlement around the lakes and Blitzen Valley and the north end of Catlow Valley. Part of the basis of French's complaint was that three of the road petitioners were not *bona fide* residents. A close look at the twenty-two signatures on French's remonstrance reveals that only four were property owners on or near the proposed road site. The rest were not property holders in the county tax rolls but were cowhands in French's employ. Despite that fact, the court in Harney City accepted the remonstrance and disallowed the road. Road Petition, October 30, 1889, and Remonstrance, November 28, 1889, Harney County Clerk's Office, Tax Rolls, 1890. The impunity with which big cattlemen diverted or closed roads already built is shown in Affidavit of N. H. A. Mason, 1890, Harney County Clerk's Office.

66. Brimlow, *Harney County*, 197.

67. See the accounts in *ibid.*, 195, 196 and *History of Baker, Grant*, 638, 639.

68. In 1893, W. C. Byrd, editor of the *Eastern Oregon Herald*, said publicly, "God speed the time when the reign of said [big] cattlemen in this valley will be brought to an end." *Harney Times*, July 19, 1893. Nine years later and five years after French had been killed the county "mug book" reflected the bias of its contributors when it said, "Burns [was] always . . . identified with the interests of the settlers . . . and . . . incurred the unrelenting enmity of the men who wished to keep the country in barbarism for the benefit of the stock interests." *History of Baker, Grant*, 638. In an interview with the grandson of a pioneer of the 1890s, the questions of the county seat issue and French's death, both of which are well known among young and old alike, brought a passionate response unusual for events more than three quarters of a century in the past: "The boys who took those records were doing what they had to do. We'd do the same today." "Peter French was ruthless—a grasping man. He was asking for it and he got it." Bob Bailey, interview with the author, Burns, Oregon, July 15, 1968.

69. The details of the story are best related in *History of Baker, Grant*, 637-640.

70. The papers were full of this scandal. See *Harney Items*, June 8, 1901, and *Blue Mountain Eagle*, February 15, 1901, and March 1, 1901. Said the Eagle scornfully, "[In] the state capital [one] . . . comes in contact with

bribe-givers and takers [who have] . . . a baneful effect always": February 15, 1901.

71. Gates, *Public Land Law*, 471-477; Marion Clawson, "Reminiscences of the Bureau of Land Management, 1947-1948," *Agricultural History* 33 (January 1959): 23. Even honest land office officials were frequently cowed into submitting to the will of powerful interests. This was true in the Burns land office, where the reluctance of the Register to thwart the will of the cattle barons put him in the position of being pro-monopolist in the eyes of the settlers. See letter from H. Kelley, Receiver, Burns Land Office, to H. Byars, State Surveyor General, Portland, Oregon, April 7, 1894, in the files of the State Land Office, Federal Records Center, Seattle.

72. O'Callaghan, *Public Domain*, 49-59; *Blue Mountain Eagle*, November 30, 1900. See also *History of Baker, Grant*, 645, 646.

73. Lo Piccolo, "Range Cattle Industry," 58-59. The following discussion is based on information in Report of Special Master, "The United States vs. the State of Oregon," 3-5, 28-30, 97, 111-116, and Brief of the State of Oregon, 3-7, 60, 61,71-73, 87-89, 90, 95-100, 103, 107-120. See also the account in *History of Baker, Grant*, 647-648.

74. According to testimony in the United States vs. Oregon, about twenty settlers followed their example between 1888 and 1895. Report of the Special Master, 114. The original surveys and maps show the location of many of these people. Map No. 4.

75. Report of the Special Master, 114, 115.

76. The story of this whole melancholy affair is well told in Lo Piccolo, "Range Cattle Industry," 62-64. See also Gates, *Public Land Law*, 334.

77. Quoted in Brimlow, *Harney County*, 150.

78. Lo Piccolo, "Range Cattle Industry," 118; Table 20, p. 410.

79. *History of Baker, Grant*, 648; Report of the Special Master, 3, 4; Brief of the State of Oregon, 3, 5-7, 71-75.

80. The following discussion, except where noted, is taken from Report of the Special Master, 29, 30, and Brief of the State of Oregon, 107-120.

81. H. Kelley, the receiver in the Burns Land Office, tried to warn the state surveyor general that Harney County settlers were in an ugly mood over the situation. He begged Surveyor-General Byars to use his influence in the settlers' favor, "as they have had a hard time of it here fighting the capital and combined capital at that without any means of their own." Kelley to Byars, April 7, 1894.

82. *Harney Items*, June 21, 1902.

83. Pertinent details of this case appear in Edward F. Treadwell and John L. Rand, "Brief in Support of Claims of Pacific Livestock Company, Before the State Water Board of Oregon, Burns, Oregon, January 24, 1923," Harney County Court House, 92-94, 129, 130.

84. For an assessment of the ill feeling stirred up by the cases reviewed, see Lo Piccolo, "Range Cattle Industry," 123-125; also *History of Baker, Grant*, 647-649, and Brimlow, *Harney County*, 75.

85. *Harney Items*, March 19, 1887.

86. Henry Nash Smith, *Virgin Land: The American West as Symbol and Myth* (New York: Vintage Books, 1950), 138.

87. Had Henry Nash Smith and Walter Prescott Webb collaborated in writing Webb's book, *The Great Plains*, perhaps it would not have dealt so harshly with Eastern lawmakers who stubbornly refused to pass land and water legislation compatible with Western conditions. Perhaps instead of looking

narrowly ignorant at best and spitefully perverse at worst, they might have emerged more true to life—sincere in large part, but shackled by Eastern farming customs and bound by the yeoman mythology that perpetuated it. See Walter Prescott Webb, *The Great Plains* (New York: Ginn and Company, 1931), 385-452, in conjunction with Smith, *Virgin Land*, 191-200.

88. Gressley, *Bankers and Cattlemen*, 160; Brimlow, *Harney County*, 201.

89. Lo Piccolo, "Range Cattle Industry," 101.

90. *Ibid.*, 42.

91. *Ibid.*, 122. Despite this incident French used restraint. When his remonstrance against the Blitzen Valley road was upheld he nevertheless cooperated generously in helping with other road changes desired by the settlers. He claimed no damages for changes made in two of his sections, though Mrs. Peter Stenger of Burns indignantly claimed and received damages for changes in one section of her land. Road Petition, Township 24, Range 31, to Township 23, Range 31, February, 1891, and Remonstrance, Harney County Clerk's Office.

92. A newspaper report accused French of duplicity. The same paper carried an account of French's assault on Smyth. *Eastern Oregon Herald*, April 11, 1889. Lo Piccolo, "Range Cattle Industry," 46, 125-127; French, *Cattle Country*, 144-156; Brimlow, *Harney County*, 177.

93. The Kidd case does not appear in the files of the docket of the county court; issues of fact are reviewed, however, in the Hearing Before the State Engineer of the State of Oregon, "In the Matter of the Determination of the Relative Rights to the Use of the Waters of Donner and Blitzen River, a Tributary of Malheur Lake," 14: 8, 9. For grand jury indictments and settlers' reaction to their dismissal see Lo Piccolo, "Range Cattle Industry," 46, 126.

94. French, *Cattle Country*, 149, 150; Typescript of the Court Reporter's Transcript of "State of Oregon vs. Ed Oliver," 1895 (property of Mrs. Esther Haugen, Burns, Oregon), 6; Diamond Jubilee Edition, *Burns Times-Herald*, January 31, 1963.

95. For French's strained relationships with his wife and French's growing irritability in general, see French, *Cattle Country* 141-143, 150. Priscilla Knuth's probing review of French's book helped in establishing some guidelines for researching the French killing. See *Oregon Historical Quarterly* 66 (March, 1965): 67, 68. Also Lo Piccolo, "Range Cattle Industry," p. 123.

96. "The State of Oregon vs. Ed Oliver," 4. For a description of the tense atmosphere in which the first survey was made see the letter from John Neal, Surveyor, to Douglas Taylor, State Surveyor General, March 16, 1888. In the files of the State Land Office, Federal Records Center, Seattle.

97. Quoted in "The State of Oregon vs. Ed Oliver," 8.

98. Compare the reports in *ibid.*, 10-12, with French, *Cattle Country*, 151, 152, and Elizabeth Lambert Wood, *Pete French: Cattle King* (Portland: Binfords and Mort, Publishers, 1951), 225.

99. The following information was taken from "The State of Oregon vs. Ed Oliver," 1-9.

100. See Dykstra's discussion of the socially functional killing in *Cattle Towns*, 241, 242, 278. The ranking given the two biggest owners in the analysis made of tax rolls in 1893 in A. A. Bardwell, D.C. Eggleston, and M.D. Palmer, "Appraisal of Land and Resources of the Malheur Indian Reser-

vation," (mimeographed) (Burns, Oregon, 1958), 76, Table 11D, shows the P ranch most valuable with an assessed valuation of $243,660, P.L.S. next at $226,440; both figures combined constituted 30 percent of the county's total evaluation. In the Harney County Tax Rolls, 1900, their respective ranking was the same except that the P ranch was worth proportionately even more (P ranch, $307,375; P.L.S., $217,578), but the two together still accounted for nearly 25 percent of the total county evaluation. See Lo Piccolo's ordering: "Range Cattle Industry," 118.

CHAPTER THREE

1. This story has been pieced together from information in George Brimlow, *Harney County, Oregon, and its Range Land* (Portland: Binfords and Mort, 1951), 207, 215, 216; Giles French, *Cattle Country* 152, 153, and Rankin Crow, *Rankin Crow and the Oregon Country* as told to Colleen Olp (Ironside, Oregon: by the author, 1970), 30-32. It took eight hours by stage during good weather to get from Burns to Drewsey. Mrs. Charley Miler, widow of P.L.S. Company Superintendent, 1900-1933, interview with the author, Miler Ranch, September 12, 1968.

2. "The only object standing in the way of a large immigration into this section . . . is its great distance from the railroad." *Harney Items* (Burns), May 23, 1903.

3. Herman Oliver, *Gold and Cattle Country*, E. R. Jackman (ed.) (Portland: Binfords and Mort, 1962), 87. See also pp. 82-96 for a richly colored description of early freighting.

4. Progress of the Sumpter Valley Railroad is reported in the *Burns Times-Herald*, July 13, 1901, and *Harney Items*, July 13, 1901. There were a greater number of postal receipts related to eastern Oregon in the post offices in Portland than in Baker City: *Blue Mountain Eagle*, February 1, 1901. "Commercial ties with Portland extend to Granite, Sumpter, and Baker City": *Blue Mountain Eagle*, February 8, 1901. Roughly ranking the amount of advertising during the spring of 1904 in terms of the towns in which an advertiser's business was located, Canyon City ranked first, Pendleton second, and Portland third. A typical edition is *Blue Mountain Eagle* (Canyon City), April 22, 1904.

5. *Harney Items*, July 20, 1901. Traveling salesmen who stopped in Canyon City were overwhelmingly from San Francisco and Portland: *Blue Mountain Eagle*, January 18, 1901. A decade later, when freight came in it was a special occasion: "One of the longest freight trains we have ever seen enter Burns at one time came in from the railroad, . . . [it] was composed of the McKinnon Brothers, Ivers and Allison's eight horse teams, eight wagons, loaded to the guards with merchandise for the already heavily stocked stores of J. Durkheimer and N. Brown": *Eastern Oregon Herald*, November 14, 1889. Freight trains nearly that big came in once a week in 1901: *Harney Items*, June 8, 1901.

6. *Eastern Oregon Herald*, February 13, 1890.

7. See advertisement in the *Blue Mountain Eagle*, December 7, 1900. The habits of salesmen, wool-buyers, farmers, and stockmen during the winter months were frequently alluded to in newspaper columns devoted to local happenings or social notes. For example, see the *Blue Mountain Eagle*,

February 8, 1901 and Brimlow, *Harney County*, 215. The introduction
of a sleigh for passengers is announced in the *Blue Mountain Eagle*,
January 11, 1901.

8. *Harney Items*, June 8, 1901. The monopoly of the Central Pacific Railroad
continued until 1910. The P.L.S. Company continued to receive rebates
on that line during that period: Edward F. Treadwell, *The Cattle King:
A Dramatized Biography* (revised edition; Fresno: Valley Publishers,
1931), 200, 201.

9. Quoted in J.B. McNamer to the state surveyor general, Portland, Oregon,
October 16, 1887, in the files of the Oregon State Land Office, Federal
Records Center, Seattle, Washington. For an account of the incredible
journey of one intrepid woman, Mrs. A. A. Austin, who took the 300-mile
trip from Burns to Eugene by way of Mckenzie Pass in a one-horse rig,
see *Harney Items*, October 17, 1901.

10. *Burns Times-Herald*, April 21, 1897; Brimlow, *Harney County*, 199, 215;
History of Baker, Grant, Malheur, and Harney Counties (Chicago:
Western Historical Publishing Co., 1902), 641. In 1890, the poor conditions of roads prevented the citizens of the Riley area from voting in the
general election in November—the reason being that no one could get
the petition for establishment of a precinct into the county court before
the prescribed deadline. See Precinct Petitions, February, 1890 and April
1890, Harney County Clerk's Office, Burns.

11. Special Term Order of the Circuit Court, February 24, 1890, Harney
County Clerk's Office. For reports of recurrent accidents, washouts, land-
slides, and actual deaths on the roads as well as the rising concern about
them, see the *Burns Times-Herald*, June 15, 1901, and *Harney Items*,
August 10, 1901, November 15, 1902, May 23, 1903, and June 6, 1903.

12. Obstructions by big owners are cited in Phil F. Brogan, *East of the Cascades*
(Portland: Binfords and Mort, 1964), p. 229. See also *Harney Items*, August
10, 1901. Roadmasters were generally accused of being lazy do-nothings
while their supervisors were accused of partiality in assigning work, of
incompetence in selecting detours, and of negligence in failing to keep
stray cattle off the roads: *Harney Items*, February 7, 1903.

13. A full-page article on the natural wonders of Harney Valley reads like a
travelogue of the entire state: *Eastern Oregon Herald*, May 16, 1888. The
neighboring Canyon City editor proclaimed in 1901 that settlers coming
to southeastern Oregon would "find a mild climate superior to that they
left, and with industry and energy they are all almost sure to better their
conditions." *Blue Mountain Eagle*, March 1, 1901.

14. Among the most energetic promoters of a railroad was Phil Smith of a
newly arrived group of three families from Plumas County, California,
which included the Youngs and the Hotchkisses. Bill Hanley was another
supporter, but Smith had much local support. Hanley, however, had personal connections with men in the railroad business and worked actively
with them to try to promote a spur line from Ontario to Juntura. Clarence
Young, interview with the author, Burns, Oregon, August 14, 1969. One
of Hanley's close friends at this time was D. J. O'Reilly, former director
of the Columbia and Southern Railroad: *Blue Mountain Eagle*, May 17,
1901.

15. *Harney Items*, March 15, 1902. C. J. Mellis was the new livestock agent
for the road: *Blue Mountain Eagle*, April 5, 1901.

16. The Portland Chamber of Commerce was complaining at the very time the Northwestern beef cattle market was experiencing a spectacular rise. The O.R. and N. story can be followed in the *Blue Mountain Eagle*, March 29, 1901, and the *Harney Items*, December 27, 1902, January 31, 1903, February 28, 1903, May 23, 1903, and April 25, 1903.
17. The company continued to experiment with dry land alfalfa and other xerophytic range grasses: *Harney Items*, June 20, 1903.
18. Roy M. Robbins, *Our Landed Heritage: The Public Domain, 1776-1936* (Princeton: The Princeton University Press, 1942), 296-298.
19. John Messing, "Public Lands, Politics, and Progressives: The Oregon Land Fraud Trials, 1903-1910," *Pacific Historical Review* 35 (February 1966): 37, 53; S. A. D. Puter and Horace Stevens, *Looters of the Public Domain* (Portland: The Portland Publishing House, 1908), 347-353. Roosevelt's commission was specifically instructed to study the prospect of leasing and, in its report, advocated such a system to the satisfaction of Western livestock interests: Paul W. Gates, *History of Public Land Law Development* (Washington, D.C.: U.S. Government Printing Office, 1968), 489-490. Robbins, *Our Landed Heritage*, 340.
20. *Harney Items*, July 2, 1902. When it appeared later that the proposed forest might curtail operations of the Sumpter Valley Railway, the *Items* changed its tune. As an organ of local business it now reflected the need for a railroad more than the need to curb monopoly in the use of the Blue Mountain forests: *Harney Items*, November 15, 1902, December 27, 1902. For general approval of federal regulatory policies in this respect, see *Times-Herald* (Burns), June 29, 1901; *Harney Items*, August 10, 1901. The advent of grazing regulation is described in detail in John T. Schlebecker, *Cattle Raising on Plains, 1900-1961* (Lincoln: University of Nebraska Press, 1963), 23, 26, 28, 35. See also Marion Clawson, *The Western Range Livestock Industry* (New York: McGraw-Hill Book Co., 1950), 96-98.
21. Powell's was the first systematic study of the problem of aridity in the West. For an assessment of Smythe's contributions, see Lawrence B. Lee's introduction of the 1969 University of Washington Press edition of William E. Smythe, *The Conquest of Arid America* (New York: Harper and Brothers, 1899). For the egalitarian ring of early pronouncements on official irrigation policy, see Gene M. Gressley, "Arthur Powell Davis, Reclamation, and the West," *Agricultural History* 42 (July 1968): 249, 250.
22. Earl Pomeroy, *The Pacific Slope: A History of California, Oregon, Washington, Idaho, Utah, and Nevada* (New York: Alfred A. Knopf, 1965), 79. For a picture of the progressive "overcoat" covering the philosophy of irrigation planners in this era, see Gressley, "Arthur Powell Davis," 245-252.
23. The *Times-Herald* carried an article from a northern California paper, which recognized irrigation as "a perfectly proper object of government expenditure": June 29, 1901. It was published not a month after the *Items* bluntly stated, "It is evident that Congress must soon take steps for national control of the whole irrigation problem": June 1, 1901.
24. *Times-Herald*, July 13, 1901. Newell's quote appears in *Harney Items*, October 5, 1901; Secretary Hitchcock's comment was reported in the *Blue Mountain Eagle*, February 1, 1901.
25. *Times-Herald*, August 23, 1902, July 13, 1901. Senator John Mitchell scored favorably with the *Items*, as did Second District Representative

Malcolm Moody. Thomas Tongue, from the First District was—if mentioned at all—shrugged off as the representative from west of the Cascades
where irrigation was neither needed nor well understood and where "even
the dogs bark when the sun shines more than two days": *Harney Items*,
January 10, 1903.

26. Most galling of all was the P.L.S. Company's refusal to allow storage reservoirs to be built on the upper Silvies River: *Harney Items*, January 6 and
October 5, 1901. See letter from one J. E. Tibbett to the *Times-Herald*,
August 3, 1901 and the editorial comments in that same paper; see also
the letter in the July 13, 1901, issue.

27. One Mrs. McGee was a newcomer then. When the P.L.S. Company built
a dam below her claim, she complained that the water thus diverted might
make another hay section out of P.L.S. pasture land, but that if it were
rightly placed, as it would be under a federal irrigation project, it would
give her a chance to irrigate her own hay land as well as the company's
land. Within a week, the P.L.S. Company cut the levee down. Edward
F. Treadwell and John L. Rand, *Brief in Support of Claims of Pacific
Livestock Company*, Before the State Water Board of Oregon, Burns,
Oregon, January 24, 1923, Harney County Court House, Burns, 86.

28. About half of the land the company wished to develop was federal land,
which the government would grant to the state upon completion of the
necessary improvements. One fifth of the remaining land was Hanley's
own, while another fifth was in the hands of the P.L.S. Company. The
smallest portion, about 10,000 acres, belonged to the Willamette Valley
and Cascade Mountain Wagon Road Company. Except where noted, the
following information on the Harney Valley Improvement Company is
taken from: Historical Notes to the William Hanley Collection, Oregon
Historical Society, Portland, Oregon, 1, 2; *Harney Items*, July 13, 1901,
October 5, 1902, October 12, 1901, November 17, 1902; *Times-Herald*,
July 13, 1901; Treadwell and Rand, Brief, 56, 56, 69, 125, 126, 128;
Brimlow, *Harney County*, 220. A concise report of the potentialities and
the pitfalls of the Carey Act appear in Johansen, *Empire*, 387-389.

29. *Harney Items*, July 25, 1903. Authors of the county "mug book" reflected
the growing dissatisfaction with Hanley's company: "so many times have
such schemes miscarried . . . that many people view this one with sus-
picion": *History of Baker, Grant*, 649. Part of the dissatisfaction people
felt stemmed from the dashed hopes of townsmen and settlers who had
been persuaded that the Silvies River was "the best natural site in
southeastern Oregon": *Harney Items*, November 15, 1902.

30. Brimlow, *Harney County*, 220. Some of the other abortive applications
under the Carey Act were by individuals: Adam George of Crow Camp
and W. E. Burke of Lawen. One corporation of townsmen filed an application under the name The Wright Point Development Company. All
were defunct by 1905. *Harney Items*, August 10, 1901, September 21,
1901, and November 22, 1901.

31. The entire Oregon delegation jumped on the bandwagon. *Harney Items*,
February 1, 1902. Of the bill's sponsors Gressley says, "Suddenly
[Newland's] fellow Western senators, who had long trumpeted the virtues of private enterprise, found themselves in the bastion of public subsidy": "Arthur Powell Davis," 241.

32. A heavy Republican majority turned out in the election of 1902. Every
state and local Republican candidate except Governor Chamberlain won

in Harney County: *Harney Items*, June 7, 1902. See also the *Times-Herald*'s support, August 23, 1902. The *Times-Herald* was uncharacteristically poetic when it guessed: "The present generation in the United States will probably live to see the congested centers of population spread out over the idle empires of an inland sea blooming with industrious farms": April 9, 1903. William Smythe's enthusiasm outstripped the others'; he called the act "that pathway of cooperation and brotherhood [that] . . . is the most shining guidepost thus far erected by the genius of our statesmanship." Smythe, *Conquest*, x.

33. *Harney Items*, December 13, 1902, June 27, August 29, 1903.
34. This was a blow to many because, unlike the Silvies Project, Silver Creek was relatively free of conflicting claims. Chief Hydrographer Newell had said openly that the government would be more interested in smaller projects since such projects would be less likely to involve conflicting property claims: *Harney Items*, January 10, 1903.
35. Brimlow, *Harney County*, pp. 220, 221; Treadwell and Rand, *Brief*, 126.
36. *Harney Items*, June 20, 1903.
37. Mary Ellen Glass, "The Newlands Reclamation Project: Years of Innocence, 1903-1907," *Journal of the West* 7 (January 1968); 55-61.
38. In a long, painstaking prepared article on the state of Harney County's fortunes in 1903, the *Harney Items* spelled out these two basic ingredients of success and praised those who persevered even without them: "The want of capital to develop our water supply and convey it upon irrigable land is the most serious drawback to general farming in this county . . . and the only object standing in the way of a large immigration into this section . . . is its great distance from the railroad . . . [These are] disadvantages common to every new country." *Harney Items*, May 23, 1903.
39. Johansen, *Empire*, 344, 345, 372, 373. Much of this general pattern has been revealed in the more recent research questioning the truth of the "safety valve" theory of immigration which was so much a part of both popular and scholarly views during the nineteenth century. The power of the vision of the West as a place to start anew has never been seriously questioned; but the notion of the West's being a place to which the destitute population created in the backwater of industrialism could come has been all but destroyed. Farmers could afford to move more readily than urban workers and farmers with more property could move more readily than farmers with less. Fred A. Shannon, "A Post-Mortem on the Labor Safety-Valve Theory," *Agricultural History* 19 (January 1945): 31-37.
40. Gates, *Public Land Law*, 495.
41. L. P. Gilman to the Oregon State Surveyor General, October 10, 1898, in the files of the Oregon State Land Office, Federal Records Center, Seattle, Washington; *Blue Mountain Eagle*, January 11, 1901.
42. Pomeroy, *Pacific Slope*, 81. Harney County records show a surprisingly cosmopolitan citizenry from the very beginning. Birthplaces of the 419 people recorded in the U.S. Census of 1880 represent thirty-one states and eleven foreign countries. After twenty years and the advent of railroad travel plus an increase in population from 419 to 2,598 people, birthplaces represent thirty-eight states and fourteen countries. *Tenth Census, Population*, 75, 76.
43. Statistics on Midwestern immigration appear in Tables 10, 11, 12, 13, 15, pp. 395-405. Brimlow refers to the influx of these so-called "Kansas suf-

ferers": *Harney County*, p. 154. A description of their difficulties appears in Gates, *Public Land Law*, 407. Midwestern-born immigrants as a whole registered a highest percentage of laborers than any other section of the country with the exception of California and the Southwest.

44. About one-and-one-half times fewer midwestern-born immigrants came to Harney County during these years than during the relatively much better times of the 1880s: Lila E. Langdon, "A History of Education in Harney County, Oregon, 1875-1940 (master's thesis, Eastern Oregon College, 1959), 72.

45. If the percentage of the midwestern-born among Willamette Valley and California immigrants was as high as in the 1880s (which it probably was not), it would have been 35 percent of all Willamette Valley immigrants and 35 percent of all California immigrants. As for those in non-agricultural pursuits, no other group except eastern-born immigrants could boast over 28 percent in such categories; among the eastern-born in non-agricultural pursuits, four of them or 35 percent were miners. Table 11, p. 397. The *Times-Herald* thought that there were more people in Malheur, Harney, and Lake counties from the Willamette Valley than from anywhere else: August 3, 1901. See Tax Rolls, 1890, 1900.

46. General County Voter Registration Book; Tables 10, 12, pp. 395, 400. Only three other groups showed as small a percentage living in the south end. For areas where midwesterners congregated, see Map No. 4, p. 428. The one exception to the dominance of midwestern and Oregon-born immigrants in the north end occurred in Island precinct, where southwesterners—mostly from Texas—constituted the majority among the small number listed in the voter registration book. These were younger men who undoubtedly worked for the P.L.S. Company in the Island Ranch. Table 11, p. 397; General County Voter Registration Book.

47. Mention of the California vaqueros who frequently drifted in and out of the south end appears in Crow, *Rankin Crow*, p. 35. Forty percent of all California immigrants were laborers, and 80 percent of all California immigrants lived in the south end. Average age for eastern immigrants was 48, nine years older than the average for all groups. Easterners were the only other group besides Californians that included more than 25 percent living in the south end. What is more, 17 percent of the New York-born listed mining as their occupation; in the next highest group only 5 percent listed mining. Tables 11, 16, 17, pp. 397, 406, 407.

48. The rate of turnover of the population in Harney County during the 1870s was over 75 percent. *Supra*, Chapter II, p. 80. During the 1890s the rate was only 51 percent, still indicating pioneer-like conditions: See William G. Robbins, "The Far Western Frontier: Economic Opportunity and Social Democracy in Early Roseburg, Oregon" (Ph.D. dissertation, University of Oregon, 1969), 248. Yet there were many more occupations listed in Harney County than in 1880. In fact the increase in their number was greater than the ratio of the increase in population, which according to the Director of the Bureau of the Census indicated a more settled community. *Tenth Census, Population*, 705.

49. Population in the region increased from 179 to 391 people between 1890 and 1900. *Twelfth Census, Population*, pp. 325, 326. For rate of turnover see Tables 7, 8, 18, pp. 390, 391, 408.

50. Drewsey was one of eight precincts out of the total thirteen in Harney County that gained in population, yet only by 5 percent. For persistence of pioneers by precinct, see Tables 7, 8, 18, pp. 390, 391, 408.

51. Drewsey grew in 1907 to nearly 500 people, most of whom were engaged in freighting or cattle and sheep buying. Mrs. Charley Miler's mother ran a hotel in Drewsey, and Mrs. Miler's early memories were of "two stages running both ways and traveling salesmen and freight wagons busting through town": Miler interview. See Tables 9, 11, pp. 392, 397.

52. Forty-three of the original sixty-three lake-area settlers noted in the survey of 1888 had moved away from that area to other parts of the county by 1900. This included fifteen of the original twenty-two squatters. The average number of acres owned by these former squatters was 2.5 acres greater than the county average with the exception of the big owners. More strikingly, the average number of cattle each owned was 89, which was 39 more cattle than the average throughout the county, again with the exception of the big owners. Original Surveys; Tax Rolls, 1880, 1890, 1900.

53. One significant community study reveals that higher rates of turnover occur not only in specific areas but within specific groups of people. The authors of the study noted clearly defined transient groups in which the immigrants of one decade would be out-migrants in the next. This element is that elusive element that sociologists and historians who are interested in community studies have difficulty tracing. The careers of those who belong to these groups are only partially known, and judgments about how they were affected by local social and economic opportunities are nearly impossible to make. Thus, the spatially fixed community-study approach is a net with holes in it, unless transients move somewhere else within the community being studied. In the present instance, transients would appear to have gained something by moving; or one might conclude, they were among the more energetic men on the make. Yet, even at that, the fact that their move within Harney County could not really be considered a change of scene might indicate that southeastern Oregon was the end of the road for them and that they were "settling down" as the western novels would have us think all transients eventually should. The story then would be closer to the older stereotype of the mover being the drifter and permanence being the key to prosperity. Much yet needs to be done with transient populations. See Sidney Goldstein, *The Norristown Study: An Experiment in Interdisciplinary Research Training* (Philadelphia: University of Pennsylvania Press, 1961), 292. Other areas of fairly high stability in Harney County were Diamond, apart from Happy Valley, and Alvord precinct in the south end. See Tables 7, 8, 18, pp. 390, 391, 408.

54. Johansen, *Empire*, 369. Some, of course, went to Alaska, where they either failed or succeeded as did their fellows who went to farm agricultural frontiers—perhaps even in equal proportions. One twenty-year resident of Burns sold his property to a newcomer and took the resulting stake to Alaska, where he lost it or squandered it, and ended by dying of smallpox in New York City. *Harney Items*, May 2, 1903.

55. *Blue Mountain Eagle*, February 22, 1901.

56. *Ibid*, March 1, 1901, April 26, 1901. Citizens of Baker City watched hopefully while over 1,500 immigrants moved through their town en route farther west. When none stopped, the jilted citizens of the town decided in retrospect that the immigrants had been "a poor looking lot": *Blue Mountain Eagle*, May 10, 1901. The *Times-Herald* noted almost hopefully, "the drought which the east [sic] is now wrestling should start a good immigration tide toward southeastern Oregon.": July 13, 1901.

57. Relative land prices can be traced in Grant County Deed Record, Book "C," pp. 22-24, 44, 146, 163, 167-169, Book "G," 734, Grant County Court House, John Day; Harney County Deed Index Indirect, Book I, Harney County Clerk's Office. Also *Blue Mountain Eagle*, November 30, 1900. The report of the Wallowa County sale appears in the *Blue Mountain Eagle*, January 18, 1901. Details of George Thompson's sale are in *Harney Items*, May 16, 1903. As to the relative unattractiveness of southeastern Oregon, evidence comes from land office reports. In 1889, the Register of the Burns Land Office reported 108 homestead and timber-culture entries comprising 5,415 acres excluding desert land entries not reported, together with total cash receipts of $17,977 for the last quarter of that year. In 1904, the same office reported 567 entries of all kinds, comprising 61,054 acres and total cash receipts of $21,075 *for the entire year*. Roughly calculating what that would represent for one quarter (141 entries, 15,263 acres, $5,268), the difference between the two sets of figures is not great. In that same year (1904) the other five land offices in the state far outstripped Burns in every category. The La Grande office alone granted 85 homesteads in one month—15 percent of Burns entries for one entire year. Reports of the Burns land office appear in the *Eastern Oregon Herald*, January 30, 1890, and the *Harney Items*, February 1, 1902; also in Brimlow, p. 193. The state reports appear in *Blue Mountain Eagle*, December 9, 1904. As the *Eagle* said, "land values here are the lowest in the country in relation to production and profits." *Blue Mountain Eagle*, February 1, 1901.

58. This is not to say that forward-looking citizens sat back calmly. Editors of southeastern Oregon's papers repeatedly complained, "we are receiving but a small percent of the immigration that is flocking to our state," and urged more active solicitation of immigrants: *Blue Mountain Eagle*, May 17, 1901.

59. The quote is from *Times-Herald*, April 9, 1904. Just such a redeeming good seemed promised by the Sumpter Valley Railroad; but the railroad company halted construction when it discovered that 30,000 acres of "fine agricultural and timber land" along the road had fallen into the hands of a single large lumber company. Notwithstanding, the *Times-Herald* said the matter of who owns the land becomes "insignificant when the development benefits that would follow the completion of the line are taken into consideration": *ibid*.

60. Allan G. Bogue, *From Prairie to Cornbelt: Farming on the Illinois and Iowa Prairies in the Nineteenth Century* (Chicago: University of Chicago Press, 1963), 43-45, 59, 175, 176.

61. Petitions for a justice of the peace, a sure sign of both growing numbers of communities and a growing sense of community within them, proliferated during the 1890s. See Petitions for Justice of the Peace, October 9, 1889, February 28, 1890, March 12, 1892, June 3, 1893, December 1, 1895, May 7 and July 9, 1897, August 28, 1898, August 10, 1899, September 21, 1900, Harney County Clerk's Office. Requests for surveys in the state land office conform to the areas mentioned: Robert A Habersham to the Surveyor General, July 10, 1895; A. A. Cowing to the Surveyor General, November 24, 1896, and February 2, 1897, in the files of the State Land Office, Federal Records Center, Seattle. For an appraisal of the extent of farm land and its availability after 1900 see Dale C. Eggleston, "Harney County, Oregon: Some Aspects of Sequant Occupancy and Land Use" (master's thesis, University of Oregon, 1970), 83, 84.

62. A concise albeit biased review of the company's career appears in *History of Baker, Grant*, pp. 644, 645. Records of Altschul's land sales appear in Grant County Record of Deeds, Book D, 367, 398; Harney County General Index of Deeds, Indirect, Book I; Harney County Mortgage Index, Indirect, Book I. See also Jerry A. O'Callaghan, *The Disposition of the Public Domain in Oregon*, (Washington, D.C.: U.S. Government Printing Office, 1960), 52, 53.

63. In 1901 both J. C. Foley and Harvey Dixon were ejected from company land that they had claimed before a survey but after the land had been withdrawn from entry by the state and granted to the company. Sentiment was such in the local land office that it allowed Foley and Dixon to bring their claims to patent. The Secretary of the Interior subsequently reversed the decision of the local office. *Harney Items*, May 2, 1903. One of the ways in which a locality struck out against speculating absentee owners was to levy excessive tax rates on them. The Wagon Road Company sent Harney County Sheriff A. A. Cowing a formal protest about Harney County rates. See Charles Altschul to A. A. Cowing, July, 1890, Harney County Clerk's Office.

64. Information on Hanley's image in Harney County has been gathered from interviews. Most helpful were those with Al Brown, grandson of merchant Nathan Brown, Burns, July 2-23, 1968; with Juan Vallejo, Burns, June 22, 1968; and with Paul Stewart, former owner of the Whitehorse Ranch, Alvord Ranch, June 24, 1968. All three knew Hanley personally.

65. This was done when C. E. S. Wood, a Portland lawyer and close personal friend of Hanley, was the road company's land agent. The capital came mostly from Wood and some of his Portland associates. One of those associates was Henry Ladd Corbett, who lent money privately in Harney County. See Harney County Index of Mortgages, Indirect, Book I. Hanley's associations with Salt Lake City and Portland financing appear in a number of letters in the Hanley Collection. A review of these associations also appears in Historical Notes to the William Hanley Collection, 1-4.

66. Bogue, *From Prairie to Corn Belt*, 51.

67. See Tables 21, 22, 23, pp. 411, 412, 415.

68. The number of smaller purchasers fell from twenty-three during the 1890s to twenty-one after 1900. Table 23, p. 415. Harney County Tax Rolls, 1890. There were 225 government land claimants recorded in the deed records of the county between 1890 and 1900. Most of these were filed at the very beginning or the end of the decade. The ratio of firstcomers who filed to newcomers who filed was approximately one to ten. Harney County Index of Deed, Indirect, Book I.

69. See Lake County old-timer Rube Long's assessment of the smugness, indeed the contempt, with which oldtimers watched newcomers trying to farm their claims after the turn of the century. E. R. Jackman and R. A. Long, *The Oregon Desert* (Caldwell, Idaho: The Caxton Printers, 1967), 26-29, 48. Information also came from Joe Fine, self-made man and last foreman of the "P" Ranch, interview with the author, Burns, August 12, 1970.

70. Nine out of the 23 smaller purchasers of the 1890s were among the 21 purchasers of the early 1900s: Harney County Index of Deeds, Indirect, Book I.

71. Table 28, p. 420; Harney County Index of Deeds, Indirect, Book I.

72. Motives behind merchants lending money or goods are discussed in Bogue, *From Prairie to Corn Belt*, p. 175. Amounts below $1,000 were in the neighborhood of $350—about the cost of a year's supplies. See Table 28, p. 420. Later, between 1904, and 1914, Nathan Brown alone loaned $31,045 to thirty-six different local citizens. Only three defaulted and these were unfamiliar names; each of those, however, had at least a town lot or a 20- or 40-acre plot of land as collateral. Harney County Index of Mortgages, Indirect, Book I.

73. Tables 2, 28, pp. 384, 420.

74. One loan comprised four-fifths of the entire amount. It was for the sum of $20,000 to the Sitz Brothers, who, from 1890 to 1912 increased their recorded land holdings by over 2,700 acres. In the ten years from 1890 to 1900, they bought 2,000 head of sheep to add to the 500 head of cattle and 30 horses already recorded in the tax rolls of 1900 under their name—an increase of 475 cattle, 2,000 sheep, and 18 horses from 1890. Table 28, p. 420; Harney County Tax Rolls, 1890, 1900. The Sitz loan is an astronomical sum for the commission to loan to one borrower since Harney County's quota of loans from the fund rarely amounted to over $20,000 annually. See *Blue Mountain Eagle*, March 1, 1901.

75. See Table 28, p. 420; Harney County Index of Mortgages, Indirect, Book I. The P.L.S. Company added only 5,000 acres to its deeded holdings during this decade. Table 20, p. 410.

76. See list of State Land Board loans, Table 29, p. 422.

77. The general tendency for private lenders to recall loans at the very time lenders could least afford to pay them, namely during hard times, is confirmed by what the grandson of old time merchant Nathan Brown, reports of credit arrangements in Harney County roughly up until the First World War. Al Brown, grandson of Nathan Brown, and son of banker Leon Brown, interview with the author, Burns, August 10, 1968.

78. A list both of tax delinquent sale notices and reports of those sales was compiled from the Burns newspapers for the years 1901-1904. There were seventeen notices during this period and eleven reports. Of the eleven reported sales, nine were to firstcomers. See also Eggleston, "Harney County," 83. As a Grant County firstcomer, Herman Oliver, relates, the bulk of his land came from homesteaders who left it for taxes or from "small farmers who did not have enough to make a living": *Gold and Cattle Country*, 99.

79. It is hard to measure in this period because most information on marriages and divorce has to be gleaned indirectly from other sources. After 1918, however, the records of marriage and divorce are complete, making measurements and correlations easier. Data for the period up until that time were gathered from: *The History of Baker, Grant*, 659-715, *The Harney Items*, and *Burns Times-Herald*, interviews, and from Brimlow, *Harney County*, especially 60, 61, 205-210. See also Tables 22, 24.

80. For an account of these particular abuses, see Gates, *Public Land Law*, 490, 491. The report of the twenty-eight claimants appears in *Harney Items*, May 23, 1903. Without land office lists it is hard to guess how many such desert claims there were, but when it is considered that the number of families in just the Riley area increased by only thirty-two from 1900 to 1910, more than likely the twenty-eight claimants in just the spring of 1903 must have included many wives even if as many as three fourths of those who filed did not stay. *Thirteenth Census, Population*, 1910, 494, 515.

81. A. A. Bardwell, D. C. Eggleston, and M. D. Palmer, "Appraisal of Land and Resources of the Malheur Indian Reservation," (mimeographed) (Burns, Oregon, 1958), 43.

82. A list of homesteaders and preemptioners and the dates of their filing appears in Treadwell and Rand, *Brief*, 70-74. The decision of the court in the case of French-Glenn vs. Sarah E. Marshall opened the door for a rush of claims. A report of five new homestead claims appeared in the *Harney Items* a week after the paper had reported that a favorable decision would be handed down. *Harney Items*, March 20, 1902.

83. Map No. 6, p. 430. This story has been pieced together from information in Treadwell and Rand, *Brief*, 66-69; Brimlow, *Harney County*, 178; *History of Baker, Grant*, 688, 689; Harney County Index of Mortgages, Indirect, Book I; Harney County Index of Deeds, Indirect, Book I; and Harney County Tax Rolls, 1890, 1900.

84. *Harney Items*, December 7, 1901. Many other examples could be cited. See for instance David Shirk's description of his own career in Martin F. Schmitt (ed.), *The Cattle Drives of David Shirk: From Texas to the Idaho Mines, 1871 and 1873* (Portland: The Champoeg Press, 1956), particularly 144, 145. I. L. Poujade prospered to the extent that he ordered wagon loads of supplies direct from Ontario just as Hanley and Miller did: *Times-Herald*, June 8, 1901. Abner Robbins continued to live in his old homestead cabin even after he built his wife a fashionable home in Drewsey: *Harney Items*, June 24, 1902. Judge Shields, on upper Silver Creek, was able to convert his family's log house into a spacious frame house by 1900, and W. C. Cecil of the same area built a convenient town house for himself and his family in Burns: *Harney Items*, August 24, 1901. Not all firstcomers succeeded. Fred Otley actually lost land between 1900 and 1912, as did J. C. Foley and J. H. Witzel: Harney County Tax Rolls, 1890, 1900, 1912.

85. *Harney Items*, August 24, 1901. On the subject of contesting claims and using scalp bounties see *Blue Mountain Eagle*, March 15, 1901, and April 22, 1904.

86. For a discussion of the hypotheses used in selecting the following data, the limitations of the data themselves, and the methods used to analyze them, see Appendix 5, p. 373. In 1900, 18 percent of the 665 tax units in the county, or 117 units, owned over half the county's taxable property. Furthermore, the 112 established families whose land ownings are recorded (i.e., 16.8 percent of the total 665 units) owned, on the average, 326 acres of land per unit. The other 495, excluding the Willamette Valley and Cascade Mountain Wagon Road Company and the big owners, owned an average of only 96 acres of taxable land per unit.

CHAPTER FIVE

1. Lee Stuart, "Men and Cattle on the Northern Plains, 1860-1887" (Ph.D. dissertation, University of Oregon, 1971), 112.

2. Gene M. Gressley, *Bankers and Cattlemen* (New York: Alfred A. Knopf, 1966), 269, 140. As has been noted, the winter of 1886-87 was the trigger that fired off many changes in the industry, but Stuart's study shows that the gun was already fully loaded: "Men and Cattle," 111-116.

3. Margaret Lo Piccolo, "Some Aspects of the Range Cattle Industry of Harney County, Oregon, 1870-1900" (master's thesis, University of Oregon, 1962), particularly 115, 116, and 127.

4. In the county "mug book" there is a revealing ambivalence. Any time the authors referred to the cattle barons in Harney County it was in disparaging terms, but when they spoke of Texas or Oklahoma cattle kings it was always in colorful, romanticized terms, denoting a mixture of admiration and dislike—the dichotomy between specific and abstract cases, all of which was probably typical of most settlers as well. See *History of Baker, Grant, Malheur, and Harney Counties* (Chicago: Western Historical Publishing Co., 1902), 687-689. See also *Eastern Oregon Herald* (Burns), November 15, 1888.

5. Hanley, for example, dealt simultaneously with a commission broker in Salt Lake City, the First National Bank in Bend, Oregon, and private credit sources in Portland. At that level of financing, large owners were in a separate category from the rest of the community. Regarding the reputation of big owners' cattle, local residents who went to eastern fairs where they were shown testified with pride to the reputation of their "homegrown cattle.": *Harney Items*, (Burns), June 21, 1902.

6. Joe Fine, ex-foreman of the P Ranch, interview with the author, Burns, November 30, 1969. Fine tells of yearly requests from important families in Portland asking about summer employment for their sons who "always wanted to be a cowboy."

7. The French empire had grown by 302 percent during the 1890s to a total taxable acreage of 190,765 acres, 45,790 acres of which was tillable land. Riley and Hardin's OO, a much smaller operation, grew by an astounding 467 percent. Hanley's rate of growth on the Bell-A Ranch alone was 266 percent. His taxable holdings in 1900 were 4,398 acres, two thirds of which were tillable land. The P.L.S. Company showed the most modest increase, only doubling its acreage during the 1890's to make a total of 73,346 acres of nontillable land and 9,343 acres of tillable land. These four held 45 percent of all the county's taxable property in 1900, representing a gross estimated value of over a million dollars. Harney County Tax Rolls, 1890, 1900, Harney County Courthouse, Burns. Also Tables 19, 20, pp. 409, 410. See also Lo Piccolo, "Range Cattle Industry," 66-68, 120.

8. Hanley's story, except where noted, was taken from Anne Shannon Monroe (ed.), *Feelin' Fine* (Garden City: Doubleday, Doran, and Co., 1931), George F. Brimlow, *Harney County and Its Range Land* (Portland: Binfords and Mort, 1951), 212-214, and Historical Notes to the William Hanley Collection, Oregon Historical Society, Portland, 1-11.

9. Some hard feelings between Bill Hanley and his brother Ed seem to have cropped up later. Ed apparently had second thoughts soon after selling and continued to draw on the Bell-A account, which Bill called a "complete breach of trust." Hanley to W. H. Stirling, January 9, 1910, Hanley Collection. For an indication of Hanley's open and friendly relationship with Lusk, see Hanley to F. C. Lusk, April 22, 1907, Hanley Collection. Lusk was a power in the American Cattlegrowers Association, serving as its president in 1901: *Burns Times-Herald*, July 13, 1901. See also Brimlow, *Harney County* 247.

10. There is no indication why Riley and Hardin sold. The case with French, however, was mostly one of fortuitous circumstances. Tax Rolls, 1890. The whole French-Glenn deal is reported in Lo Piccolo, "Range Cattle

Industry," 19, 20. See also Hanley to William Miller, February 27, 1907, Hanley Collection.

11. Brimlow, *Harney County*, 177. Big owners of the nineteenth century would never have understood Hanley's approach. The difference, of course, was that Hanley owned most of the land he used and many of the large owners before him did not. Development in the county could not but enhance the value of Hanley's property.

12. See Edward F. Treadwell and John L. Rand, *Brief in Support of Claims of Pacific Livestock Company*, Before the State Water Board of Oregon, Burns, Oregon, January 24, 1923, Harney County Court House, Burns, 3, 9, 66, 69, 86, 121, 124.

13. The headquarters building is now a private home in Burns located a block north of main street on what is labeled the "P.L.S. Block." It was the home for many years after his retirement of the company accountant. Clarence Young, former County Sheriff, interview with the author, Burns, Oregon, August 19, 1969. When Gilchrist spoke, the community was evidently disposed to listen. His remarks on range leasing were judiciously serialized in the *Times-Herald* in 1901. Gilchrist's policies are recounted in Treadwell and Rand, *Brief*, 64, 65. Information comes also from Mrs. Charles Miler, wife of former P.L.S. Superintendent Charles Miler, successor to Gilchrist, interview with the author, Burns. September 12, 1968. Information on the pump appears in Harney County Commissioner's Journal, Volume A, Harney County Court House, 515.

14. The story was first told to me over a cup of coffee by Pete Praeger, an old-time buckaroo at the Sod House Ranch, French's former ranch headquarters in the north end near Malheur Lake. Praeger had "buckarooed" for the P.L.S. Company on both the Island and the Whitehorse ranches and later on the P Ranch under Joe Fine. The story was tested on others and, though versions were different, the gist was the same. Interview with Pete Praeger, Sod House Ranch, August 10, 1969. It may be argued that Miller's approach was, at that time, very possibly the only sensible one. In 1904 a rustler caught stealing a P.L.S. steer in the south end was found not guilty by a jury that sat a mere twenty minutes: *Times-Herald*, April 9, 1904. In 1914 the P.L.S. Company compromised with the state in a suit over swamp land acquisitions turning back 18,000 acres to the state of which 9,057 acres were thrown open to settlement. Brimlow, *Harney County*, 231, 233.

15. The categorization appears in Ernest S. Osgood, "The Cattleman in the Agricultural History of the Northwest," *Agricultural History* 3 (July 1929), 125. For his categorization of cattlemen on the high plains after 1886 see Osgood, *The Day of the Cattleman* (Minneapolis: University of Minnesota Press, 1928), 226. Regarding the techniques of John Devine, Lo Piccolo cites the uncomplimentary tone of *Westshore* magazine. Lo Piccolo, "Range Cattle Industry," 118. See also Brimlow, *Harney County*, 220.

16. J. Orin Oliphant, *On the Cattle Ranges of the Oregon Country* (Seattle: University of Washington Press, 1968), vii, 346, 342.

17. The Ryegrass District and the peripheral dry farms are described in Dale C. Eggleston, "Harney County, Oregon: Some Aspects of Sequent Occupancy and Land Use" (master's thesis, University of Oregon, 1970), 84. The matter-of-fact predictions of rain for "the grain growers" in Harney County who should have "an abundant harvest" in the *Harney Items*, in light of prolonged subsequent dry spells, appear naive in the extreme: June 1, 1901.

18. Some ranchers, of course, could recklessly and needlessly overspend on machinery. All data from Tax Rolls, 1890-1912.

19. Among the big owners themselves, the most progressive in these terms was Hanley, whose land was 89 percent hay land by 1912. The P.L.S. Company converted 69 percent of its land to hay in 1912, and the former French land holdings were 47 percent hay in 1912—up 23 percent from 1900. Bill Brown's horse and sheep ranch near Riley kept and needed only 18 percent of its acreage in hay. Thus the P.L.S. Company and Hanley, along with firstcomers, were well situated in terms of potential feeding capacity by 1912. Table 26, p. 418.

20. The O.R. and N. Company had been promoting the use of dry-land alfalfa in eastern Oregon with some success among ranchers like Cecil and Poujade and among the stock-feeder spreads in Grant and Morrow counties, especially the Butler Creek Ranch in Morrow County: *Blue Mountain Eagle*, (Canyon City), April 22, 1904: Paul Stewart, early settler and former owner of the Whitehorse Ranch, interview with the author, Alvord Ranch, June 22, 1968. Even the Butler Creek Ranch started feeding some time in December or January: *Blue Mountain Eagle*, January 18, 1901. Hanley did not get his cattle on feed in 1907 until January 4: Hanley to Henry Welcome, January 8, 1907, Hanley Collection. A statement exhibiting the fact that most cattle-country people might have been (to twist a phrase from Richard Hofstadter) wise with the wisdom of their age but certainly ignorant with its ignorance was the comment in the *Blue Mountain Eagle* in January that "the stock men have begun feeding their cattle . . . since the last snow fall." *Blue Mountain Eagle*, January 4, 1901. The same paper told in as commonplace a way of the Izee rancher who "expects in a week or so to turn his cattle out on the range." The date of the paper and the quote are in *Blue Mountain Eagle*, March 22, 1901. Green ranges were more subject to overgrazing and quick kill than a more mature range in late April or May. Most knew this, but few operated on that knowledge during these years: Fine interview.

21. For the method used to formulate these categories and the source materials used to substantiate them, see Appendix 7, p. 378. For the numerical tabulation in each category, see Table 27, p. 419.

22. These distributions can be seen in Table 27, p. 419.

23. Interviews with the author by Art Sawyer, Manager of the Harney County Chamber of Commerce and first Harney County Extension Agent, December 30, 1969, and Lloyd Hill, long-time resident and prominent rancher, Burns, November 14, 1969. For the story of the prodigious improvements Hanley made on the P Ranch including his construction of a drainage canal which reclaimed 25,000 acres of swamp land, see Brimlow, *Harney County*, 219, 247; Lo Piccolo, "Range Cattle Industry."

24. Reference to Hanley's steer-feeding operation appears in *Blue Mountain Eagle*, April 29, 1901. County extension agents beginning in the period between 1910 and 1912 propagandized the concepts of progressive and efficient operations and applied them to better-operated spreads both large and small; to the extent they did so, these agents helped identify the values of the cattleman's subculture more closely with middle-class farmer values, emphasizing the quality of an operation before the quantity of products it produced, and thereby attaching worth to individual merit rather than merely to wealth. Interviews with the author by Sawyer, and with Ray Novotny, September 19, 1969. Hanley's advice to a young rancher just

starting who had written Hanley asking him of his methods was "open up more cultivated land, put in alfalfa, and expand." Hanley to Burr Wood, April 21, 1910, Hanley Collection.

25. Brimlow, *Harney County*, 208.

26. There were not yet "traction machines" to pull rakes, mowers, harrows, and ditchers; but horse- or mule-drawn versions of such equipment were used by most of the better-off owners. The P.L.S. Company, however, did not go further than enclosing vast, well-watered acreages in its control around Camp Creek and Jump Creek, which were then used as pastures during all but the hardest part of the winter. Such rough feeding grounds cost little in upkeep, while they supported 4,000 to 5,000 head of cattle for two or three months of the year. Treadwell and Rand, *Brief*, 18, 19; Stewart interview.

27. Shirk could remember his own tribulations during the winter of 1889 and 1890 too well to hold much by casual or slipshod methods. See Martin Schmitt (ed.), *The Cattle Drives of David Shirk: From Texas to the Idaho Mines, 1871 and 1873* (Portland, Oregon: The Champoeg Press, 1956), 141, 142. See also interviews with the author by Hill, Stewart, Fine, Sam Dunn, rancher and son of the homesteader from the 1890's, The Narrows, July 20, 1968; and Joe Altnow, rancher and son of firstcomer Albert Altnow, Drewsey, July 23, 1968. All ranchers corroborate these values as having existed and having been important during this period as well as today.

28. On importation of blooded stock by big owners see Oliphant, *Cattle Ranges*, 201. The most popular breed was still the Durham, though eastern Oregon livestock growers were becoming interested in the Hereford strain. There was an occasional "sour grapes" tone to newspaper reports of large cattlegrowers importing cattle and leaving smaller owners in the lurch. See *Blue Mountain Eagle*, January 4, 1901. See also Brimlow, *Harney County*, 231.

29. The Chicago prices for blooded stock are quoted from a sale made by Grant County cattle-buyer J. D. Combs in 1901: *Blue Mountain Eagle*, March 1, 1901.

30. In Hanley's records are several Bull Pedigree Certificates from the American Hereford Association acquired in the years between March 8, 1905 and August 6, 1908, Hanley Collection. Also, Stewart interview. The rise of the firstcomers is attested to in Lo Piccolo, "Range Cattle Industry," 98. See also prices given by cattle buyer J. D. Combs for cattle belonging to firstcomers in *Harney Items*, August 31, 1901, and August 15, 1903. When the Sitz brothers bought two Durham bulls in April, 1904, the *Harney Times* took the occasion to upbraid others who had not yet joined what was by then beginning to look like a campaign to encourage the production of better stock: April 9, 1904. The O.R. and N. Company campaign to introduce Herefords is mentioned in *Harney Items*, March 15, 1902.

31. Interviews with the author by Clarence Young, former Watermaster and Surveyor, Burns, August 13, 14, 1969, and James McEwen, former ranch hand, sheep herder, and rancher, Sod House Ranch, June 23, 1968; Fine interview.

32. Praeger and Fine interviews. The same is true today of the cowboy's distaste for farm work: "Red" Leavitt, ranch worker, interview with the author, Rinehart Ranch, July 16, 1968. On this subject see also Stuart, "Men and Cattle," 115. See also Sylvester L. Lahren, "Cowboy Economics:

Traditionalism, Adaptation, and the Future," presented at the 24th Northwest Anthropological Conference, Moscow, Idaho, 1971 (mimeographed).

33. Shirk's account appears in Schmitt, *David Shirk*, p. 144. I. L. Poujade contracted for the haying on the Island Ranch: *Harney Items*, August 1, 1903. Machines, of course, were not what they are today and much hand work was still necessary. Hanley, for instance, had to hire as many as 75 hands during haying season. Brimlow, *Harney County*, 270.

34. John Robertson of the Robertson family, firstcomers in Drewsey, worked for Hanley mostly during spring roundups as a foreman. In a letter to Hanley under a heading entitled "Labor Account" he listed the names of men who had worked for him in 1907. None was familiar except for Clarence Mace, who had worked only during the spring roundup that year. John Robertson to Hanley, November 28, 1909, Hanley Collection.

35. Bill Brown of the Gap Ranch felt the secret of keeping good hands was to give them good food of their own choosing: Brimlow, *Harney County*, 214. The quote is from the testimony of a transient hand given in 1895 during the trial of Ed Oliver for the killing of Pete French. Transcript of "State of Oregon vs. Ed Oliver," 1895 (Property of Mrs. Esther Haugen, Burns, Oregon), 8.

36. See Lo Piccolo, "Range Cattle Industry," 92, 93. Record per capita consumption is told of in Schlebecker, pp. 17, 18. Rising prices are reflected in newspaper accounts of marketing transactions after 1900. See, for example, *Times-Herald* (Burns), August 3, 1901; *Harney Items*, August 3, 1901; *Blue Mountain Eagle*, June 7, 1901. A concise review of these market conditions as they affected large corporations appears in Gressley, *Bankers and Cattlemen*, 109-111.

37. Dorothy Johansen, *Empire of the Columbia: A History of the Pacific Northwest* (New York: Harper and Row, 1967), 377. The O.R. and N. Company livestock agent's report appears in *Harney Items*, November 22, 1901. See also Brimlow, *Harney County*, 178, 231. Indeed, so rapidly had the northwestern market grown that some cattle growers actually became complacent about it. When a Seattle buyer went to the south end of Harney County to pick up feeders in advance of the fall market, he was snubbed by ranchers too busy with haying to give him their time. *Harney Items*, August 3, 1901.

38. Lo Piccolo, "Range Cattle Industry," 95. A cattle sale to a Portland buyer in late winter, 1901, grossed the seller an average of $47 per head for 167 head: *Blue Mountain Eagle*, February 15, 1901. Stockyards in Portland advertised prices for both Chicago and Portland markets, and they were roughly the same, ranging from 4¢ to 6¢ per pound: *Blue Mountain Eagle*, November 30, 1900. For effects of Alaskan market, see *Blue Mountain Eagle*, January 4, January 18, March 15, April 19, 1901.

39. On the subject of the spring market see Stuart, "Men and Cattle," 51, 52; *Harney Items*, May 2, 1903; *Blue Mountain Eagle*, January 4, 1901, February 15, 1901.

40. P.L.S. Company activities, for example, were regularly noted in both the Grant and Harney county papers, and the seasonal ritual was invariably the same. The Agency Valley, Harney Valley, and Silvies Valley herds were put to pasture in March with about one quarter of them being trailed on to Ontario in mid-April for shipment to the California market. An October shipment was also made of slaughter animals that had summered in the Blue Mountains. By contrast the Malheur River and Whitehorse Valley

herds were all sold in the fall in one massive shipment to California. The shipment of October, 1901, was not unusual: it numbered thirty-nine carloads of cattle bound for the California market. *Blue Mountain Eagle*, November 30, 1900; *Harney Items*, October 12, 1901. Despite the preoccupation of large owners throughout the West with the market, few if any seemed able to gear for other than the fall market. See Gressley, *Bankers and Cattlemen*, 130.

41. Ira Stubblefield's odyssey is told in *History of Baker*, Grant, 665. Information also from Stewart interview. For herding methods see *Harney Items*, June 1, 1901.

42. The story comes from newspaper sources and records in the Hanley Collection. For related materials on marketing see Lo Piccolo, "Range Cattle Industry," 96-99; Oliphant, *Cattle Ranges*, 196-198; and Brimlow, *Harney County*, 178. See the label applied to Blackwell in *Blue Mountain Eagle*, March 29, 1901.

43. Lo Piccolo, "Range Cattle Industry," 96; Brimlow, *Harney County*, 178. Though the Hanley correspondence does not show it, there was a report that Parsons had bought the Warm Springs Ranch just north of the Nevada line for $200,000 and had made Hanley manager: *Harney Items*, May 9, 1903.

44. The foregoing is from Brimlow, *Harney County*, 178, and *Harney Items*, June 1, July 13, 1901. Economic intercourse between Hanley and the older established families was not only in the area of buying and selling cattle; there is evidence that Hanley leased out pasture land to groups of better established ranchers (Varien, Craddock, McLaren, and Egli, for instance). These men helped hay the Bell-A as well. Whether this was done as partial payment for the lease or as a continuing commitment for which the leases might have been given in the first place is not known. Hanley to W. H. Stirling, July 22, 1918, Hanley Collection.

45. See *Blue Mountain Eagle*, March 29, May 31, 1901.

46. See *Harney Items*, November 15, 1902, May 2, September 12, 1903. Frank Sweetser, formerly in partnership with Tom Overfelt in Silvies Valley, turned to the lucrative business of cattle buying in southeastern Oregon and became a large dealer out of Winnemucca in the partnership of Stauffer and Sweetser. See Oliphant, *Cattle Ranges*, 198; *Harney Items*, July 13, 1901. Feedlot auctions took place on other ranches outside Harney County. Heppner had a county market. Canyon City and John Day had active markets. Bill Butler's auctions in Grant County drew buyers and sellers from nearly every eastern Oregon county, mostly for trade with the Union Meat Company and the Pacific Meat Company—both Northwest concerns. more names could be listed and to them should be added the buyers for the O.R. and N. Company, the Union Pacific Railroad, and the U. S. Army. See *Harney Items*, September 21, December 21, 1901; *Blue Mountain Eagle*, November 30, 1900, March 1, April 5, May 17, 1901.

47. *Blue Mountain Eagle*, May 24, 1901.

48. Tax Rolls, 1896, 1907. Table 19, p. 409.

49. See Oliphant, *Cattle Ranges*, 345, 346.

50. They were neither numerous nor powerful enough to form a separate special interest group, nor would they have been likely to do so since their interests were clearly identified with one side or the other of the fight between big and little owners.

51. Grant County sheepraisers enjoyed exceptionally good market conditions; ranges were in good shape and buyers from as far east as Boston were bidding up to 13¢ per pound for wool. The Heppner market catered to all salable stock but soon dealt with sheep far more than cattle. Pendleton, of course, became a national symbol for fine woolen products largely because of this "wool boom" of the early twentieth century. The *Blue Mountain Eagle* followed the sheep market closely: see issues for January 4, 11, and 18, February 8, 22, March 8, 15, and 29, April 5, May 3, 10, and 24, 1901. See also *Harney Items*, June 8, 1901, June 13, 1903. Sheep shearing became a steady part of the spring and summer employment picture: See *Harney Items*, January 6, 1901, May 9 and 16, 1903; *Blue Mountain Eagle*, February 15, 1901, April 22, 1904.

52. Carson's comment appears in *Blue Mountain Eagle*, March 1, 1901. A note on the closing of the trails appears also in Brimlow, *Harney County*, 218. Closing the trails was partially responsible for the tremendous increase of sheep on the ranges of southeastern Oregon; it in effect built up what amounted to a false surplus. *Harney Items*, June 24, 1902. For a well-informed account of sheep raising in Harney County see E. R. Jackman, John Scharff, and Charles Conkling, *Steens Mountain in Oregon's High Desert Country* (Caldwell: The Caxton Printers, 1968), 136-142.

53. *Oregonian* (Portland), September 9, 1902. Governor Chamberlain's comment appears in *Harney Items*, July 25, 1903. Notations of increasing numbers of sheep and fears concerning them appear in *Harney Items*, July 27, December 7, 1901; *Blue Mountain Eagle*, January 11, May 17, 1901; McEwen interview.

54. Except where noted the following story is taken from an interview by the author with Bill Davies, early sheep herder for the Jenkins Brothers, Mud Flat Ranch, September 10, 1968.

55. There was a "western circle" as well from Warner Valley in Lake County to the Steens and back. In time the western circle came to be dominated by Irish herders, while the eastern circle was becoming more and more the territory of Basques. McEwen interview; John Scharff, early resident and former Director of the Malheur Wildlife Refuge, interview with the author, Malheur Wildlife Refuge Headquarters, July 9, 1968. See also Jackman, et al., *Steens Mountain*, 140; Brimlow, *Harney County*, 270.

56. Reports of fighting on the mountain appear in *Harney Items*, August 15, 1903.

57. One could say that the conflict was between home-seekers and the would-be monopolists, though transient sheep herders were monopolists mostly in wish: they were notably unaggressive and largely on the defensive, coming as late as they did in most areas of the West. Typical examples of the journalistic deference paid resident sheepmen appear in *Harney Items*, June 22, 1901, July 25, August 8, 1903. Local merchants like Nathan Brown advertised goods and equipment for the sheepmen: *Harney Items*, March 14, 1903. King's comment appears in *Harney Items*, September 5, 1903. The difficulty with the general histories treating the open-range era and the subsequent transition to the era of stock farming is that sheepmen are presumed in nearly every case to be transients.

58. Oliphant is more accurate when he refers to the clash as "the problem of two conflicting interests on unpoliced lands open without cost to each of these interests." Yet the basis for his statement still rests upon the assumption that these interests were separate because the differences

between the animals made them so. Oliphant, *Cattle Ranges*, 337, 338. Even in 1901 the argument was being exposed in Harney County. "As to cattle not grazing with sheep, it is true they won't but in this country they occupy the ranges shortly after the sheep are driven to the higher ranges . . . ": *Harney Items*, August 24, 1901.

59. Hanley to Herr Bayley Wilson and Smith of Seattle, Washington, June 22, 1910, Hanley Collection. Also Tax Rolls, 1900.

60. Others have pointed these things out before, but Clawson's work should have been the last word on the subject, though it has long been out of print and copies have not found their way into college and university libraries as one would expect they should; when they have, they are often kept in special collections subject to rigid library restrictions. Marion Clawson, *The Western Range Livestock Industry* (New York: McGraw-Hill Book Co., 1950), 128, 194, 195.

61. The quote above appears in Gretta Gossett, "Stock Grazing in Washington's Nile Valley: Receding Ranges in the Cascades," *Pacific Northwest Quarterly* 55 (July 1964), 126. A letter from small owner Charles Becker pertaining to the range leasing controversy to be discussed further on shows at least one man's feeling about government regulation of the ranges. "I believe that, with the exception of those tramp sheepmen who with their immense herds of sheep roam from place to place reducing our best ranges to a dusty desert, all stockmen are in favor of a law to protect our ranges from certain quick destruction." *Harney Items*, August 10, 1901.

62. *Harney Items*, August 15, 1903.

63. For information on the impulse behind no-fencing, see Paul W. Gates, *History of Public Land Law Development* (Washington, D.C.: U.S. Government Printing Office, 1968), 488. Hanley hired lawyers to fight these inspectors. In one of their briefs they stated that the grand jury "seemed to have lacked discretion. Surely the United States does not wish to try men criminally when no good purpose can be served." Miscellaneous Papers, 1910, Hanley Collection. The *Harney Items* saw through all this. "It is not just the big fry, but the small fry who would like to be classed with them, who opposed it.": June 27, 1903.

64. Johansen, *Empire*, 403, 404. Some history of these associations appears in Oliphant, *Cattle Ranges*, 246, 247.

65. There is some divergence between accounts of the origin and growth of the Harney County Stockgrowers Association. Brimlow states there was no such organization until 1947; newspaper sources plainly contradict him. Brimlow, *Harney County*, 279; *Times-Herald*, June 8, 1901.

66. The professional men most active were attorney Archie McGowan and Doctor Marsden: *Harney Items*, April 9, 1904. Mention of locals in the state Wool Association appears in *Harney Items*, October 12, 1901. A full list of the membership of the stockgrowers' association appears in *Times-Herald*, June 8, 1901. See also Appendix 3, p. 366.

67. Gressley, *Bankers and Cattlemen*, 235. Information below comes from *ibid.*, 235, 237.

68. Quoted in *ibid.*, 236. The leasing controversy was followed locally with close interest and can be followed as well by those interested in the *Times-Herald*, June 19, July 13, and August 3, 1901, and the *Harney Items*, June 8, June 15, July 27, 1901. See also Gates, *Public Land Law*, 489, and Clawson, *Western Range Livestock Industry*, 107-110.

69. The leasing issue as it involved the National Livestock Association can be followed in *Blue Mountain Eagle*, March 8, 1901; *Harney Items*, August 10, November 9, and December 7, 1901.
70. The above quotes appear in *Times-Herald*, June 6, and June 15, 1901.
71. *Ibid.*, January 20, 1901. News of the vote of the association against leasing appears in *Harney Items*, September 28, 1901.
72. Forest regulation and the grazing-fee system were under way by 1905 and helped to reduce the threat of overgrazing. Yet the stockgrowers' association met in special session before the system was introduced to consider the "grave threat" it constituted. *Harney Items*, January 10, 1903. As the years went by, the only true threat forest regulation represented to cattlegrowers was that it worked to emphasize greater reliance on farming phases of the industry by allowing privileges on the basis of how much winter feed a rancher could raise on his home property. During the price decline between 1911 and 1914 some marginal and submarginal outfits were squeezed out. See Clawson, *Western Range Livestock Industry*, 261, 262. Brimlow, *Harney County*, 231. The federal government, of course, was interested in improving agricultural techniques. A more direct reflection of this interest was in the passage of the Hatch Act and the growth of agricultural experiment stations, as well as the work of the new Bureau of Animal Husbandry in producing Blackleg vaccine. Johansen, *Empire*, 375; Oliphant, *Cattle Ranges*, 254; *Blue Mountain Eagle*, March 8, April 26, 1901.
73. The quotes above appear in *Blue Mountain Eagle*, June 14, 1901. For the federal engineer's report, see Brimlow, *Harney County*, 220.
74. J. H. Kolb and Edmund deS. Brunner, *A Study of Rural Society* (Boston: Houghton Mifflin Co., 1946), 79, 380, 381.
75. When the *Blue Mountain Eagle* praised the "strict honesty and fidelity" of Herbert Spencer, it did so as though its readers would know the author and agree with his theories: *Blue Mountain Eagle*, April 22, 1904.
76. Hanley to Tim Wood, Portland, June 22, 1910, Hanley Collection. See also the veritable paean to the salubrious effects of the desert on a man's character in E. R. Jackman and R. A. Long, *The Oregon Desert* (Caldwell: The Caxton Printers, Ltd., 1967), 4, 10, 11, 54.
77. Hanley's correspondence over the period of just one month in 1910 shows the dichotomy. In a letter to his ranch manager he calls for more teamwork on the OO spread because "the organization is the thing.": Hanley to William Stirling, Burns, March 1, 1910, Hanley Collection. Just over a month later he wrote to one Mrs. Farnham stating he would not "fall in line" on irrigation until other members of his company "are prepared to give their support to an irrigation ditch." Hanley to Mrs. Farnham, April 20, 1910, Hanley Collection. An incisive comment on this subject appears in Allan Bogue, "Social Theory and the Pioneer," *Agricultural History* 34 (January 1960), 23.
78. The comments attributed to various professions came from interviews, except the colorful description of bankers which appeared in a letter from Hanley to C. F. Adams, Security Savings and Trust Company, Portland, November 15, 1925, Hanley Collection. On schooling in general, see Jackman and Long, *Oregon Desert*, 29, 30. See also the contempt two rural witnesses had for a school teacher in his case for libel against the *Harney Times*: State vs. J. C. Roberts, Circuit Court, October 26, 1894. Hanley referred to a local attorney as "Sweek and his crooked fossils": Hanley

to C. E. S. Wood, Portland, October 2, 1916. Even more scathing and to the point is Hanley's diatribe, "I do resent this damned cheap law advice and the man that sets [sic] up behind a little sign Attorney at Law has any right to write any letter to a citizen who makes no pretence of knowing anything but what is right between men.": Hanley to W. Lair Thompson, Lakeview, April 21, 1910.

79. Stubb Currey, interview with the author, Cow Creek Ranch, August 31, 1969.

80. One cattleman who enjoyed bird hunting publicly accused homesteaders of stealing game-bird eggs and feeding them to chickens and hogs: *Harney Items*, November 22, 1901. For a broader picture of homesteader-cattlemen relations see Jackman and Long, *Oregon Desert*, 24-26, 37-40. For the classic range-baron attitude see Treadwell and Rand, *Brief*, 3, and Schmitt, *David Shirk*, 145.

81. The differences, strictly speaking, were between "civilized" and "uncivilized" people. See the references to uncivilized Indians in *Blue Mountain Eagle*, April 19, 1901. Of Japanese and Chinese the *Harney Items* claimed: "The American people have no use for either": August 3, 1901. As for blacks, the only one mentioned was a barroom entertainer named simply "Smith" of whom it was said he was of "more than ordinary intelligence and a pretty good musician": *Harney Items*, May 16, 1903.

82. *Harney Items*, April 18, 1903. Hanley's attitude is revealed in a letter to one Webster, June 23, 1910, Hanley Collection.

83. Interviews with the author by Scharff and by Titus Garrett, rancher and descendent of firstcomers, Johnny Temple, rancher and second-generation resident, and Johnny Crow, former cowhand, bootlegger, and retired rancher, Crow Ranch, July 25, 1968. Also personal experiences in Harney County as participant-observer and past experiences on the B-4 Ranch, Cooke City, Montana, and the TE Ranch, South Fork, Wyoming. The two Anderson brothers were black homesteaders south of Folly Farm in the south end. The fact that they proved up in that part of the country and actually made a living earned the respect of their neighbors. "Both of them could ride with the best of them": Stewart interview. A legend among cowpunchers and oldtimers was the great black bronc rider Jess Stahl, whose exploits during the late 1920s on the local rodeo circuit are spoken of with awe even today. His picture appears in Rankin Crow, *Rankin Crow and the Oregon Country*, as told to Colleen Olp (Ironside, Oregon: by the author, 1970), p. 203. The Indian buckaroo who worked for Jim McEwen earned special respect for his roping, and legends built up around the Mexican vaqueros Juan Redon, Cheno Berdugo, and "Tebo."

84. Read particularly the preparations for, and the events planned, as a part of the Fourth of July celebration in 1901. *Harney Items*, June 1, 1901. See Hanley to C. R. Horney, April 20, 1910 and Hanley to Seneca Beach, April 20, 1910 both Hanley Collection. In Harney County the phrase used to describe a government agent who knows little of the country is: "He's a man who won't open his own gate."

85. Official Register of Elections, Harney County Court House, 1912, 1918, 1934, 1938. On the act itself, see Roy M. Robbins, *Our Landed Heritage: The Public Domain, 1776-1936* (Lincoln: University of Nebraska Press, 1962), 421-423. Local response to the act appears in *Burns Times-Herald*, May 1, 1934. For a more technical but illuminating study of the intention and effect of the act see A. Doyle Reed, Stephen C. Smith, Philip S.

Parsons, "A Brief Analysis of Livestock Grazing on the Public Lands," Department of Agricultural Economics, University of California, Berkeley, July, 1959 (mimeographed), 4.

86. Virginia McEwen, special Indian representative and wife of second-generation rancher Walter McEwen, interview with the author, Sod House Ranch, June 16, 1968. For a description of similar roles assigned to "hispanos" in Texas, see D. W. Meinig, *Imperial Texas: An Interpretive Essay in Cultural Geography* (Austin: University of Texas Press, 1969), 88-90.

87. Two such herders, Losarica and Gray, reportedly made over $18,000 in two short years and had credit limits in local banks higher than many of the stable, permanent residents: Scharff interview.

88. Information on Hanley comes from *Blue Mountain Eagle*, February 1, 1901; Hanley Company Statement, Miscellaneous Papers; Hanley to William Miller, February 27, 1907; Hanley to D. O. Lively, March 26, 1910, Hanley Collection.

89. See Brimlow, *Harney County*.

90. Above information in Hanley to Brooks Manufacturing Company, Saginaw, Michigan, November 10, 1909; Hanley to Covey Motor Car Company, Portland, July 12, 1910; Hanley to Clara Hanley, October 20, 1910, Hanley Collection. See also *Blue Mountain Eagle*, May 24, 1901.

91. Bill Hirsch, old-time homesteader, interview with the author, Burns, December 29, 1969. The envy many felt for Bill is described in Monroe, *Feelin' Fine*, xii: xiii.

92. The rash of town-house building was, of course, not solely motivated by attempts to emulate Hanley, who actually had no town house in Burns since the Bell-A was only two miles out of town. It was just as likely firstcomers were also trying to emulate each other. It is merely intended to show that firstcomers wished by 1912 to signify their worth—something Hanley, the community's leading figure, did with gusto. On the quality of firstcomers' town houses, see reports in *Harney Items*, August 24, October 12, 1901, August 12, 1902, *Times-Herald*, July 13, 1901.

93. Interview with the author by Mrs. Forrest Sneva, wife of experiment station biologist, Squaw Butte Experiment Station, August 12, 1968; by Mrs. Ron Shelley, rancher's wife, Sod House Roundup, July 20, 1968; by Art Sawyer. Two suicides, both by drowning, were both reported as motivated by "ill health": *Blue Mountain Eagle*, March 15, 1901.

94. Jackman and Long, *Oregon Desert*, 50-52; interviews with the author by Art Sawyer; Bill Hirsch; and Mel Kundert, homesteader in Catlow Valley, Burns, July 4, 1968.

95. Jackman and Long, *Oregon Desert*, 46, 91.

96. *Ibid.*, 32, 44, 46, 48-50. A popularized survey appears in Jackman, et al., *Steens Mountain*, 32, 175-176. The best sources are the few former homesteaders who remain in Harney County. Analysis of assessment rolls shows the pattern of increased land holdings. For forty representative families, increases of thirty-six acres per family were reported in thirty-one cases over a period of eleven years from 1907 to 1918: Harney County Tax Rolls, 1907, 1912, 1918. Average farm size for the entire county decreased rapidly between 1910 and 1920 from 1269.1 acres to 890.8 acres but increased again between 1920 and 1925 from 890.8 acres to 1012.2 acres: 1948 Report of Harney County's Agricultural Planning Conference, February 21, 1948, in the files of the County Extension Agent, Burns, 8.

97. An automobile on the streets of Burns in 1903 "drew a fair-sized crowd." *Harney Items*, June 13, 1903. Complaints were voiced about Burns's first public telephone, which was located in a store so that everyone who wished to use it "had to publish his business to all who [chanced] to be in the store": *Blue Mountain Eagle*, January 11, 1901. The first telephone company was the Inland Telephone Company, which was in business in 1901; Home Telephone Company set up shop in December, 1902: *Harney Items*, July 15, 1901, December 20, 1902. See also Brimlow, *Harney County*, 207. Local taxpayers, by a thin margin, voted down a Pacific Electric Company electric light and water works bid in 1901, and were plagued with power failures, inadequate lighting, and overloaded machinery and equipment from the inadequate facilities of a series of local companies, until 1924. See *Harney Items*, November 22, 1901, and May 9, 1903. The local nickelodeon was driven by a sputtering gas engine that often could not be kept running through a full-length feature. Brimlow, *Harney County*, 260.

98. Grain production in 1900 was 34,500 bushels—enough to keep three gristmills going full-time for a year. All of this, however, was for local consumption. On milling see *Harney Items*, June 24, 1902, May 16, 1903; *History of Baker, Grant*, 640; Brimlow, *Harney County*, 207, 219. L. L. Sitz bought goods for a general store at Lawen, while Charlie Haines, the most successful of the new country store owners, began a profitable merchandise and grocery store at the Narrows: *Harney Items*, April 4, 1903. One of Haines's shrewd contracts was the provisioning of all of the Harney Valley Improvement Company ranchers: Stirling to Charlie Haines, April 1, 1910, Hanley Collection. Two other stores in other parts of the county were C. O. Bedell's at Silver Creek and O. W. Porter's, Miller's, and Sitz's at Drewsey: *Harney Items*, November 17, 1902; Hanley Company Statements, Miscellaneous Papers, Hanley Collection.

99. On lumber mills see *Harney Items*, May 23, 1903; Brimlow, *Harney County*, 219; Bardwell, *et al.*, "Appraisal of Land," 30-34. One other extractive industry, mining, had burgeoned into a relatively permanent industry with three absentee-owned company mills working in the Pueblo district gold and copper fields. See letter from Thomas Jones to the State Surveyor General, October 29, 1897 and miscellaneous correspondence in the files of the State Land Office, Federal Records Center, Seattle, Washington: *History of Baker, Grant*, 640; *Harney Items*, June 22, November 9, 1901; *Blue Mountain Eagle*, February 1, February 22, May 3, 1901.

100. The extraction was done by the Rose Borax Company. See Crow, *Rankin Crow*, 33, 34; Eggleston, "Harney County," 20; *Times-Herald*, May 23, 1903.

101. *Harney Items*, August 15, 29, 1903; Scharff interview.

EPILOGUE

1. Transient sheepmen were notorious gamblers after cattlemen could no longer afford to be. This trait may help explain in part the friction between the two. In exasperation Bill Hanley wrote, "It is just pig-headed, short-sightedness and any one of them can well afford to use [the hay]

even at the price we have to get for it." Hanley to Henry Welcome, September 18, 1925, Hanley Collection, Oregon Historical Society, Portland. Referring to declining cattle prices in 1924, Bill Hanley wrote to his commission agent: "Agricultural conditions look bad again. Everything from the west to [sic] the corn belt is tied up for the lack of market." Hanley to M. K. Parsons, Salt Lake City, Utah, December 12, 1924, Hanley Collection.

2. Under the management of Joe Fine, the great P Ranch, then owned by Swift and Company, turned exclusively to sheep raising during this period. Joe Fine, interview with the author, November 30, 1969. See also E. R. Jackman, John Scharff, and Charles Conkling, *Steens Mountain in Oregon's High Desert Country* (Caldwell: The Caxton Printers, Ltd., 1968), p. 161. In 1922 Hanley tested the wind with regard to sheep: "we need some for feeding this winter and it seems to be the coming fashion to contract them. We are going to try to get ourselves up to a point to go in." Hanley to Henry Welcome, April 20, 1922, invoices dated August, 1922, Hanley Collection.

3. Interviews with the author by former sheepmen; by Art Sawyer, former Harney County Extension Agent (1936-1952) and director of the Harney County Experiment Station (1952-1969); and by John Scharff, former superintendent of the Malheur National Wildlife Refuge, 1936-1971, July 9, 1968. Hanley observed as early as 1925: "and so much of it left that does not produce much feed any more it is getting down to a pretty bad factor in the grazing problems." Hanley to M. K. Parsons, September 1, 1925, Hanley Collection. "All the land has been so badly grazed over as to have become common waste": *Burns Times-Herald*, January 24, 1930. Jackman, *et al.*, *Steens Mountain*, 136, 140, 142.

4. Henry Ausmus, interview with the author, Ausmus Ranch, June 22, 1968. Ausmus's father's claim to 2,500 acres of exposed shoreline was settled for $25,000 in 1939. When asked what the claim was based upon, Ausmus answered, "my father simply took advantage of a confused situation to buy some cows."

5. A. Doyle Reed, Stephen C. Smith, Philip S. Parsons, "A Brief Analysis of Livestock Grazing on Public Lands," Department of Agricultural Economics, University of California, Berkeley, July, 1959 (mimeographed) 4.

6. Official Register of Elections, 1934, 1938. Local response to the Taylor Act appears in *Burns Times-Herald*, May 1, 1934. Interviews.

7. Burns's population in 1920 was 1,022; in 1930 it was 2,599. *Fifteenth Census, Population*, p. 635. The *Burns Times-Herald*, January 31, 1930 talks of the "new era." Howell Howard, Chairman of the Board, Howard Enterprises, of which E. A. Hines Lumber Company is a subsidiary, interview with the author, July 29, 1968.

8. Interviews with the author by Dale Eggleston, former city councilman and former owner of the Harney County Land Title and Abstract Company, December 7, 1969; "Corky" Corbett, city councilman, August 5, 1968; Jack Slade, former CCC volunteer, September 3, 1968. Not surprisingly, council minutes do not contain this kind of entry, nor does the police docket. The problems of displaced sheepmen were revealed in interviews with the author by William Hirsch, Jess Ereno, Basque storeowner, Burns, September 9, 1968, Julio Urizar, Burns, September 4, 1968.

9. County Commissioner's Journals, Book G, pp. 321, 405, 412, 522, Harney County Courthouse, Burns; George F. Brimlow, *Harney County, Oregon and Its Rangelands* (Portland: Binfords and Mort, 1951), 264, 277. At the same time, county school districts were consolidating; many, in fact, were abandoned as a result of declining rural populations in the 1930s: Lila E. Langdon, "A History of Education in Harney County, Oregon, 1875-1940" (master's thesis, Eastern Oregon College, 1959), 36, 38, 64, 65.

10. Burns grew from 2,566 to 3,523 from 1940 to 1960, Hines from 677 to 1,207 during the same period: *Sixteenth Census, Population, Volume 1*, 889; *Seventeenth Census, Population, Volume 1*, 37-46; *Eighteenth Census, Population, Volume 1*, Part A, 39-45. The changes discussed above were corroborated by interviews with the author by Newton Hotchkiss, County Judge, August 6, 1969; Mark Anderson, County Juvenile Counselor, July 11, 1968. With respect to transportation, the greater use of trucking along the state highways east and west made the southern parts of the county more dependent on Burns. The road to Nevada through Denio is mostly a gravel and dirt road.

11. The increase in value per acre in Harney County was from $7.00 in 1945 to $39.57 in 1969: Bureau of the Census, *U.S. Census of Agriculture: 1945, Volume 1*, Part 32, 103; *U.S. Census of Agriculture: 1969, Volume 1*, Part 47, 105.

12. Interviews with the author by Joe Fine, Burns, November 30, 1969; R. E. Naftzger, owner of the Whitehorse Ranch, August 23, 1969; Paul Stewart, former owner of the Whitehorse Ranch and former owner of the Mann Lake Ranch, June 22, 1968; Robert Wilson, former owner of the Alvord Ranch, July 18, 1968.

13. Cuts were made in the spring of 1960. Two meetings of the Harney County Stockgrowers Association immediately followed. The second one, in March, with three B.L.M. men present, was a protracted, occasionally bitter session. The cattlemen professed support of "multiple use" in theory, especially when the subject under discussion was the Wilderness Bill. Minutes of the Special Meeting, March 8, 1960, Harney County Stockgrowers Association.

14. A father with two or more sons has added complications. Primogeniture is the informal rule, but, no matter what the rule, minor tragedies are enacted in every home where the question of inheritance becomes embroiled with the question of commitment to the ranch: interviews, 1968-1969. As for declining numbers of ranches and rising prices, top cattle prices rose gradually from $29.68 per cwt. to $32.45 per cwt. from 1950 to 1964. The number of ranchers decreased from 436 in 1940 to 311 in 1960, while the average size of ranches increased from 2,005.6 acres in 1940 to 4,521.7 acres in 1960. Harney County Assessment Rolls, 1948-1969; 1948 Report of Harney County's Agricultural Planning Conference, 6, 8: Harney County Program Planning Conference, *Vision of the Future*, March 22, 1957; 4, 5, 9; Analysis of Average Top Livestock Prices Paid by the Portland Union Stock Yards Company, 1950-1964.

15. The local rancher expresses pride at being among the only agriculturists in America who "do not accept subsidies." Yet he considers emergency grain feed relief and grazing fees themselves as free from the taint of subsidy: interviews with cattlemen, 1968-1969; Leonard Grimes, Agricultural Soil and Conservation Service Agent, interview with the author, Burns, Oregon, November 17, 1969; A.S.C.S. Emergency Grain Feed Relief Files,

1961-1970. Two quotes separated by sixty-eight years of Harney County history are illustrative: "We must not give the opportunity for controlling vast areas of land to any one man, which might make homes for thriving communities. It is not American," *Burns Times-Herald*, January 20, 1901; "Whenever ownership of the land falls into the hands of a few, prosperity and independence disappear . . . ," memorandum to the members of the Harney County Stockgrowers Association, Lee Williams, President, 1968, in the files of the County Extension Agent, Burns.

A P P E N D I X E S

APPENDIX 1

Malheur River and Blitzen River Water Rights

Albert Altnow	1883	Warm Springs Creek
J. H. and E. V. Anderson	1884	Calamity and Wolf Creek
W. L. Blaylock	1887	Middle Fork Malheur River
Clarence T. Carey	1884	Crane Creek
Vern Cawlfield	1886	Calamity Creek
George W. Clark, et al.	1885	Crane Creek
Tom Cleveland	1886	Wolf Creek
I. M. Davis	1885	Calamity Creek
Jesse C. Davis	1883	Little Muddy Creek
Drewsey Reclamation Company	1884	Middle Fork Malheur River
Clarence W. Drinkwater	1884	Otis Creek
Harry Fairman	1887	Malheur River
G. W. Fletcher	1884	North Fork Malheur River
William Fredericks	1883	Otis Creek
Margaret A. Gearhart	1883	Wolf Creek
Margaret A. Gearhart	1883	Calamity Creek
J. A. George	1886	Big Muddy Creek
Deane Goodman	1885	North Fork Malheur River
John V. Hoffman	1885	North Fork Malheur River
Edward J. Howard	1883	Middle Fork Malheur River
William H. Howard	1883	Little Stinkingwater River
Jason S. Hunter	1883	East Fork Ben Deer Creek
Malinda A. Hunter	1883	East Fork Ben Deer Creek
Clara B. Jones	1887	North Fork Malheur River
Jones Land and Livestock Co.	1883	North Fork Malheur River
Juntura Investment Company	1884	North Fork Malheur River
Eunice R. Luckey	1883	North Fork Malheur River
James F. Mahon	1886	Camp Creek
David McKenzie	1884	North Fork Malheur River
William W. Miller, et al.	1883	Gould Creek
August Muller	1884	Griffin Creek
John Murphy	1883	Warm Springs Creek
Frank Newman	1897	Alder Creek
Oregon and Western Colo. Co.	1887	Crane Creek
P.L.S. Company	1884	Little Muddy Creek
P.L.S. Company	1881	Camp Creek
P.L.S. Company	1881	Middle Fork Malheur River
Charles R. Peterson	1884	Alder Creek
Charles R. Peterson	1884	Crane Creek
Mrs. M. C. Peterson	1886	South Fork Malheur River
Joseph Robertson Estate	1885	Cottonwood Creek
W. A. Robertson	1888	North Fork Malheur River
M. W. Scott	1885	North Fork Malheur River
J. L. Sitz	1888	Middle Fork Malheur River
Charles A. Spurlock	1889	Malheur River

L. N. Stallard	1885 Otis Creek
Charles Thompson	1883 Warm Springs Creek
Thomas Turnbull	1888 Swamp Creek
W. T. Van Der Veer	1883 Pine Creek
J. A. Williams	1883 Middle Fork Malheur River
S. S. Williams	1884 Otis Creek
Tom R. Woodward	1884 Middle Fork Malheur River

Decreed Water Rights—Blitzen River and Tributaries

Priority Dates	Acre Feet
1872	22,756
1874	2,064
1876	223
1877	537
1880	2,296
1881	640
1882	573
1883	687
1884	162
1885	5,995
1886	2,226
1887	13,239
1888	3,272
1889	2,038
1890	3,906
1891	1,503
1892	1,230
1893	2,221
1896	204
1897	346
1899	713
1900	165
1901	61
1902	196
1904	88
1906	25
1908	250
1909	66
Total	62,942
1872-1880	27,877
1881-1888	26,796
Total	54,674

APPENDIX 2

Major Breeds of Range Beef Cattle

Shorthorn Considered a superior beef animal. Early maturing. Used mostly for upgrading native stock. Not as durable or dependable as the Durham on the trail, though adaptable to the range. Often called "roan" because of their distinctive color.

Durham Strong resemblance (especially color) to shorthorn, from which it came. Longer legs than shorthorn and not as high-quality beef. The durham was an excellent trail animal, and oxen on the Oregon trail were mostly of this breed. It is adaptable to range, although it does not cross with other animals as readily as does the shorthorn.

Moorish Progenitor of the bullring bull. Tough and "gamey" meat. Great range adaptability. When allowed to run wild they were more difficult to hunt than deer. Often dangerous, they were handled in California by the Spanish and Mexican vaqueros, the only ones who were consistently successful in doing so. Descendants of black Andalusian cattle of Spain.

Texas longhorn Unique American breed. Originated in Texas from crosses between Moorish and Mexican (Castillian and "scrub" Durham cattle from Louisiana). Tended to preserve the temperament of Moorish with extra size and longer horns of Mexican cattle. Superb range adaptability (Texans were so prejudiced in their favor that they kept out the average rather than the better bulls in order to maintain the strain). Alert, fast, and difficult to handle when not trail broken. Could be any color from blue and black to red or dun. Spare, tough meat.

APPENDIX 3

Membership List: Harney County Stockgrowers Association, 1901

George D. Hagy, of Burns, accustomed range is Emigrant and also west and northwest of Burns, cattle.
B. R. Porter, of Burns, Emigrant Creek and northwest of Burns, cattle.
Peter Clemens, Burns.
I. C. Grout, Burns, horses and cattle.
Mel Fenwick, Burns, horses and cattle.
J. O. Bunyard, Burns, cattle.
J. P. Withers, Harney, horses and cattle.
Martin Brothers, Burns, cattle.
O. I. Shingledecker, Burns, horses and cattle.
Fred Denstedt, Burns, horses and cattle.
R. J. Williams, Riley, horses and cattle.
H. H. Elliott, Narrows, horses and cattle.
Silvester Smith, Narrows, horses and cattle.
P. G. Smith, Burns, horses and cattle.
A. E. Young, Burns, horses and cattle.
C. P. Rutherford, Burns, horses and cattle.
Michael Moylan, horses and cattle.
Thomas Wingfield, Burns, horses and cattle.

John Craddock, Silvies, horses and cattle.
W. E. Smyth, Burns, cattle.
Green Hudspeth, Burns, cattle.
Simon Lewis, Burns, cattle.
T. V. Kribs, Burns, cattle.
John Witzell, Burns, horses and cattle.
D. M. McMenamy, horses and cattle.
Varien Brothers, horses.
C. W. Jones, Burns, cattle and horses.
J. A. Williams, Van, horses and cattle.
H. Elliott, Burns, horses and cattle.
C. S. Johnson, Van, horses and cattle.
C. J. Johnson, Riley, cattle.
W. B. Johnson, cattle.
W. A. Camel, Narrows, horses and cattle.
John Buoy, Burns, horses and cattle.
Mrs. I. N. Hughet, Warm Springs, cattle.
John Whitman, Burns, horses and cattle.
Sam King, Burns, cattle.
J. P. Dickenson, Narrows, cattle.
Rose Sitz, Narrows, horses and cattle.
D. Finnemore, Burns, horses and cattle.
A. Egli, horses and cattle.
J. T. Ware, Narrows, cattle.
J. W. Biggs, Burns, horses.
H. B. Timmons, Narrows, horses and cattle.
Joel H. Howard, Burns, horses and cattle.
W. W. Brown, Fife, horses.
W. D. Hanley, Burns, horses and cattle.
J. C. Cressman, Burns, cattle.
L. L. Clark, Narrows, horses.
John Gilchrist (P.L.S. Company), Burns, horses and cattle.

APPENDIX 4

Cattle Marketing Terms

Too often historical accounts of the cattle industry fail to include an explanation of some basic but not very well-known terms related to marketing. This is true even of those works devoted solely to the economic aspects of the industry in which an understanding of such terms is essential. Thus the "tenderfoot" is left to "lasso" the meaning of a term from the context—a loose rope in any rodeo. Throughout this study the following terms are used: bull, cow, dry cow, and replacement heifer. These are functional terms referring to the breeding characteristics of animals, or, to put it another way, the production phase of the industry. The terms calf and yearling, as well as terms like two-year-old, three-year old, etc., are all terms designating the age of cattle and are functional in the sense that they often apply to the market characteristics of cattle as well as to their breeding capabilities. In other words, these are operational terms. Steer, heifer, weaner stocker, feeder, and slaughter, are terms dealing *exclusively* with the market function of beef cattle. All of the foregoing are terms applied to the production and marketing of beef and are separate and apart from any considerations of types of breeds.

A bull is a male breeding animal and is usually the most expensive animal in a cowman's herd. If a stockman wishes to "upgrade" his herd, he may buy purebred bulls of one or another breed, depending on the qualities of breed that the cattleman believes are best suited to his operation and to the demands of the market. A rule of thumb used to be roughly one bull to every forty or fifty cows; it is now approximately one to every twenty-five or thirty cows.

The cow is the heart of the cattleman's herd. She is the herd producer whose calves (baby cattle not yet weaned) are sold or otherwise used by the cowman in his operation. A good breeder cow, or "brood" cow, will produce a good calf yearly for as many as fifteen years. Her calves are either male (bull calves) or female (heifer calves).

A weaner calf is a calf or either sex that has been weaned from its mother. Usually weaning occurs when the calf is six to eight months old. At this time or earlier—depending on the needs of the cattleman—the male calf meant for market is castrated and thereby becomes a non-breeding male, or "steer." In former days, the rare bull calf of good breeding and configuration (raised now exclusively on purebred farms) was kept as a breeding bull, or rented or sold to others for that purpose. In the latter case, it would be called a "stocker" animal: that is, an animal used either to start or to build up another herd.

The heifer calf, if it is the product of good breeding (in this case a calf dropped from a good brood cow), may be kept as a "replacement" heifer to replace older cows when they are past their prime, or cows no longer able to produce regularly for reasons other than age. All such cows are called dry cows. A good replacement heifer can also be sold as a stocker animal. Dry cows are slaughter cattle of inferior quality because they are usually older and their meat less tender.

The heifer used for market and the steer, which is always a market animal, can both be raised for "stocking" purposes. Technically, they would be feeder animals used by the purchaser for "stocking" his range with some readily marketable cattle. In the late nineteenth and early twentieth centuries, such heifers and steers were sold when the animals were one year old, or yearlings. The term yearling, then, applies to any one-year-old animal, regardless of age, sex, or function.

Non-replacement heifers and steers are generally sold as either feeder or slaughter animals. A feeder is an animal sold to any individual or concern engaged in feeding and fattening rather than in producing cattle. Steers usually bring higher prices as feeders because of their better fleshing and weight-gaining potential. In the 1880s, feeders were usually sold at three or four years of age. Slaughter animals, among non-replacement heifers and steers, are sold directly to meat-packing houses or other slaughtering facilities. Before the turn of the century, these animals were usually kept an additional year to be fed and fattened by the cowman on his own ranges and pastures. Today, feeders, and slaughter cattle are generally sold as either weaners or yearlings.

APPENDIX 5

Methodology: County Tax Rolls

There are limitations in the data used to show land consolidation that stem from the fact that the information in the tax rolls was of public record and was instrumental in the functions of land transfer, taxation, and the verification of contracts. Thus, there are distortions resulting from the rather universal practice by both small and large owners of declaring only the minimum amount of land they owned; this usually did not include either leased land or land in the name of another, which was used within families on an informal basis. Naturally, land being squatted upon—or even in some cases the land of a government claim that had not yet been proved up—escaped being recorded on the rolls. In many cases land ownership already declared for some years was inexplicably omitted for certain other years, although this happened less frequently as years went by. Still, since distortions were quite universal, they do not radically alter the proportional relationships between owners. Thus the data provide a fair appraisal of size of the holdings of landowners relative to each other.

A system was used in collecting these data that it was thought would help minimize the time of collection without obscuring the patterns being sought. Certain years were selected to illustrate distinguishable periods in this epoch of the county's history: 1890, the first year of the county's independent existence and the beginning of the decade when the acquisition of land became more difficult for newcomers; 1900, one of the four or five years during the transition from the leaner years of the 1890s to the better years at the beginning of the homesteader period; and 1912, two years after the census records a 56-percent rise in the population from 1900 and five years before it records the rapid decline of population that signaled the end of the homestead era— i.e., the median year of the ten growing years.

These three selected years encompassed the total so-called transition period in the cattle industry in Harney County, and it was calculated that they would most likely show the rise of the early persistent settlers as well as the stabilization of the larger outfits as they ceased to expand rapidly. It was also expected that the increasing disadvantages for those wishing to start from scratch after 1890 would show up as well.

Not all taxpayers were noted. Instead an arbitrary figure for personal property was used based upon the accepted axiom of the transition period that one must have hayland in his control if he wished to raise more than a few head of cattle. It was also surmised that if one had more than a few head of cattle he would be more likely to declare that hayland with which he supported them, since the assessor would not be able to ignore the implications of owning more than a few head. Data were collected for the county on land, farm machinery, horses, cattle, sheep, swine and goats, and automobiles, where applicable, after which data were collected on each individual taxpayer owning either 5 or more cows or 500 or more sheep. In addition, individual case records were kept for each year for 101 tax units representing families in certain dominant segments of the county's social and economic structure.

APPENDIX 6

Methodology: Implements, Machinery, and Tillable Land

Many difficulties attend these data: The category for machinery includes merchandise in stores and manufactured products used for other than agricultural purposes. Thus only the data from 1900 to 1912 that mean only farm machinery and implements can be used comparatively. Tax evasion is an uncontrollable variable in all assessment figures, but in the category of farm implements and machinery there is a suspicious sameness to the entries; nearly all are in round numbers and differences between the first- and secondcomers relative to the newcomer group are almost negligible when compared with the differences that appear between these groups in land ownership. One can only guess that assessors were not strict with these values, and as a consequence they are of rather limited use.

As to tillable and nontillable land, the distinction was a new one after 1896 and assessors were as ready to take a man's word for which kind of land he had as he was to exercise his own judgment in the matter. Consequently newcomers may have labeled land one or the other before it was well known which in fact it was. High hopes often made marginal hayland tillable land, while undue pessimism or a desire to lower one's tax rate made tillable land the opposite. The distinctions themselves meant land one could harvest as opposed to land one could not, when in fact it would on first impression seem to have meant land actually cultivated as against land that was not. This explains how over 46,000 acres of Willamette Valley and Cascade Mountain Wagon Road Company land could be listed as tillable land in 1912.

Essentially, however, these distinctions in land did, in fact, reflect relative amounts of hayland in the hands of taxpayers as opposed to rangeland; and this, in turn, was the primary distinction between self-sustaining year-round operations and marginal or submarginal operations.

APPENDIX 7

Methodology: Categories of Cattlegrowers, 1900

To introduce these categories of ranchers simply in terms of the relative size of their holdings as it is recorded in the assessment rolls, they were (1) the large owners with 1,000 head of cattle or over and with over 4,000 acres of land; (2) the well-off owners with 120 to 1,000 head of cattle and anywhere from 330 to 400 acres of land (averaging 588.9 acres per unit); (3) the smaller owners with 25 to 120 head of cattle who owned from 160 to 330 acres of land (averaging 278.4 acres per unit); and (4) the marginal and submarginal owners who owned less than 25 head of cattle and under 160 acres of land (averaging 121.4 acres per unit). These are arbitrarily assigned categories based upon two criteria: the gaps in the distribution of acreage and number of cattle owned, and an assessment of what was deemed by people living at the time to be the equivalent of "well off," "small," and "poor," or "marginal" and "submarginal."

Mention is made frequently in newspapers and in private correspondence, as well as in official records, of the number of acres of land individuals in the county owned. Assessed acreage works out to be between 50 percent and 80 percent of the same acreage mentioned unofficially, but the ratio between the holdings of individual owners, where it can be checked, scarcely varies at all from official to unofficial sources. The case with the number of cattle is different. Few if any unofficial sources mention the number of cattle people owned and assessment records are, as has been said elsewhere, notoriously poor sources of information about actual herd sizes. United States census schedules help to balance the figures in the tax rolls but only for 1880, the last year for which original schedules were available at the time of the study. However, the ratio between the number of cattle reported on these schedules and the numbers of cattle recorded on the assessment rolls of 1880 is consistent. What is more, cattle numbers in the assessment rolls for later years when the schedules are not available at least correlate well with the amount of land that individual cattle owners reported—i.e., the ratio between cattle and land seems to show enough land to maintain the number of cattle declared. Thus, even without other sources of information, it can be assumed that the number of cattle owned by individuals is a proportionally accurate representation of the actual number owned, even though the actual number is impossible to discover.

The discrepancy between real and reported numbers of cattle was probably greater among large owners for two reasons: (1) their herds were so extensive and scattered over so many acres that assessors would have had great difficulty counting them accurately even if they had gone onto the land to do so, which they rarely did in Harney County; and (2) large owners themselves never knew the exact number of cattle they owned at any one time and often guessed long because of the bookkeeping methods they used at the same time they estimated short for tax purposes. These two factors led to confused counts almost universally throughout the West.

This same tendency to estimate low was common among small owners, except that their holdings were more compact and thus more visible to an assessor should he pay them a visit; thus the relative discrepancies were probably not as great—a fact that, of course, wore a sore spot between big and little owners. Both, however, shared the same reluctance a cattleman feels today to divulge the real size of his herd to anyone; cattle are his liquid assets and represent both his income potential and an important part of his overall worth. He would no more wish to have the number of his cattle broadcast than a city dweller today would wish to have his precise net worth known to all. Probably the closest count was in the hands of his creditors; but most credit was from private sources, and the county no longer has its records of personal property or chattel mortgage loans before 1918.

BIBLIOGRAPHY

MANUSCRIPTS

Bingham, Edwin R. "Charles Erskine Wood: An Era and a Realm. Part I. Three Vignettes." (typescript)

Garoian, Leon, James Youde, and Forrest Baker. "Impact of Transportation on Trends in Marketing Western Agricultural Products." Paper presented to the meeting of the Transportation Committee of the National American Cattlemen's Association. San Francisco, California, October 5-6, 1966.

Ladies Guild of the First Baptist Church. "History of the Burns First Baptist Church." (mimeographed)

Lahren, Sylvester L. "Cowboy Economics: Traditionalism, Adaptation, and the Future." Paper presented at the Twenty-fourth Northwest Anthropological Conference, Moscow, Idaho, 1971. (mimeographed)

Novotny, Ray. "Social Change Aspects of Vertical Integration." (typewritten)

Olcott, Fred. "History of the Olcott Family and Genealogy: Father to Son." 1957. (typewritten)

Pomeroy, Earl. "Has the Pacific Coast an Identifiable Culture? A Memorandum on Backgrounds." (mimeographed)

Reed, A. Doyle, Stephen C. Smith, and Philip S. Parsons. "A Brief Analysis of Livestock Grazing on the Public Lands." Department of Agricultural Economics, University of California, July, 1959. (mimeographed)

Searl, Gary H. and Harvey O. Bennett. "The Whitehorse Ranch in Southeastern Oregon." (mimeographed)

Simpson, Peter K. "The Wine Industry in Mittlebergheim." Geography Seminar Paper, 1965. (mimeographed)

Thompson, W. G. ("Uncle Billy"). "Reminiscences." (typewritten)

William F. Hanley Collection. Oregon Historical Society, Portland, Oregon.

THESES AND DISSERTATIONS

Burton, Robert Earl. "A History of the Democratic Party in Oregon, 1900-1956." Ph.D. dissertation, University of Oregon, 1969.

Eggleston, Dale C. "Harney County, Oregon: Some Aspects of Sequent Occupancy and Land Use." Master's thesis, University of Oregon, 1970.

Langdon, Lila E. "A History of Education in Harney County, Oregon, 1875-1940." Master's thesis, Eastern Oregon College, 1959.

Lo Piccolo, Margaret J. "Some Aspects of the Range Cattle Industry of Harney County, Oregon, 1870-1900." Master's thesis, University of Oregon, 1962.

Robbins, William Grover. "The Far Western Frontier: Economic Opportunity and Social Democracy in Early Roseburg, Oregon." Ph.D. dissertation, University of Oregon, 1969.

Stuart, Leland Everett. "Men and Cattle on the Northern Plains, 1860-1887." Ph.D. dissertation, University of Oregon, 1971.

ATLASES AND MAPS

The Cattle Country of Peter French. Portland, Oregon: Binfords and Mort, Publishers, 1964.
Espenshade, Edward B. (editor). *Goode's World Atlas.* Twelfth edition. Chicago: Rand, McNally and Company, 1964.
Highsmith, Richard and John Leverens. *Atlas of the Pacific Northwest.* Fourth edition. Corvallis, Oregon: Oregon State University Press, 1968.
Kogan, Hilde Heun (editor). *The American Heritage Pictorial Atlas.* New York: American Heritage Publishing Company, 1966.
Metsker, Thomas. *Map of Harney County, Oregon.* Seattle: Thomas Metsker, 1966.
Preston, R. N. *Historical Maps of Oregon.* Corvallis: Treasure Chest Maps, 1970.

GOVERNMENT DOCUMENTS AND RECORDS

Bardwell, A. A., D. C., Eggleston, M. D. Palmer. "Appraisal of Land and Resources of the Malheur Indian Reservation." U. S. Department of the Interior. Burns, Oregon. (mimeographed)
Federal Cooperative Extension Service. Annual Reports. Oregon State Agricultural College Extension Service, 1936-1963. Oregon State University, 1963-1969.
Grant County, Oregon. County Clerk's Office. Assessment Rolls, 1885-1889. (John Day)
_____. County Clerk's Office, Deed Record, Books C and G.
_____. County Clerk's Office. County Commissioner's Journals, Books A-G.
Harney County. County Clerk's Office. General Index of Deeds, Indirect, Book I.
_____. County Clerk's Office. Index of Mortgages, Indirect, Book I.
_____. County Clerk's Office. Official Register of Electors, 1906, 1908, 1910, 1912, 1914.
_____. County Clerk's Office. Precinct Petitions, 1890.
_____. County Clerk's Office. Record of Deeds, Books A-F.
_____. County Clerk's Office. Record of Election, Volumes 1-4 (1908-1969).
_____. County Clerk's Office. Record of Marriage Certificates, 1918-1936.
_____. County Clerk's Office. Road Petitions, 1889-1892.
_____. County Clerk's Office. Special Term Order of the Circuit Court, February 24, 1890.
_____. County Clerk's Office. Tax Rolls, 1889-1936.
_____. County Clerk's Office. State vs. Oliver, Transcript of Trial Held in Harney County (Mrs. Esther Haugen).
_____. County Clerk's Office. Claims Certificates, Witness Circuit Court, 1931-present.
Harney County, Oregon. County Court House. Claims Certificates, Witness Grand Jury, 1898-present. (Burns)
_____. County Extension Service. Analysis of Average Top Livestock Prices Paid Portland Union Stockyards Company, 1910-1948.

_____. County Extension Service. Report of Harney County's Agricultural Planning Conference, February 21, 1948.

_____. County Extension Service. *Vision of the Future*. Program Planning Conference, March 22, 1957.

_____. Patents and Deeds. Abstract of Title, Lot 4, Section 34, Lot 1, Section 35, Township 26, South, Range 31, East.

_____. Stockgrowers Association, Minutes, November 20, 1951 to 1969.

_____. Easement Dedication: Town of Narrows, July 31, 1906.

National Association of County Officials and Federal Agencies. "A Discussion of the Public Land Problems of the Eleven Western States by County Officials and Representatives of State Associations of County Officials." Salt Lake City, Utah, January 20, 1941. (mimeographed)

O'Callaghan, Jerry A. *The Disposition of the Public Domain in Oregon*. Washington, D.C.: U.S. Government Printing Office, 1960.

Schultz, John L. "Socio-Cultural Factors in Financial Management Strategies of Western Livestock Producers—Final Report." Economic Research Service, Farm Production Economics Division, U.S Department of Agriculture. Washington, D.C., 1972.

State of Oregon. Agricultural Experiment Station. State Bulletin 604, "Effects of Selected Changes in Federal Land Use on a Rural Economy." Oregon State University, March, 1968.

_____. State Engineer. Hearing, "In the Matter of the Determination of the Relative Right to the Use of the Waters of Donner and Blitzen River, a Tributary of Malheur Lake." Volumes I-XVIII. Harney County Court House.

_____. State Engineer. Hearing, "In the Matter of Determination of the Relative Rights to the Use of the Waters of Silvies River, a Tributary of Malheur Lake." Volumes I-XXXVIII. Harney County Court House.

_____. State Land Office. General Land Office Correspondence. Federal Records Center, Sand Point, Seattle, Washington.

State of Oregon. State Land Office. Miscellaneous Letters of the Surveyor General. Federal Records Center, Sand Point, Seattle, Washington.

_____. Secretary of State. *Oregon Blue Book*, 1965-1966.

_____. Secretary of State. *Oregon Blue Book*, 1969-1970.

_____. State Water Resources Board. Hearing, "In the Matter of a Water Resource Program for the Malheur Lake Basin." Burns, Oregon, January 19, 1966. Harney County Library.

_____. State Water Resources Board. In re: Silvies River, "Brief in Support of Claims of Pacific Livestock Company." Water Division Number 2, Grant and Harney Counties, January 24, 1923.

United States Army. Department of the Columbia. *General Orders, 1869*.

_____. Military Division of the Pacific. *Outline Descriptions of the Military Posts in the Military Division of the Pacific, 1870*.

_____. Department of the Columbia. Assistant Adjutant General's Office. *Roster of Troops Serving in the Department of the Columbia*, 1877.

United States Bureau of the Census. *Tenth Census of the United States: 1880. Population*, Volume I, Schedule I.

_____. *Tenth Census of the United States: 1880. Agriculture*, Volume III.

_____. *Eleventh Census of the United States: 1890. Population*, Volume I.

_____. *Eleventh Census of the United States: 1890. Agriculture*, Volume V.

_____. *Twelfth Census of the United States: 1900. Population*, Volume I.

_____. *Thirteenth Census of the United States: 1910. Population*, Volume III.

_____. *Fourteenth Census of the United States: 1920. Population*, Volume III.

_____. *Historical Statistics of the United States: 1789-1945*. Washington, D.C.: U.S. Government Printing Office, 1949.

United States Bureau of the Census. *U.S. Census of Agriculture: 1945*. Volume I, Part 32.

_____. *U.S. Census of Agriculture: 1969*. Volume I, Part 47.

United States Bureau of Land Management. Case Files and Correspondence. Federal Records Center, Sand Point, Seattle, Washington.

_____. Government Survey Maps and Field Notes. Oregon District Office, Portland, Oregon.

United States Supreme Court. United States vs. the State of Oregon. Brief of the State of Oregon, October Term, 1934. Harney County Library.

_____. United States vs. the State of Oregon. Report of the Special Master, October Term, 1934. Harney County Library.

INTERVIEWS

Anderson, Mark, Harney County Juvenile Counselor, July 11, 1968, Burns.

Ausmus, Henry, June 22, July 12, 1968, Ausmus Ranch.

Bailey, "Bob," July 15, 1968, Burns.

Berrington, Marvin, Owner, Wildhorse Ranch, July 9, July 17, 1968, Wildhorse Ranch.

Berrington, Mrs. Marvin, Wife of Owner, Wildhorse Ranch, July 9, 1968, Wildhorse Ranch.

Brown, Alfred, Realtor, July, August, 1968, July, August, 1969, July, 1970, Burns.

Corbett, "Corky," Burns City Councilman, August 5, 1968, Burns.

Crow, John, July 14, 1968, Crow Ranch.

Culp, Marianna, County Assessor, July 19, 1968, Burns.

Currey, Stubb, August 31, 1969, Cow Creek Ranch.

Davies, Bill, September 10, 1968, Mud Flat Ranch.

Day, Orin, June 23, 1968, Sod House Ranch.

Dunn, Sam, July 20, 1968, Sod House Ranch.

Eggleston, Dale, Former Owner of the Harney County Land Title and Abstract Company, December 7, 1969, Eugene.

Ereno, Jess, September 9, 1968, Burns.

Fine, Joe, Former Foreman of P Ranch, November 30, 1969, Burns.

Grimes, Leonard, Agricultural Soil and Conservation Service Agent, November 17, 1969, Burns.

Hayes, Ilda Mae, July 23, 1969, Burns.

Hill, Lloyd, November 14, 1969, Burns.

Hinshaw, Dwight, Publisher, *Burns Times-Herald*, June 23, 1968, Burns.

Hirsch, Bill, December 29, 1969, Burns.

Hotchkiss, Newton, Harney County Judge, August 6, 1969, Burns.

Howard, Howell, Chairman of the Board, Howard Enterprises, July 29, 1968, Hines Mill Headquarters.

Kundert, Mel, July 4, 1968, Burns.

Lavin, Verdie, Field Man, Bureau of Land Management, July 8, 1968. Burns.
Leavitt, "Red," July 16, 1968, Sod House Ranch, July 28, 1968, Rinehart Ranch.
McEwen, Jim, June 23, 1968, Sod House Ranch.
McEwen, Virginia, June 16, 1968, Sod House Ranch.
McEwen, Walter, Owner of Sod House Ranch, September 1, 1968, Sod House Ranch.
Meiers, Harold, M.A.I., May 10, 1967, Eugene.
Miler, Mrs. Charley, Wife of Former P.L.S. Company Superintendent, 1900-1933, September 12, 1968, Miler Ranch.
Novotny, Ann, Wife of County Extension Agent, July 9, 13, 1968, Hill Ranch.
Novotny, Ray, Extension Agent, Harney County, July, August, 1968, August, 1969, Burns.
Otley, Charley, July 29, 1969, Diamond.
Perkins, Charles, Former Rector, St. Andrew's Episcopal Church, November 15, 1969, Burns.
Praeger, Pete, August 10, 1969, Burns.
Sawyer, Art, Manager of Harney County Chamber of Commerce and first Harney County Extension Agent, December 30, 1969, Burns.
Scharff, John, Former Director, Malheur Wildlife Refuge, July 9, 14, 1968, Malheur Wildlife Refuge Headquarters.
Shelley, Ron, July 20, 1968, Sod House Roundup.
Slade, Jack, June 20, 1968, Burns.
Sneva, Mrs. Forrest, August 12, 1968, Squaw Butte Experiment Station.
Stewart, Paul, June 22, 23, 1968, Whitehorse Ranch.
Stott, John, Owner of Frenchglen Store, June 29, 1968, Frenchglen.
Taylor, Elta, June 25, 1968, Taylor Ranch.
Taylor, Rex, July 20, 1968, Sod House Roundup.
Toelle, Don, June 17, 23, July 1, 3, 4, 15, 1968, Sod House Ranch.
Vallejo, Juan, June 22, 1968, Burns.
Wilson, Bob, Owner of Alvord Ranch, June 22, 1968, Alvord Ranch.
Woodell, Larry, Officer, U.S. National Bank, June 17, 1968, Burns.
Young, Clarence, Former County Sheriff, Watermaster and Surveyor, July, August, 1968, August, 1969, July 24, 1970, Burns.

NEWSPAPERS

Blue Mountain Eagle (Canyon City, Oregon), November, 1900-April, 1904, May, 1904-January, 1910.
Burns Times-Herald (Burns, Oregon), March, 1890, June 6-December, 1901, December, 1902-April, 1904, January 31, 1963.
Eastern Oregon Herald (Burns, Oregon), May-November, 1888, March-November, 1889, February 1890, October, 1893.
Harney Items (Burns, Oregon), February-May, 1887, July, 1888, October, 1888, March, 1897, June-October, 1901, March-November, 1902, January-June 1903.
Harney Times (Harney, Oregon), March 1890, July, 1893, June, 1901-October, 1903.
Morning Oregonian (Portland, Oregon), November 12, 1902.

BOOKS

Adams, Ramon. "The Old-Time Cowhand." *The American West: An Appraisal*. Robert G. Ferris, editor. Santa Fe: Museum of New Mexico Press, 1963. pp. 15-24.

Bogue, Allan G. *From Prairie to Cornbelt: Farming on the Illinois and Iowa Prairies in the Nineteenth Century*. Chicago: University of Chicago Press, 1963.

Brimlow, George F. *Harney County, Oregon, and Its Range Land*. Portland: Binfords and Mort, 1951.

Brogan, Phil F. *East of the Cascades*. Portland: Binfords and Mort, 1964.

Buck, Solon Justus. *The Granger Movement: A Study of Agricultural Organization and Its Political, Economic, and Social Manifestations, 1870-1880*. Cambridge: Harvard University Press, 1913.

Clark, John G., editor. *The Frontier Challenge: Responses to the Trans-Mississippi West*. Lawrence: The University Press of Kansas, 1971.

Clawson, Marion. *The Western Range Livestock Industry*. New York: McGraw-Hill Book Company, Inc., 1950.

Cleland, Robert Glass. *The Cattle on a Thousand Hills: Southern California, 1850-1880*. San Marino: The Huntington Library, 1951.

Cochran, Thomas C., and William Miller. *The Age of Enterprise: A Social History of Industrial America*. New York: Harper and Row, 1961.

Coleman, James S. *Community Conflict*. New York: The Free Press, 1957.

Crow, Rankin. *Rankin Crow and the Oregon Country*, as Told to Colleen Olp. Ironside, Oregon: by the Author, 1970.

Curti, Merle. *The Making of an American Community: A Case Study of Democracy in a Frontier County*. Stanford: Stanford University Press, 1959.

Dale, Edward Everett. *The Range Cattle Industry*. Norman: University of Oklahoma Press, 1962.

Dicken, Samuel N. *Oregon Geography: The People, the Place and the Time*. Fourth edition. Ann Arbor, Michigan: Edwards Brothers, 1965.

Dillon, Richard H., editor. *California Trail Herd: The 1850 Missouri to California Journal of Cyrus C. Loveland*. Los Gatos, California: The Talisman Press, 1961.

Dobie, J. Frank. *The Longhorns*. Boston: Little, Brown and Co., 1941.

Drago, Harry Sinclair. *Great American Cattle Trails*. Norman: University of Oklahoma Press, 1920.

Dykstra, Robert R. *The Cattle Towns*. New York: Alfred A. Knopf, 1968.

Edwards, Col. Philip L. *California in 1837: An Account of a Trip to the Pacific Coast*. Sacramento: A. J. Johnston and Company, 1890.

Fite, Gilbert C. *The Farmers' Frontier, 1865-1900*. New York: Holt, Rinehart and Winston, 1966.

French, Giles. *Cattle Country of Peter French*. Portland: Binfords and Mort, 1965.

Gates, Paul W. *History of Public Land Law Development*. Washington, D.C.: U.S. Government Printing Office, 1968.

Goldschmidt, Walter. *As You Sow*. New York: Harcourt, Brace and Co., 1947.

Goldstein, Sidney. *The Norristown Study: An Experiment in Interdisciplinary Research Training*. Philadelphia: University of Pennsylvania Press, 1961.

Gressley, Gene M. *Bankers and Cattlemen*. New York: Alfred A. Knopf, 1966.

Higham, John. *Strangers in the Land: Patterns of American Nativism, 1860-1925*. New Brunswick: Rutgers University Press, 1955.

History of Baker, Grant, Malheur, and Harney Counties, Oregon. Chicago: Western Historical Publishing Company, 1902.

Jackman, E. R. and R. A. Long. *The Oregon Desert*. Caldwell, Idaho: The Caxton Printers, Ltd., 1967.

Jackman, E. R., John Scharf, and Charles Conkling. *Steens Mountain in Oregon's High Desert Country*. Caldwell, Idaho: The Caxton Printers, Ltd., 1968.

Jackson, W. Turrentine. *Wagon Roads West: A Study of Federal Road Surveys and Construction in the Trans-Mississippi West, 1846-1869*. New Haven: Yale University Press, 1965.

Johansen, Dorothy O. *Empire of the Columbia: A History of the Pacific Northwest*. Second edition. New York: Harper and Row, 1967.

Kilkenny, John F. *Shamrocks and Shepherds: The Irish of Morrow County*. Portland: Glass-Dahlstrom Printers, 1969.

Kolb, J. H. and Edmund de S. Brunner. *A Study of Rural Society*. Boston: Houghton Mifflin Company, 1946.

Meinig, D. W. *Imperial Texas: An Interpretive Essay in Cultural Geography*. Austin: University of Texas Press, 1969.

Monroe, Anne Shannon, editor. *Feelin' Fine*. Garden City: Doubleday, Doran and Co., 1931.

Mourant, A. E. and F. E. Zeuner. *Man and Cattle: Proceedings of a Symposium on Domestication at the Royal Anthropological Institute, 24-26 May, 1960*. Royal Anthropological Institute Occasional Paper No. 18. Glasgow: Robert MacLehose and Co., Ltd., the University Press, 1963.

Oliphant, J. Orin. *On the Cattle Ranges of the Oregon Country*. Seattle: University of Washington Press, 1968.

Oliver, Herman. *Gold and Cattle Country*. Portland: Binfords and Mort, 1962.

Osgood, Ernest Staples. *The Day of the Cattlemen*. Minneapolis: University of Minnesota Press, 1929.

Paul, Rodman Wilson. *Mining Frontiers of the Far West, 1848-1880*. New York: Holt, Rinehart and Winston, 1963.

Pelzer, Louis. *The Cattleman's Frontier: A Record of the Trans-Mississippi Cattle Industry from Oxen Trains to Pooling Company, 1850-1890*. Glendale: The Arthur H. Clark Co., 1936.

Pomeroy, Earl. *The Pacific Slope; A History of California, Oregon, Washington, Idaho, Utah, and Nevada*. New York: Alfred A. Knopf, 1965.

Puter, S. A. D. and Horace Stevens. *Looters of the Public Domain*. Portland: The Portland Publishing House, 1908.

Riegel, Robert Edgar. *The Story of the Western Railroads*. New York: The Macmillan Company, 1926.

Robbins, Roy M. *Our Landed Heritage: The Public Domain, 1776-1936*. Princeton: The Princeton University Press, 1942.

Schlebecker, John T. *Cattle Raising on the Plains, 1900-1961*. Lincoln: University of Nebraska Press, 1963.

Schmitt, Martin F., editor. *The Cattle Drives of David Shirk: From Texas to the Idaho Mines, 1871 and 1873*. Portland: The Champoeg Press, 1956.

Shannon, Fred A. *The Farmer's Last Frontier: Agriculture, 1860-1897*. New York: Holt, Rinehart and Winston, 1945.

Smythe, William E. *The Conquest of Arid America*. Reprint edition. Seattle: University of Washington Press, 1969 [1899].

Towne, Charles Wayland and Edward Norris Wentworth. *Cattle and Men.* Norman: University of Oklahoma Press, 1955.

Treadwell, Edward F. *The Cattle-King: A Dramatized Biography.* Revised edition. Fresno: Valley Publishers, 1966.

Webb, Walter Prescott. *The Great Plains.* New York: Grosset and Dunlap, 1931.

Westermeier, Clifford P. "The Modern Cowboy—An Image." *The American West: An Appraisal*, Robert G. Ferris, editor. Santa Fe: Museum of New Mexico Press, 1963. pp. 25-34.

Wright, Louis B. *Culture on the Moving Frontier.* New York: Harper and Brothers, 1961.

Wyllie, Irvin G. *The Self-Made Man in America: The Myth of Rags to Riches.* New York: The Free Press, 1954.

ARTICLES

Adams, Ramon. "The Cowman's Philosophy." *The American West: An Appraisal.* Robert G. Ferris, editor. Santa Fe: Museum of New Mexico Press, 1963. pp. 15-24.

Anderson, George L. "From Cattle to Wheat: The Impact of Agricultural Developments on Banking in Early Wichita," *Agricultural History* 33 (January 1959): 3-15.

Baker, Neal A. "Red River County, Texas, in the 1920's: A Landlocked Frontier," *Southwestern Historical Quarterly* 70 (January 1967): 442-460.

Bogue, Allan G. "Social Theory and the Pioneer," *Agricultural History* 34 (January 1960): 21-34.

Brandhorst, Carl L. "The Panacea of Irrigation: Fact or Fancy," *Journal of the West* 7 (October 1968): 491-509.

Burns, Robert H. "Beef Makers of the Laramie Plains," *Annals of Wyoming* 36 (October 1964): 185-197.

Carter, George E. "The Cattle Industry of Eastern Oregon, 1880-1890," *Oregon Historical Quarterly* 67 (June 1966): 139-159.

Clawson, Marion. "Reminiscences of the Bureau of Land Management, 1947-1948," *Agricultural History* 33 (January 1959): 22-28.

Dale, Edward Everett. "The Cow Country in Transition," *Mississippi Valley Historical Review* 24 (June 1937): 3-20.

Dobie, J. Frank. "The First Cattle in Texas and the Southwest Progenitors of the Longhorns," *Southwestern Historical Quarterly* 42 (January 1939): 3-29.

Fite, Gilbert C. "The American West of Farmers and Stockmen." In *Historians and the American West*, edited by Michael P. Malone. Lincoln: University of Nebraska Press, 1983. Pp. 209-233.

Fletcher, Robert S. "That Hard Winter in Montana: 1886-1887," *Agricultural History* 4 (October 1930): 123-130.

Fugate, Francis L. "Origins of the Range Cattle Era in South Texas," *Agricultural History* 35 (July 1961): 155-158.

Gates, Paul W. "Cattle Kings in the Prairies," *Mississippi Valley Historical Review* 35 (December 1948): 389-397.

Glass, Mary Ellen. "The Newlands Reclamation Project: Years of Innocence, 1903-1907," *Journal of the West*, 7 (January 1968): 84-95.

Gossett, Gretta. "Stock Grazing in Washington's Nile Valley: Receding Ranges in the Cascades," *Pacific Northwest Quarterly* 55 (July 1964): 118-127.

Gressley, Gene M. "Arthur Powell Davis, Reclamation and the West," *Agricultural History* 42 (July 1968): 241-257.

Kingston, C. S. "The Introduction of Cattle into the Pacific Northwest," *Washington Historical Quarterly* 14 (July 1923): 163-185.

Knight, Oliver. "The Owyhee Avalanche: The Frontier Newspaper as a Catalyst in Social Change," *Pacific Northwest Quarterly* 58 (April 1967): 74-81.

McArthur, Lewis O. "Devine Monument Dedication," *Oregon Historical Quarterly* 29 (September 1928): 229-236.

Meinig, Donald W. "American Wests: Preface to a Geographical Interpretation," *Annals of the Association of American Geographers* 62 (June 1972): 159-184.

Messing, John. "Public Lands, Politics, and Progressives: The Oregon Land Fraud Trials, 1903-1910," *Pacific Historical Review* 35 (February 1966): 35-66.

Oliphant, J. Orin. "The Cattle Herds and Ranches of the Oregon Country, 1860-1890," *Agricultural History* 21 (October 1947): 217-238.

. "The Cattle Trade from the Far Northwest to Montana," *Agricultural History* 6 (April 1932): 69-83.

. "The Eastward Movement of Cattle from the Oregon Country," *Agricultural History* 20 (January 1946): 19-43.

. "Winter Losses of Cattle in the Oregon Country, 1847-1890," *Washington Historical Quarterly* 23 (January 1932): 3-17.

Osgood, Ernest S. "The Cattlemen in the Agricultural History of the Northwest," *Agricultural History* 3 (July 1929): 117-130.

Paul, Rodman W. "The New Western History: A Review of Two Recent Samples," *Agricultural History* 43 (April 1969): 297-300.

Peterson, Ottis. The Story of a Bureau," *Journal of the West* 7 (January 1968): 84-95.

Pomeroy, Earl. "Rediscovering the West," *Agricultural History* 12 (September 1960): 20-29.

. "Toward a Reorientation of Western History: Continuity and Environment," *Mississippi Valley Historical Review* 41 (March 1955): 579-600.

Shroyer, Peter A. "Oregon Sheep, Wool, and Woolens Industries," *Oregon Historical Quarterly* 57 (June 1966): 125-138.

Swierenga, Robert P. "Land Speculation and Frontier Tax Assessments," *Agricultural History* 44 (July 1970): 253-266.

Ulph, Owen. "Cowboy's Lament or the Dilemma of the Twentieth Century Buckaroo," *Arizona and the West* 9 (Winter, 1962): 357-368.

Whitaker, James W. "Agriculture and Livestock Production." In *American Frontier and Western Issues: A Historiographical Review*, edited by Roger L. Nichols. Westport, Connecticut: Greenwood Press, 1986. Pp. 51-67.

Wohld, Mike. "Squaw Butte—Cow-Calf Research Center of the West," *Oregon Farmer* 92 (September 1969): 6-8.

Winther, Oscar Osburn. "The British in Oregon Country: A Triptych View," *Pacific Northwest Quarterly*, 58 (October 1967): 179-186.

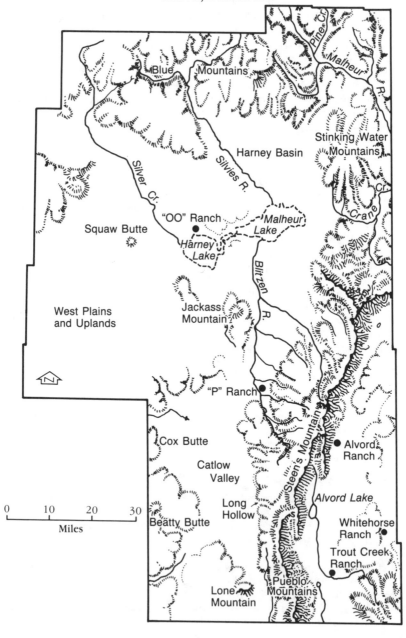

Harney County: Major Physiographic Regions,
with Major Ranch Sites

Blue Mountains

Pine Cr.

Malheur R.

Harney Basin

Silvies R.

Silver Cr.

Stinking Water
Mountains

Crane Cr.

"OO" Ranch

Malheur
Lake

Squaw Butte

Harney
Lake

West Plains
and Uplands

Jackass
Mountain

Blitzen R.

N

"P" Ranch

Cox Butte

Alvord
Ranch

Catlow
Valley

Steen's Mountain

Alvord Lake

Long
Hollow

Beatty Butte

Whitehorse
Ranch

Trout Creek
Ranch

Lone
Mountain

Pueblo
Mountains

0   10   20   30

Miles

Areas of First Class Soil, and Major Towns*

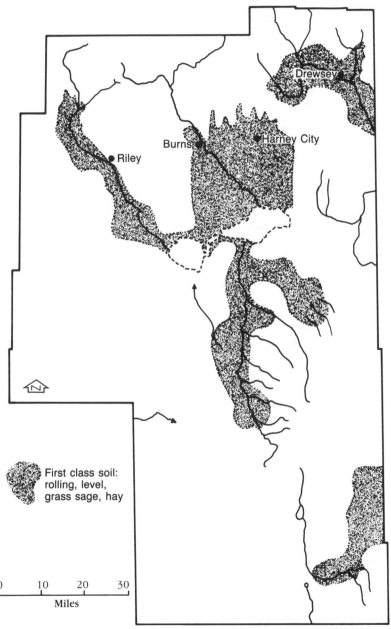

*Taken from Original Survey Field Notes;
1873, 1875, 1880, 1882-1884, 1891, 1895, 1896, 1902, 1911.

INDEX

Act of 1921 (Oregon), 78
Agency Valley, 32, 66
Alfalfa, feed crop, 52
Altschul, Charles, 106-107
Alvord Lake, 6
American Cattlegrowers Association, 92; leasing bill, 142
Atherton, Lewis, 61

Bell-A Ranch, 119, 126, 147, 202n.92
Big owners, defined, 114
Biographies, Southeastern Oregon Counties, 43. *See also* "Mug Books"
Blitzen Valley Land Company, 120
Blue Mountain Eagle, 99; defamatory articles on David Shirk, 73
Blue Mountain Reserve, 92
Brand registration law, 68
Brown, Nathan, 147, 166n.82, 175n.31
Brown, William (Bill), 35
Bureau of Animal Husbandry, 200n.72
Bureau of Land Management, 154-55, 179n.71
Burns, town of, 62-67, 70-71, 152, 154-55; professional services in, 63-64
Burns Eastern Oregon Herald, 58, 65, 71-72
Burns Times-Herald, 93, 105-106, 142-43
Byrd, Julian, 142-43

California "Herd Laws." *See* "Herd Laws"
California, settlement from, 101
Camp Curry, U.S. Army, 12, 46
Camp Harney, U.S. Army, 9
Camp C.F. Smith, U.S. Army, 17
Canyon City, 17-18
Carey Act of 1894, 55, 94-95. 107, 120, 184n.30
Catlow, John, of Silver City, Idaho, 21, 158n.18
Catlow Valley, 7, 25

Cattle: breeds, 1-3, 12, 38-39, 90, 114, 128; market outlets, 38, 130; "pilgrim," 39; prices, 3, 31, 38, 153, 196n.38, 205n.14; stocker, 38-39
Cattle and sheep wars, 134, 170n.122
Cattle Barons, 117-121 and *passim*
Cattle breeding, 127-128
Cattlemen's association in the Harney country, 67
"Cattlemen's frontier," 1
Cattle raising, 123-27; "cow-calf" operation, 126, 132; open-range, 53, 116; "reservation system," 29; stock farming, 53, 116
Census, U.S., 100
Chamberlain, George E., Governor, 135
"Chicago Market," 130
Clemens, Peter, 112-114
Cleveland, President Grover, 67-68
Colorado Gold Rush of 1859, 3
Coolidge, Calvin, 153
Coville, Frederick, U.S.D.A. Inspector, 141
Cowhands, 148
Crow, Frances, marries David Shirk, 26
Crook, General George, commander of Fort Harney, 18
Crow, James Rankin, 25
Crook County, 134

Daily Oregonian, 93
Dalles Military Wagon Road, 17; Company, 105
Dances, social, 65, 175n.35
Desert Land Act of 1877, 22, 32-34, 91-92, 112; and land acquisition, 24; modification of, 91
Devine, John, 6, 13, 21, 23, 27, 33, 37, 52, 57, 64, 128, 171n.132. 175n.30; death of, 122; swampland holdings, 113
Diamond Valley, 45, 102-103
Donation Land Act of 1850, 19
Drewsey, town of, 66, 186n.50, 187n.51; settlement patterns, 103